"An Insect View
of Its Plain"

"An Insect View of Its Plain"

Insects, Nature and God in Thoreau, Dickinson and Muir

Rosemary Scanlon McTier

McFarland & Company, Inc., Publishers
Jefferson, North Carolina, and London

The following poems are reprinted by permission of the publishers and the Trustees of Amherst College from *The Poems of Emily Dickinson: Variorum Edition*, edited by Ralph W. Franklin, Cambridge, MA: The Belknap Press of Harvard University Press, Copyright © 1951, 1955, 1979, 1983 by the President and Fellows of Harvard College.

I prayed at first a little girl (J576/F546), Of course I prayed (J376/F581), Mama never forgets her birds (J164/F130), Nature the gentlest mother is (J790/F741), Ourselves we do inter with sweet derision (J1144/F1449), My faith is larger than the hills (J766/F489), "Faith" is a fine invention (J185/F202), A toad can die of light (J583/F419), Longing is like the seed (J1255/F1298), To be alive is power (J677/F876), Awake ye muses nine (J1/F1), A spider sewed at night (J1138/F1163), How lonesome the wind must feel nights (J1418/F1441), A fuzzy fellow without feet (J173/F171), These are the signs to nature's inns (J1077/F1106), The bee is not afraid of me (J111/F113), It would have starved a gnat (J612/F44), They shut me up in prose (J613/F445), Nobody knows this little rose (J35/F11), Bee! I'm expecting you (J1035/F983), The fairest home I ever knew (J1423/F1443), I went to heaven (J374/F577), A little road not made of man (J647/F758), A soft sea washed around the house (J1198/F1199), Some keep the sabbath going to church (J324/F236), Heaven is so far of the mind (J370/F413), The butterfly obtains (J1685/F1701), A coffin is a small domain (J943/F890), The opening and the close (J1047/F1089), Spring is the period (J844/F948), My cocoon tightens, colors teaze (J1099/F1107), Ungained it may be, see Each life converges to some (J680/F724), Growth of man like growth of nature (J750/F790), This consciousness that is aware (J822/F817).

Selections from *John of the Mountains: The Unpublished Journals of John Muir*. Ed. Linne Marsh Wolfe. Madison: University of Wisconsin Press, 1979. John Muir Papers, Holt-Atherton Special Collections, University of the Pacific Library. © 1984 Muir-Hanna Trust.

LIBRARY OF CONGRESS CATALOGUING-IN-PUBLICATION DATA

McTier, Rosemary Scanlon, 1970–
 "An insect view of its plain" : insects, nature and God in
Thoreau, Dickinson and Muir / Rosemary Scanlon McTier.
   p.   cm.
 Includes bibliographical references and index.

 ISBN 978-0-7864-6493-7
 softcover : acid free paper ∞

 1. Thoreau, Henry David, 1817–1862 — Knowledge —
Insects. 2. Insects in literature. 3. Dickinson, Emily,
1830–1886 — Knowledge — Insects. 4. Muir, John, 1838–
1914 — Knowledge — Insects. 5. Nature in literature.
6. Naturalists — United States. I. Title.
 PS3057.E6M38   2013
 810.9'36257—dc23   2012029674

BRITISH LIBRARY CATALOGUING DATA ARE AVAILABLE

© 2013 Rosemary Scanlon McTier. All rights reserved

No part of this book may be reproduced or transmitted in any form or by any means, electronic or mechanical, including photocopying or recording, or by any information storage and retrieval system, without permission in writing from the publisher.

Front cover image © 2013 Shutterstock

Manufactured in the United States of America

McFarland & Company, Inc., Publishers
 Box 611, Jefferson, North Carolina 28640
 www.mcfarlandpub.com

For Grandma Rose, who never lost hope.

And for Pam and Shea, who continue to live in joy.
May they always find Leah in the rainbows.

Acknowledgments

This book has been years in the making, and more people have extended their support and knowledge than I can possibly begin to recognize here. I must extend my gratitude to the members of my dissertation committee, Dr. Frederick Newberry, Dr. John Dolis, Dr. Elaine Parsons, and Dr. Linda Kinnahan, for their time and assistance in helping me clarify the ideas and overall presentation that formed the foundation of this study, and to Dr. Albert Labriola and Dr. Magali Michael for believing in me and my project. Dr. Tammy Horn very kindly allowed me to peruse the notes for her forthcoming book, and I am thankful for her thoughtfulness, encouragement, and input. I would also like to thank my grandmother, Rosemary Arrisher, my mother, JoAnn Scanlon, my aunt, Diane McLaughlin, my spouse, James Lindstrom, and, most of all, my daughter, Moiya McTier, for their support and confidence. I will always appreciate the help of the staff at Eberly Library for their swift attention to my many requests and queries, and I will never forget the kindness and encouragement of my colleagues and friends, Dr. Jamie Dessart, Dr. Marilyn Roberts, Dr. Jenny Jellison, Jan Teagarden, Pam Abbe, Charles Beiter, Jennifer Foradori, Elizabeth Williamson, Regina Davis, Beth Merry, Jill Sunday, Susan Biddle, Ella Belling, Lance Smith, Christopher Stewart, Phillip Coss, Heather Cummings, Donna Carcella, Carol Salai, Jet'aime Gantt McTier, Aaron Youngblood, Cass Eaton, Vern Toland, Dawn and Ethan Phillips, Kristi Smouse, and Annabel Moats. I am most especially indebted to Dr. Nicole Andel, who offered invaluable advice and assistance and, above all else, kept me (somewhat) sane.

Table of Contents

Acknowledgments — vi
Preface — 1
Textual Abbreviations — 4
Introduction — Henry David Thoreau, Emily Dickinson, and John Muir: Interpreting the Language of Nature — 5

I. Insects and the Nineteenth Century — 27
II. "With Microscopic Eye": Thoreau's Insect Perspective — 70
III. "A Minor Nation": Emily Dickinson and the Insects' Society — 104
IV. John Muir: Translating "Nature's Book" — 145

Chapter Notes — 177
Works Cited — 185
Index — 193

Preface

A discussion of how insects are woven into the fabric of nineteenth-century American culture and more specifically into the nature writing of the period fills an important critical gap in both ecocriticism and literary entomology. As I note in the Introduction of this book, several ecocritics and other researchers have emphasized the importance of listening to the "voice" of nature and recognizing that all elements of creation, no matter how insignificant they appear to be, contribute to a planetary "dialogue" between equal members. Investigation of how writers developed unique methods of peering into microscopic environments in order to comprehend and translate those minute presences and voices has evolved into an important branch of ecocritical studies. In addition, while increased interest in cultural and literary entomology has inspired animated discussions about the appearance and function of insects in literature, very few revolve around nineteenth-century writers. A study of insects in the works of Thoreau, Dickinson, and Muir contributes to the understanding of their work as nature writers, their abilities as natural scientists, entomologists, and botanists, and their intimate and highly spiritual relationships with nature.

Thoreau, Dickinson, and Muir share many essential beliefs about the nature of our connection to insects and what they have to teach us about creation and our place in it. While each writer approaches the idea from the points of view of different insects, they come to the same essential conclusion: ecstatic "joy is the condition of life" (NH 4) and, more than any other creature in creation, insects exist to celebrate. Thoreau discovers the universal joy in the songs of all insects, but especially in the chorus of the crickets and the swarms of insects that endlessly dance above Walden Pond. The chorus of the crickets also captures Dickinson's ear, a song that has the power to set the sun as they "celebrat[e]" their "unobtrusive Mass" (J1068/F895]. Dickinson also focuses on the joyous experiences of individual insects, reflecting on the pleasures bees or butterflies might experience as they flit from bud to bud. Like Thoreau, Muir is entranced by the innumerable insects that endlessly dance in joyous celebration under the gaze of God, and he believes every speck of creation participates in that dance, from the trees over our heads to the microscopic particles under our feet. Only mankind seems divorced from the song of creation, the harmonic pulses that direct the chorus of crickets and the deep rolls of thunder that rumble across the mountains, and Thoreau and Muir in particular share a belief that the exuberant dancing and singing of insects are acts of worship, of reverence for creation and its Creator.

Insects remind Thoreau, Dickinson, and Muir that all members of creation are equally vital to creation and to God; that life, no matter what its form, matters and has a purpose. While Thoreau recognizes this equality in the universal chorus, in the infinite eyes reflecting from the shores of Walden, and in the eyes of the water-skater, Dickinson and Muir are much more direct about their belief that all organisms are equal to mankind. Because of her intimate relationship with the insects and plants in her garden, Dickinson regards the insects she meets as "people" or "citizens" of nature, members of a closely interrelated and interdependent society that inspire her to believe in the dignity and essential purpose of every unique life, deliberately created and fiercely loved by God, no matter how small and seemingly unimportant, reassuring her that her life is meaningful and her spirit is already residing in an earthly Eden or Heaven. Muir expands upon this idea of interrelatedness, earnestly believing that all members of creation, grasshoppers, houseflies, ants, squirrels, microbes, rocks, trees, are "brothers," equal in the eyes of God.

At times, Thoreau, Dickinson, and Muir attempt to imagine how insects might experience their own existence, how they might relate to their environment or even possibly understand their position within it. Dickinson most frequently imagines what it might *be* like to be an insect or another one of Earth's citizens, but Thoreau and Muir also used this technique to further explore the world from an insect point of view. Throughout her poems, Dickinson attempts to discover what the experience of being a bee, a butterfly, a stone, a gnat, a caterpillar, a worm, "a Hay" [J333/F379], a field of grass, or a gust of wind, might be like, what purpose each might offer. Thoreau most consciously and deliberately tries to comprehend what it might be like to be an insect when he stretches himself across the frozen surface of Walden, attempting to imitate the water-skater's experience of gliding along the margin between water and sky. Unsurprisingly, of the three, Muir most easily envisions the possible points of view of an insect when he attempts to envision the flower fields at the foot of the Sierras from a bee's perspective in his elaborate discussion of how California was a paradise when viewed from a bee's perspective.

When I began this project, I thought that an examination of how Thoreau, Dickinson, and Muir took "an insect view of its plain" would focus on how they attempted to adopt the perspective, the point of view, of insects when they engaged in their examination and description of nature, how they would relay what they thought an insect might see from its unique vantage point. Instead, I discovered that in addition to relating to how they literally *looked* at nature, taking "an insect view" encouraged each of these writers to appreciate the evidence of divine order and love written in the book of nature and to understand that even the smallest "particles" of creation are significant and important in the eyes of God.

Textual Abbreviations

B   John Muir, *The Story of My Boyhood and Youth*, in *John Muir: Nature Writings*, ed. William Cronon. New York: Library of America, 1997.

E   Ralph Waldo Emerson, "Nature," in *Essays and Lectures: Nature: Addresses and Lectures/ Essays: First and Second Series/ Representative Men/ English Traits/ The Conduct of Life*. New York: Library of America, 1983.

F   John Muir, *My First Summer in the Sierra*, in *John Muir: Nature Writings*, ed. William Cronon. New York: Library of America, 1997.

G   John Muir, *A Thousand Mile Walk to the Gulf.* 1916. Ed. William Frederic Bade. New York: Mariner Books, 1998.

JM   John Muir, *John of the Mountains: The Unpublished Journals of John Muir*, ed. Linnie Marsh Wolfe. Madison: The University of Wisconsin Press, 1979.

L   Emily Dickinson, *The Letters of Emily Dickinson* in 3 Volumes, ed. Thomas H. Johnson with Theodora Ward. Cambridge: Belknap Press/Harvard University Press, 1955.

MC   John Muir, *The Mountains of California*, in *John Muir: Nature Writings*, ed. William Cronon. New York: Library of America, 1997.

NH   Henry David Thoreau, "Natural History of Massachusetts," in *"A Natural History of Massachusetts," "Wild Apples" and Other Natural History Essays*, ed. William John Rossi. Athens: University of Georgia Press, 2002.

NP   John Muir, *Our National Parks*. 1901. San Francisco: Sierra Club Books, 1991.

W   Henry David Thoreau, *Walden*, in *Walden, Civil Disobedience, and Other Writings*. Third Edition. Ed. William Rossi. Norton Critical Edition. New York: W. W. Norton, 2008.

WW   John Muir, "Wild Wool," in *John Muir: Nature Writings*, ed. William Cronon. New York: Library of America, 1997.

Numeration of Emily Dickinson's Poems

F   Emily Dickinson, *The Poems of Emily Dickinson*, ed. R. W. Franklin. Cambridge: The Belknap Press of Harvard University Press, 1998.

J   Emily Dickinson, *The Complete Poems of Emily Dickinson*, ed. Thomas H. Johnson. Boston: Little, Brown, and Company, 1960.

Introduction — Henry David Thoreau, Emily Dickinson, and John Muir: Interpreting the Language of Nature

In "The Natural History of Massachusetts," the short essay often overshadowed by the more extensive and celebrated *Walden*, Henry David Thoreau declares, "Nature will bear the closest inspection; she inspires us to lay our eye level with the smallest leaf, and take an insect view of its plain" [NH 4]. Thoreau returns many times to the idea of attempting to imagine and view the world as an insect might in both his excursions into nature and his literary efforts, delighted by the beauty, brutality, order, ubiquity, fecundity, and divine presence and will revealed in the insect world. Thoreau was not alone in his enthusiasm and praise for nature's "smallest Citizens" [J1374/F1407], as Emily Dickinson once describes them; indeed, insects became a very popular and at times even fashionable subject of study in the nineteenth century. However, despite the textual prevalence and societal importance of insects in the nineteenth century and an increased contemporary interest in ecocriticism and literary and cultural entomology, the presence of insects in nineteenth-century literature has been largely ignored; this book addresses that gap by examining how insects are featured in the works of Henry David Thoreau, Emily Dickinson, and John Muir.

Thoreau, Dickinson, and Muir perceived that insects offered a unique angle, a rare opportunity to explore and understand the "intensities and subtleties" of the environment surrounding them and their relationship with it.[1] They approach insects through the various lenses of scientific examination, natural history, fiction, theology, and personal experience drawn from their immersion in and fascination with nature, closely observing insects in order to understand their role and function in nature or the stages of their lifecycles, considering their position in and impact on human culture and society, and at times imagining, if only briefly, what the experience, the point of view, of an insect, something tiny and of no consequence, might be like. At some level, each author attempts to "take an insect view of its plain" to investigate the purpose and imagine the experience of the most insignificant, misconstrued, and nonhuman creatures of all: insects. This study explores three interrelated issues connected to their encounters with and explorations of the microscopic and unacknowledged position of insects in nature, encounters informed by their consideration of insects' place and function within their ecosystems and by their interest in the symbolic messages revealed by their observations: first, how insects factor into their growing knowledge about nature and ecology; second, how nature serves as a conduit to or inspiration for spirituality, revealing in its intricate processes the messages of the divine; and third, how insects are important not only for their critical ecological function but also for their symbolic value in suggesting the possibility of a renewed connection and relationship with the natural world and God, either through an awareness of ecological integration, an acknowledgement that all life participates in a joyous celebration of creation and has a right to exist, or a metamorphic process that seeks to unite the physical and spiritual in an attempt to transcend earthly experience.

The cultural bias against insects is a primary reason why so few scholars have investigated the role of insects in culture and more specifically literature. Our modern instinct, when confronted with a fly or ant or cockroach, is usually to smash it, quickly, before running for the can of Raid or dialing the Orkin man. While some insects are considered beautiful or useful, such as butterflies and ladybugs, dragonflies and bees, most insects are regarded as pests to destroy, miniature monsters to despise or fear. Attempting to address our cultural aversions to and prejudices against insects, cultural entomology explores the many ways humans used insects in, for example, religion, art, folklore, or even medicine, asserting that whether we regard them as pests, benefactors, beautiful or exotic curiosities, or even subjects of study, insects are inextricably connected to human culture and experience. Literary entomology, a subdivision of cultural entomology concerned with the treatment of insects in literature, examines how the insect has always served as a very useful device, a convenient symbol. Even though by the nineteenth century there was a wealth of literary, biblical, mythological, artistic, historical, and scientific entomological images and meanings from which writers could select for varying purposes, very few critics have addressed insects in the literature of the period.[2]

An exploration of the critical tenets of ecocriticism introduces several key ways in which previous assumptions about nature and nature writing must be reexamined and redefined that are essential to the subject of this book.[3] First, ecocriticism explores the possibility of changing cultural presuppositions about and attitudes toward nature, challenging the basic premise that nature exists only for human use. Second, ecocriticism attempts to reduce textual human presence and concern and amplify the interests of the nonhuman, proposing a world view that asserts that all of nature has a right to exist and a function to perform that is separate from human interest. Third, by emphasizing the importance of developing new ways of speaking about, relating to, learning from, and interacting with nature, ecocriticism maintains that nature has a presence and a voice that must be acknowledged. By insisting that nature must be seen as more than an object, ecocriticism encourages a relationship with nature that demands sympathy, understanding, and respect for every organism, even insects.

It is first important to recognize that ecocriticism has three central aims, expressed most succinctly by Cheryll Glotfelty in the introduction to *The Ecocriticism Reader*; Glotfelty likens the evolution of ecocriticism, "the study of the relationship between literature and the physical environment," to that of feminism, arguing that Elaine Showalter's "model of the three developmental stages of feminist criticism" can be usefully applied to delineate the principal interests and aims of ecocriticism. The first phase is concerned with how nature is "represented" or imagined in literature, the second revolves around discovering and "rediscover[ing]" literary traditions, and the third examines the symbolic construction of nature in literary discourse. This book contributes to the "fertile, weedy field of ecocriticism" not only by approaching Dickinson and Muir from an ecocritical perspective but also by investigating how Thoreau, Dickinson, and Muir literally and symbolically represent insects, especially in relation to how their awareness of the ecological role of insects influences their understanding of their own position in and relationship with nature.[4]

Most ecocritics agree that an essential element of ecocriticism involves radically changing how we represent, perceive, and approach the environment, believing that without a conscious shift in the way we regard nature and our role in developing and protecting it, an ideology that maintains that the environment is just as important as we are, if not more so, will never develop. Historically, Americans have always been torn between developing natural resources as quickly and inexpensively as possible, without regard to potential environmental impact, and earnestly believing the myth that the great outdoors is just beyond our doorstep, infinite, always within reach. Culturally, "we are superior to nature, contemptuous of it, willing to use it for our slightest whim"; according to Daniel G. Payne, we "assum[e] our resources to be endless" and our world a forgiving, "virtually limitless storehouse where [we] can dispose of waste and alter the landscape with little concern for the ways in which these actions will affect the local or global environment."[5] Nature is a thing to be used, developed, or sold for profit and entertainment; it has no identity or function beyond its usefulness to humankind. Payne observes that even recent conservation efforts are more often concerned with preserving humanity's interests rather than nature's, essentially an anthropocentric, not an eco- or bio-centric point of view.[6]

Whether inspired by a growing concern over global environmental vulnerability or increased ecological awareness of the delicate balance between multiple, interrelated ecosystems, redefining humanity's relationship with the natural has always been of central concern to ecocritics. Lynn White, for example, noted in 1967 that the anthropocentric stance of the Judeo-Christian tradition is partially responsible for current environmental problems, claiming that no change would be possible without "reject[ing] the Christian axiom that nature has no reason for existence save to serve men."[7] Joseph Meeker observed in 1972 that literature "perpetuate[s]" and "defines human relationships" to the natural world and "should be examined carefully and honestly to discover its influence upon human behavior and the natural environment." Calling for a multidisciplinary approach that would "reconcil[e] [literature] with the forms and structures of nature as they are defined by scientific ecologists," he perhaps hoped that this new "literary ecology" would accomplish more than an unmasking of "cultural ideologies that have contributed to the modern ecological crisis."[8] Echoing White, Glen Love maintains that society must "outgrow" its belief in "human dominion" and reject the concept that "the earth exists for our comfort and disposal alone," replacing anthropocentric and egocentric assumptions with eco-conscious models of reality. In addition, he insists that ecocritics must also reorganize literary studies "to redirect human consciousness to a full consideration of its place in a threatened natural world."[9] More recently, Lawrence Buell reiterates the idea that society must discover better ways of dealing with environmental problems, beginning by "finding better ways of imaging nature and humanity's relation to it." Approaching literature from a perspective imbued with concern, respect, and admiration for the environment forces readers to reconsider "assumptions about the nature of representation, reference, metaphor, characterization, personae, and canonicity." Like Glotfelty and Love, he believes that establishing an ecocritical literary canon of environmentally aware texts is an important step in reconfiguring social attitudes toward nature.[10]

Unlike other literary perspectives, which assume the superiority of the human point of view, ecocriticism "negotiates between the human and nonhuman," attempting to diminish the human presence in a text in favor of the nonhuman.[11] As awareness of and interest in ecocriticism grew, critics began to seek out texts that explore the "*nonhuman environment ... as a presence*" that is as much involved with and "*implicated in natural history*" as are humans.[12] In *Reading the Earth: New Directions in the Study of Literature and the Environment*, a collection of essays edited by Michael P. Branch, Rochelle Johnson, Daniel Patterson, and Scott Slovic, ecocriticism is defined as "a move toward a more biocentric world-view, an extension of ethics, a broadening of humans' conception of global community to include nonhuman life forms and the physical environment."[13] In "Surveying the Emergence of Ecocriticism," the Introduction to the *ISLE Reader*, Scott Slovic suggests that examinations of "the explicit treatment of human-non-human relationships" allows for an environmental, ecocentric "reading of any work of literature."[14] Similarly, for Buell, the establishment of the nonhuman as a presence, not a backdrop or setting, and the elevation of the interests of the nonhuman to the level of human interests are essential characteristics of an ecocritical text.[15]

Contrary to traditional outlooks on nature as something to be explored, conquered, settled, developed, landscaped, and thus as something always Othered, an ecocritical perspective affirms that nature "belongs to" itself, has "a what" and a "way of being" quite aside from human interest and manipulation. As Christopher Manes notes in "Nature and Silence," nature is traditionally a "silenced subject" in a culture that privileges human speech as the only true, legitimate language; several critics have in fact compared the evolution of ecocriticism to the emergence of Gender, Racial, and Gay Studies, all of which depend on the recognition and celebration of voices previously silent in mainstream culture.[16] A key step in breaking this silence is recognizing that, like human society and culture, "environment has a history, that it is not simply 'out there' waiting to either be destroyed or preserved." Ecocriticism explores this history, examining the "interdependent communities, integrated systems, and strong connections" in nature, human and nonhuman, in order to find new approaches to existing harmoniously within it.[17]

Recognizing and acknowledging the presence and interests of the nonhuman involves "learning a new language ... even if it puts at risk the privileged discourse of reason — and without a doubt, it does."[18] Even though reasonably we can never expect to understand completely the nonhuman experience no matter how exactly and precisely we attempt to replicate physical and environmental conditions, immerse ourselves into ecosystems, or imagine what it might be like to possess senses and abilities we lack, even the attempt to do so contributes to the formation of a more inclusive world view. Learning this "language" involves not only challenging our linguistic and philosophical approaches to exploring nature but also accepting the possibility that language itself is not an exclusive ability of mankind. Essentially, ecocriticism accepts the possibility that everything in nature — trees, bats, mosses, ponds, dogs, fungi, rocks, insects — has a voice, an individualized point of view, a position and purpose both unique and worthy. Just as the human experience consists of infinite interaction with a multitude of voices, perspectives, and cultures, so does nature's experience, for the natural world is not a static, uniform thing but a living, growing, mutating, evolving process comprised of interdependent yet discrete presences capable of responding to each other. One of the goals of establishing an ecocentric perspective for literature is to recognize, translate, interpret, and somehow relate to these presences within a text, a corollary to continually reestablishing and redefining humanity's relationship with and influence on nature.

Listening to and communicating with nature is certainly not a new idea; as Manes points out, animistic cultures flourished in pre-Christian times, believing that communication with the natural world was not only possible but essential to understanding humanity's place in the cosmic order. Language was not an exclusive prerogative of humanity but a gift granted to all creation. As Christianity asserted the belief that the natural world existed only for the benefit of mankind, the voices of nature were muted. In American society, these muted voices are currently most often depicted in fantasy and children's literature, cartoons and movies, genres generally not taken seriously by reasonable adults and scholars. Except for the literature of naturalism, which displays at best an indifferent nature, unconcerned with and unconnected to human interests, in most literature the environment usually figures only as a backdrop, a symbol or metaphor, a measure of human progress and experience, rarely representative of its own concerns and interests. Even though a handful of researchers have been successfully teaching primates such as apes and bonobo chimpanzees sign language for decades, have already partially decoded the messages embedded in the dancing of bees, and are attempting to crack the language barriers between humans and dolphins and whales, other members of the scientific community still debate whether animals have the ability to express themselves through any form of language, to experience emotions or exhibit emotional responses, or even to feel and respond to pain on some level or in some way commensurate with that of humans. Religiously, literarily, and scientifically, modern culture rejects most forms of communication with nature as meaningless, childish, ridiculous, or impossible — a myth or fairy tale or superstition in a ideological system manifested in anthropocentric Christianity, consumerism, and science, and thus an obstacle which makes it all the more difficult to formulate let alone accept an ecocentric world view.[19]

Our cultural prejudice in favor of anthropocentrism naturally leads to a bias against anthropomorphism; as Jeffrey Moussaieff Masson and Susan McCarthy observe in *When Elephants Weep: The Emotional Lives of Animals*, "[p]lacing humans at the center of all interpretation, observation, and concern ... has led to some of the worst errors in science, whether in astronomy, psychology, or animal behavior." In science especially, anthropomorphism is considered to be a "contagion," a "sin," "a forgetting of the line between subject and object," violating clinical detachment and objectivity by relying on undependable and often emotional "'anecdotal evidence'" rather than "experimental evidence." Field studies and observations are generally believed to be less reliable, more susceptible to the errors of personification and emotional attachment, than studies and experiments conducted in the carefully considered and controlled environment of a laboratory. Masson and McCarthy identify a sexist slant to this reasoning, claiming that some believe that, because more women are drawn to field than to laboratory research, its objectivity is questionable because women are considered more likely to form unacceptable and unreasonable emotional connections to their subjects. Masson and McCarthy also explain that, for many people, the ability to experience emotions and to express those feelings and thoughts in spoken and written language is what sets us apart from and above the rest of creation, assumptions anthropomorphism can at times severely undermine. Accepting that animals share emotional lives and can "communicate information through posture, vocalizations, gestures, and actions both to other animals and to humans who are attentive" and are capable of exhibiting behavior and emotions usually believed to only be found in humans, is an important step toward understanding and redefining our own place in nature.[20]

It is becoming increasingly for difficult for those who believe that language is an exclusive ability of humans to defend their beliefs, thanks to ongoing and increasingly successful research in the fields of language learning and animal research. Some of the most inspiring work in the field of teaching "beings from different worlds [to] communicate in a human language," has been the result of the relationship between the chimpanzee Washoe and Allen and Beatrix Gardner, her first caretakers, and Roger Fouts, arguably her best friend of forty years, the story of which is told in *Next of Kin: My Conversations with Chimpanzees*. Fouts' work with Washoe and other chimpanzees, including Washoe's children, was instrumental in revising scientific understanding about the process of language acquisition in primates, both human and chimpanzee. Within a few years of beginning to learn American Sign Language (ASL), Washoe "was handling longer [word] combinations, Wh-questions, prepositions, and other elements of grammar that were comparable to children in [Roger] Brown's Stages II and III" of language development and progression. Using ASL, Washoe often invented word combinations when she did not know a specific term; she called a swan a "WATER BIRD" and a Brazil nut a "ROCK BERRY," for example. By the time she was five years old, Washoe could accurately use 132 signs and understood many more, and was able to understand and follow directions that depended on an awareness of grammar and context. While working with Washoe and extending his experiences with her to his work with two autistic children, he discovered that there is an incontrovertible link between the development of gestural language and spoken language, later learning those two seemingly very different modes of communication are controlled by the same region of the brain that control precision movement. Fouts' and others' work with autistic children and ASL, strongly influenced by his work with Washoe, revolutionized the way autistic children were approached in terms of language acquisition and socialization by researchers, physicians, teachers, and parents.[21]

After many years of fighting for the rights of Washoe and other chimpanzees and primates victimized by both a scientific and public community unable or unwilling to change research-oriented and environmental practices and standards, Fouts and co-researchers attained funding for the Chimpanzee Human Communication Institute, a safe haven for chimpanzees who might otherwise be trapped in environmentally and emotionally inadequate research facilities. The CHCI is currently the home of three chimpanzees, Loulis, Washoe's adopted son, Tatu, and Dar, and offers a rare opportunity for students of anthropology, language studies, primate studies, and a variety of other fields to interact and communicate with another species. One of CHCI's goals is "to promote quality, humane research on the communication and behavior of the chimpanzees in [their] care," emphasizing both their interest in further exploring the implications of chimpanzees' use of ASL in connection with humanity's development of a spoken language and the ever-increasing importance of incorporating ideals of humane treatment and standards for all animals, especially primates, our closest kin, into the scientific and other research communities. In an interview, Fouts makes it clear that the most important lesson he has learned in his forty year relationship with Washoe is ecocritical in nature, that humanity's "arrogance" and "ignorance," not its superior intellect or capacity for language, is all that divides us from the rest of the natural world: "Washoe has taught me that we are both a part of the natural world we share with all our fellow animals. She has taught me that personhood is something we share, and that personhood goes beyond species classifications. She has taught me that human arrogance is very lethal to our fellow beings on this planet, especially when it is combined with human ignorance. She has taught me that the most profound scientific discoveries are often based on the most humble approach. She has taught me that compassion is one of our dearest traits, and that we should value it above all others, including intelligence. She helped me to realize that if we humans do not embrace and respect our fellow species on this planet, then we stand a good chance of destroying the whole thing."[22] Communicating with another species at a level previously thought impossible and even ridiculous makes even more evident the importance of reimagining and redefining our relationships with and assumptions about "Other" life to acknowledge that emotions such as compassion, humility, and love should be afforded and extended to all life, not just *Homo sapiens*.

Apiarists have long known that bees communicate, but the root elements of their language eluded researchers until well into the twentieth century, and the debate as to whether they actually have a "language" at all is still challenged today. Karl von Frisch was the first to suggest that the elegantly strange "waggle dance" of the bees communicated meaning, that the "runs and turns of the dance were correlated with the distance and direction of the food source from the hive"; in the 1960s, Adrian Wenner and Harald Esch simultaneously discovered that bees "emit faint low-frequency sounds ... that ... might play a critical role in the bees' communication." More recent research conducted by Wolfgang Kirchner and Axel Michelsen have successfully constructed a robotic bee that they manipulate to convey, successfully, using the researchers' understanding of the motions and rhythms of the waggle dance and the role of sound in honeybee communication, the location of a specific food source the bees had never visited. In the course of their studies, they have learned that bees are capable of telling their hive-mates not only the distance and location but also the quality and quantity of a nectar source. In light of the recent mysterious deaths of honeybees and other critical pollinators, called Colony Collapse Disorder, the cause and cure of which continue to elude beekeepers and scientists, further examination of the grammar and limits of the movements and sounds of the waggle dance can only benefit the quest to find a cure. The loss of honeybees and other pollinators will irreparably alter our food choices and supplies, and could very well herald significant and maybe even permanent environmental damage. Albert Einstein claimed "[i]f honey bees become extinct, human society will follow in four years"; while it is easy to consider this statement to be hyperbole, it is clear that the loss of honeybees would quite literally change our approach to food production and consumption as we know it.[23]

Dolphins present a unique opportunity and challenge for researchers of language acquisition and communication; like some primates, they are capable of learning cues and following directions, but they cannot physically duplicate what they learn or what they might want to say, and like bees, they have a language of their own, but we as yet have no effective way of using it for meaningful conversation. Most of the research on dolphin language, which parallels the emergence of primate language studies, emphasizes teaching dolphins to follow directions using a gestural language similar to ASL. Researchers Louis Herman, Douglas Richards, and James Woltz were the first to present "results showing convincingly an animal's ability to process both semantic and syntactic information in interpreting language-like instructions[,] ... considered core components of any human language." They created directional "sentences," using the same subjects, objects, and prepositions in different patterns, and Akeakamai, a bottlenose dolphin, was able to correctly follow directions dependent on both "word meaning and word order.... For example, the sequence of five gestures glossed as *left basket right ball in* asks the dolphin to place the ball on her right into the basket on her left. In contrast, the rearranged sequence *right basket left ball in* means the opposite, 'put the ball on the left into the basket on the right.'" Akeakamai also had an awareness of grammar, as Louis Herman, Stan Kuczaj, and Mark Holder proved in a series of tests that consisted of giving Akeakamai a series of "sentences that violated the syntactic rules of the language or the semantic relations among words.... For example, the researchers compared the dolphin's responses to three similar gestural sequences: *person hoop fetch, person speaker fetch,* and *person speaker hoop*. The first sequence is a proper instruction; it violates no semantic or syntactic rule of the learned language. It directs the dolphin to bring the hoop to the person, which the dolphin does easily. The second sequence is a syntactically correct sequence but is a semantic anomaly inasmuch as it directs the dolphin to take the underwater speaker, firmly attached to the tank wall, to the person. The dolphin typically rejects sequences like this, by not initiating any action. The final sequence is a syntactic anomaly in that there is no sequential structure in the grammar of the language that provides for three object names within a sequence. However, embedded in the four-item anomaly are two semantically and syntactically correct three-item sequences, *person hoop fetch* and *speaker hoop fetch*." Akeakamai, instead of not acting or responding to directions that were anomalous, was able to "process the entire sequence, apparently searching backward and forward for proper grammatical structures as well as proper semantic relationships, until she found something she could act on, or not. This analytic type of sequence processing is part and parcel of sentence processing by human listeners." Akeakamai was also able to process "references to absent objects" and successfully follow directions provided on a television screen in her tank the first time she was ever exposed to a screen. Clearly, dolphins have an extraordinary capacity to learn and process language as we know it, abilities that will become more and more useful as oceanographers and marine biologists search for new ways to explore the ocean both to satisfy curiosity and assess environmental damage.[24]

Interpreting the natural language of the dolphins is the other fascinating aspect of studying dolphins and their relationship with language, and scientists are only beginning to crack the code. Peter Tyack learned that dolphins have, in essence, names, called "signature whistles," and can even reproduce the signature whistles of other dolphins, and will whistle a name apparently to get the attention of an individual in the pod. Researchers are only beginning to translate the cacophony of other noises dolphins make, ranging from "yelps," "pulsed squeaks," and "buzzing clicktrains." Dolphins also have a complicated system of body language, but scientists are still uncertain of the relationship between that body language and their vocalizations. Much still has to be learned about dolphins and their language, but given the new understanding of the evolutionary relationship between dolphins and primates, it is evident, in the words of Herman, that "any demonstration of language-learning competency by dolphins would bear on questions of the origins of human language, shifting the emphasis from the study of precursors in other hominoid species to common convergent characteristics in ape and dolphin that might lead to advanced communicative and cognitive capacities."[25]

Despite these advances, we are a very long way away from having meaningful conversations with anything other than other human beings, which leads to yet another obstacle to accepting the possibility that anything in nature has a voice and identity of its own: the belief that only through *human* experience, perspective, and language can we begin to describe and interpret that which is essentially not human, not Us, but Other. Inasmuch as we can never escape our humanity to experience what it is like to have gills or wings or webbed feet, we can never truly understand what it means, what it is, to be a fish, a bat, a platypus, a dolphin, a bee, a chimpanzee. Limited by our inability to experience, understand, and explain what we perceive beyond the human experience of any event, we can ultimately rely only on imagination to interpret what the individual entities within nature have to say. Human experience, including imagination, is inseparable from language, which inevitably can represent only human values and ethics. Personification of nature is acceptable as long as it reflects human emotion and desire; any attempt to do more than that is merely a retreat into fancy, a "Romantic indulgence."[26]

A small number of scientists, theorists, and critics have attempted to counter the belief that any attempt to imagine the experience of another creature is impossible. For example, biologist Julian Huxley, in his 1961 introduction to Joy Adamson's *Living Free*, proposed "that to imagine oneself into the life of another animal is both scientifically justifiable and productive of knowledge." Thomas Nagel, in his landmark essay, "What Is It Like to Be a Bat?" admits that "[a]t present we are completely unequipped to think about the subjective character of experience without relying on the imagination — without taking up the point of view of the experiential subject." For Nagel, however, this presents an interesting "challenge," not an insurmountable obstacle: "This should be regarded as a challenge to form new concepts and devise a new method — an objective phenomenology not dependent on empathy or the imagination. Though presumably it would not capture everything, its goal would be to describe, at least in part, the subjective character of experiences in a form comprehensible to beings incapable of having those experiences." In "The Bakhtinian Road to Ecological Insight," Michael J. McDowell provides a simple solution to the "pathetic fallacy": he reappropriates it. Instead of "condemn[ing]" language for its inadequacies and inaccuracies, its unavoidable human slant, we should "acknowledge and celebrate" our ability to "inspirit" the natural world with human characteristics and emotions. Of course "every literary attempt to listen to the voices in the landscape ... is ... anthropocentric"; how could it be otherwise? Our unavoidable inability to fully relate to or truly understand something that is Other than us should not prevent or prohibit the attempt to do so. In this light, scientists who attempt to communicate with chimps, bees, and dolphins are making the same leap of faith and imagination as ecocritical writers who are able to "dissolve their egos" and transcend the cultural representations of environment as a silenced subject or commodity. Both have learned how "to enter the private worlds of different entities in the landscape," readjusting and reconsidering their perceptions of science, nature, and language with every encounter. Researchers who seek to teach "beings from different worlds [to] communicate" with us and writers who address "how the mind sees nature, and ... how the mind sees itself" are both essentially attempting to reconcile how the human mind continually translates and reinterprets its relationship to the nonhuman perspectives, viewpoints, and voices they encounter in the landscape, whether literal or literary.[27]

Describing Mikhail Bakhtin's theories as "the literary equivalent of ecology," McDowell explains that "the ideal form to represent reality ... is a dialogical form, one in which multiple voices or points of view interact.... For Bakhtin as for [Charles] Darwin, every creature defines itself and in a real sense becomes a 'self' mentally, spiritually, and physically by its interaction with other beings and things." Within any text, the "interacting voices," both human and nonhuman, are "infinite" and unique. Referring to an essay by Jacob von Uexkull, "A Stroll through the Woods of Animals and Men," which asserts that the sensory abilities of a species help create "bubbles" (Umwelten) of experience unique to that species, McDowell suggests that recreating or "imitat[ing an animal's] Umwelt by confining our sensory perceptions to those of the animal, and imagining the perceptions of those senses in which we're deficient" is one way of skirting the pitfalls of the "pathetic fallacy."[28] While this technique is limited, it is by no means unique or unusual. In fact, we are often asked to imagine ourselves in the experiences of others, to put ourselves in someone else's shoes, as it were, in order to evoke sympathy for and understanding of the dangers and prejudices others endure: organizers of sexual harassment awareness seminars and marriage counselors ask men and women to reverse roles, charitable organizations ask us to imagine our own children suffering from starvation, abuse, or illness, and volunteers interested in working with the blind are often asked to blindfold themselves in a public place in an attempt to learn what it might be like to physically and emotionally negotiate a world dominated and ordered by visual cues and assumptions. By using scientific fact, imagination, observation, intuition, reason, sympathy, and compassion to recreate what it might be like to be another organism, a relationship with nature that equally considers both human and nonhuman experiences and interests begins to develop.

As ecocriticism narrowed the focus of literary study to include the interests and presence of nature and the nonhuman, it became evident that many writers, including Henry David Thoreau, Emily Dickinson, John Muir, Mary Austin, Rachel Carson, John Janovy, Jr., and Annie Dillard, to name a few, were interested in "creat[ing] landscapes in which obscure or overlooked objects become magnified or more densely rendered than they would be in the ordinary experience of them" in order to amplify and explore the nonhuman elements of their environments. Buell begins to address this intricate visualization of the natural world by attributing it to a "sense of accountability ... intensified by a moral or even religious conviction as to the rightness of artistic conception being shaped by what the environment offers it," citing as one example Emerson's idea of correspondence as presented in "Language," which "validated the authority of the inspired creative imagination as the means by which nature's meanings were to be read." Yet Buell seems more satisfied with an answer proposed by Norman Bryson in a paper entitled "Looking at the Overlooked: Four Essays on Still Life Painting," which declares that exaggeration or magnification of the obscure compels "a 'renunciation of normal human priorities' and humbl[es] the self by 'forcing the eye to discover in the trivial base of life intensities and subtleties which are normally ascribed to things of great worth.'" After providing a brief historical and critical overview of the "depiction of trivial objects" and the "grotesque," Buell offers several examples of writers who "[saw] things differently than the average person," because they were "caught up in the quest for environmental literacy."[29]

While the magnification of seemingly insignificant, obscure objects certainly does have the effect of displacing and decentering the reader or viewer, forcing a "renunciation" of Self, a recognition of Otherness even in the trivial, the point of view that is offered for inspection, for translation, is usually ignored. In *Interpretation of Otherness: Literature, Religion, and the American Imagination*, Giles Gunn notes that "modern man tends to view the encounter with 'otherness' ... as a mode of access to possibilities of change and development within the self and the self's relation to whatever is experienced as 'other,'" a perspective that is oriented only to what the human self has to gain from the encounter.[30] By focusing only on the experience and sensation of displacement, by emphasizing the Otherness of nature in relation to human experience, the point of view, the voice, of the inconspicuous and overlooked, briefly risen to the surface of literary discussion, is cast aside. For writers like Thoreau, Dickinson, and Muir, however, encounters with nature do not end with confrontations with the nonhuman; they often begin there.

Thoreau, Dickinson, and Muir repeatedly attempt to cross the boundary between human and nonhuman in order to better understand their own position in and relationship with nature, to explore their spiritual connection to nature, and to recognize the presence and legitimacy of the voices and experiences of nature. Even as they regretfully acknowledge that, ultimately, language can never fully escape itself, never escape imagination as the fundamental way of approaching the experience of the nonhuman, they still search for new ways of comprehending and explaining that experience. As they become more at home in nature, in wildness, as they come to know nature familiarly, personally, intimately, beyond humanity's usual experience of it as commodity or mythic landscape or "symbolic reinforcement of the subservience of disempowered groups," they begin to discern the nearly imperceptible but individual presences within it.[31] By "vacillat[ing] ... between aesthetic celebration and scientific explanation," at times observing, recording, fictionalizing, and imagining objects more "magnified or more densely rendered than ... the ordinary experience of them," they reduce human and elevate nonhuman presence and influence in the environment; this "equilibrium ... results in the prized tension of awareness," a state in which the observer "dissolves" into the landscape, conscious only of the multiple processes of nature.[32]

Thoreau, Dickinson, and Muir were especially interested in dissolving into nature, exploring, mapping, and creating microcosms that acknowledged and somewhat represented those exaggerated glimpses into tiny ecosystems, magnifying their environments as a way to perceive, translate, and comprehend nonhuman experiences. Their deliberate and patient scrutiny of nature, informed and influenced by scientific knowledge and method as well as by imagination and wonder, increases their "awareness" of and respect for the delicate and fragile bonds that unite all life and reinforces their belief in a creation deliberately designed and orchestrated by God. For example, after spending years immersed in the study and practice of botany, in "To be alive — is Power" [J677/F876] Dickinson proclaims that the mere fact of "Existence," the most unpretentious pulse of life, is "Omnipotence — Enough —" [J677/F876] to justify a life with seemingly no "further function —," a perspective and belief that echoes Thoreau's eagerness to adopt an "insect view." Similarly, Muir's botanical studies led him to the idea that he "has only to examine plants to learn the harmony of their relations" because "the Creator in making the pea vine and the locust tree had the same idea in mind" [B 139], an idea that closely resembles Thoreau's revelation that "The Maker of this earth but patented a leaf" [W 207]. For Muir as well as for Thoreau and Dickinson, nature is "essential unity with boundless variety" and offers "glorious traces of the thoughts of God" [B 139] in every petal and leaf, feather and scale. As they fluctuate between "explanation" and "celebration," Thoreau, Dickinson, and Muir realize that the smallest elements of creation, even insects, usually overlooked and underappreciated, have a function, a place, in the divine plan.

At first, this grouping of Thoreau, Dickinson, and Muir may appear to be arbitrary except for their common use of insect imagery, but they also share philosophical, literary, and cultural concerns. Thoreau, Dickinson, and Muir had mutual interests in the relationships between science, culture, and nature, relationships that they were partly able to explore and express through the observed habits and experiences of insects. Sharing the belief that nature was a reflection of God's intention, an idea abandoned and scorned by late-eighteenth and early-nineteenth-century theologians and philosophers and later revisited by many scholars and writers, including the Transcendentalists, they recognized that insects, like every other particle of nature, were lovingly created by God to serve a unique purpose. Each was a writer who deliberately lived, at one time or another, outside of normal cultural contexts, using that distance both to critique society and its values and to uphold the values they found in nature. They shared a strong interest in ecology and the processes of nature, especially in relation to humanity's assumption of superiority to nature and as evidence of divine intention and order. All three constructed elaborate visions of exaggerated landscapes, and they were intrigued and inspired by the insect's place within the microcosms that they were inspired to imagine and create. Thus, as Buell says, they were able in some measure to exceed a mere assigning of "something like human subjectiveness" to the beings they encountered, creating personal, private relationships extending beyond scientific observation.[33] It was their tendency to accept Nature's "invit[ation ...] to lay [their] eye[s] level with the smallest leaf, and take an insect view of its plain" [NH 4] as Thoreau recommends, noticing the insignificant and trivial life surrounding them and appreciating its critical and uncelebrated position in creation, that assisted their achieving intimate connections with nature and establishing their position within it.

An examination of how insects relate to the ways Thoreau, Dickinson, and Muir juxtapose the larger issues of ecological and environmental awareness and faith and spirituality in order to reevaluate and redefine their understanding of and relationship with nature and the divine engenders interesting questions: What is the extent of their knowledge of insects? From what literary, scientific, historical, and cultural perspectives do they write? From which angles do they observe their subjects, and what do they finally learn about the processes of nature, the function of insects, and their connection to human experience and culture from these vantage points? How does the insect — normally considered trivial, insignificant, and repugnant — influence and inform their understanding of the divine purpose they discover in the patterns of nature? Essentially, how do insects help to enhance and redefine their understanding of the natural world and humanity's relationship with it?

Chapter I, "Insects and the Nineteenth Century," provides a social and cultural summary of the position and image of insects in the nineteenth century in order to establish what information and assumptions about insects Thoreau, Dickinson, and Muir very likely shared. By the nineteenth century, according to the *OED*, the term insect was popularly used to denote a wide variety of small creatures, referring to both insects that were zoologically categorized as members of the class Insecta and many other arthropods, invertebrates, and vertebrates, including spiders, centipedes, earthworms, and even frogs. Because of their education in natural sciences, Thoreau, Dickinson, and Muir would have been aware of the scientific characteristics of the class Insecta, but, like other scholars of their time, would have used the word insect less formally. Interest in entomology blossomed in the early half of the century; building on René Antoine Reaumur's belief that "insects deserved to be studied for their own sake, as a matter of pure scientific interest, rather than because of their importance to agriculture," and Carl Linnæus' "seven great insect orders," early nineteenth-century entomologists competed with European natural scientists to discover and catalogue new species. By 1842, the first organization devoted to the field of entomology, the Entomological Society of Pennsylvania Insects, was founded, dedicating itself to "the improvement of insect systematics rather than ... displaying insects as objects of beauty or demonstrating the habits of injurious species."[34] Several entomological texts were already widely available, including William Kirby and William Spence's *Introduction to Entomology*, to which Thoreau specifically refers in *Walden*; advances in printing technology led to volumes devoted to insect classification and imagery, some featuring a technique that combined illustrated bodies with actual wing specimens, antennae, and other preserved body parts pressed directly into the pages.[35] As entomology expanded into a legitimate science, it became a profession rather than a gentleman's hobby, and practical applications, namely, the benefits to agriculture, were explored more thoroughly. By the 1850s, farmers were clamoring for "effective solutions" to insect-related problems, asking for more information about "the identification, habits, and life histories of injurious insects," but they did not achieve any real control over insect infestations until arsenic insecticides were introduced in the 1870s.[36]

Scientific curiosity about insects naturally blended with mainstream interests; for example, in the fashion industry, by 1840, fabrics imported from India embellished with beetle wings were popular; by 1860, hats embellished with preserved beetles, butterflies, hummingbirds, mosses, bird nests, and small animals were introduced in Paris; and by 1880, ladies of fashion were adorning themselves with iridescent, colorful beetles ensnared alive in delicate gold cages attached to chains and brooches.[37] Dickinson certainly would have been aware of these trends. Stephen Nissenbaum reports that barley sugar molds of beetles and other insects, secreted in Christmas stockings, were particularly coveted by children in the 1840s and '50s.[38] Bug collecting was a popular hobby throughout the century, and amateur and professional collectors alike approached their expeditions as safaris on a diminutive scale, stalking their prey and proudly mounting specimens in cabinets and wall displays; by the latter half of the century, entomology had become a legitimate and somewhat profitable profession. Clearly, the nineteenth-century attitude toward insects in many ways was very different from current thoughts and therefore must be considered when discussing the entomological knowledge Thoreau, Dickinson, and Muir might have shared.

Chapter II, "'With Microscopic Eye': Thoreau's Insect Perspective," focuses on insects in Thoreau's "Natural History of Massachusetts,"

Walden, and selected sections from his *Journal*. Thoreau refers to insects and entomology several times in "Natural History of Massachusetts," asserting that "an insect view" offers an ideal vantage point, both literally and symbolically, for the close observation of nature. This idea is also very evident in *Walden* and the *Journal*; several critical points in *Walden* concern insects, the most famous of which is certainly the popular "The Battle of the Ants," and the *Journal* is riddled with references to insects and entomological images. Even though very few critics address the insect imagery directly, several have provided useful foundations from which to view the microcosmic universes Thoreau creates. The "The Battle of the Ants" appears most prominently in critical discussion and a few authors discuss the mysterious insect in the "Conclusion" chapter of *Walden* or the cosmic mosquito in "Where I Lived, and What I Lived For," but most of the other insects in *Walden* are completely ignored; similarly, the importance of, for example, crickets or cocoons in the *Journal* has interested a few scholars, but how these images relate and compare to Thoreau's overall use of insects has not attracted much critical attention.[39] Comparatively, most insect references appear to be textually insignificant, rhetorical caterpillars inching across the pages; but others, especially the choir of crickets, the swarms of innumerable insects, the heroic ants, the noble, musical mosquito, the water-skaters skittering across the ripples of Walden Pond, the ova and chrysalides of burgeoning insect life, and the patient, magnificent bug in "Conclusion," clearly invite more serious consideration.

This chapter establishes and examines the presence and voice of the insect in the works of Thoreau in relation to his ecological awareness, his spiritual interests, and his belief in the possibility of transcendence. My discussion of Thoreau's interest in and examination of insects begins with his exploration of the participation of the crickets in what he describes as a universal "quire" orchestrated by God's hand, a chorus that some can perceive but few aspire to join. Insects reinforce for Thoreau his belief that "Joy is the condition of life" [NH 4], and he finds examples of this natural exuberance and ecstatic praise in the song of crickets, the buzz of a mosquito, and the swarms of insects so numerous that they can afford to be sacrificed. He becomes especially entranced by the water-skaters that skim along the surface of Walden, existing in a perfect space, balanced between earth and heaven, water and sky, at one point so interested in their point of view and perspective that he slides his body onto the frozen surface of Walden, hoping somehow to get closer to their experience, their point of view. As he develops the image of Walden as the eye of the world, the eye of God, he depends on the circles of the water-skaters and the eyes reflected in the concentric waves to assist his navigation across the surface. The process of metamorphosis also intrigues Thoreau, and he at times shifts his focus from the "myriads of life" surrounding him to the solitary experience of metamorphosis, discovering in the miraculous transformations of larvae to insect humanity's potential to transcend a common, grubbish existence and develop a new understanding of the language of the universe and the Creator.

Insect imagery in the poems of Emily Dickinson is the focus of the third chapter, "'A Minor Nation': Emily Dickinson and the Insects' Society." Despite her continual use of vivid and precise images of nature, critics have only recently begun to examine Dickinson's work in light of current ecocritical concerns, and only a handful of them have explored the insects featured in her poetry.[40] Dickinson is one of the few authors to surpass Thoreau in the number of insects that creep across her pages. Bees, butterflies, spiders, and crickets appear more often in her poems than people, and, like Thoreau and Muir, she continually immerses herself in their landscape and culture. Individually, each insect might not appear to be particularly important within a poem, but collectively, as images to which Dickinson repeatedly turns, they acquire unmistakable textual significance.

This chapter first explains that Dickinson's understanding of the ecological significance of insects enhances her belief in a divinely ordered creation in which every organism matters, no matter how small or insignificant it may appear to be, and then moves on to a discussion of Dickinson's literal and symbolic interest in metamorphosis. Dickinson's approach to insects mirrors her approach to her garden; as she gains knowledge about the plants in her garden through her academic and personal readings, friendships with natural historians and other scholars, and personal observations and experiments, she also begins to understand the complex network and fragile bonds which exist between plants and insects. For Dickinson, her flowers and the insects that live among them are individual members of a vital community, each individual bee or butterfly having an essential role in the life cycle of specific plants that depend upon them for survival. She often endeavored to visualize herself as another being in creation, attempting to discern the experience and purpose of being a blade of grass, a gnat, or a butterfly. Like Thoreau, Dickinson heard a universal chorus of crickets in the grass which has the power to set the sun, and like Muir, she hears the eternal music echoing in the sighs of the wind. Her efforts to develop both a microscopic vision that includes the insect point of view and a macroscopic gaze that encompasses the landscape and all living within it also led her to discover the divine intention behind the intricate balances that unite every member of creation. Her respect for the power of life represented in her garden allows her to see in the processes of nature and metamorphosis the possibility of change and transformation, of renewal and resurrection, which eases her uncertainties about her own purpose and potential, alleviates her fear of death, and leads to a reaffirmation of her faith in God.

John Muir, the central figure of the fourth chapter, "John Muir: 'Translating Nature's Book,'" has appeared most prominently in critical history as an environmentalist, naturalist, and children's writer; but increasing interest in nature writing and the establishment of an ecocritical literary canon has encouraged critics to approach Muir's work as more than travel journals and tales for children. Despite the significant chronological gap between them, the connections between Emerson, Thoreau, and Muir are becoming more obvious, and it is important to recognize that, while Muir did not begin publishing his journals until later in the century, primarily as an attempt to increase support for his preservationist interests, the experiences he writes about took place much earlier.[41] Muir is particularly adept at adopting perspectives that were not his own; perhaps more than any other writer of the late nineteenth and early twentieth centuries, he is able to readjust his vision in an effort to imagine what he believes nature might see and experience. For Muir, as Buell states, speaking of nonhuman creatures as "people ... was no metaphor,"[42] for, perhaps even more than Thoreau and Dickinson, he genuinely believed in the legitimacy and significance of every unique voice nature had to offer. *My First Summer in the Sierra*, like *Walden*, swarms with insects, some relatively unimportant, many textually significant; the same is true of *Our National Parks, The Mountains of California, A Thousand Mile Walk to the Gulf*, and the collection of journal entries compiled by Linnie Marsh Wolfe in *John of the Mountains*. However, no one has written about Muir's interests in and relationships with insects, even though he creates intensely intimate relationships with every living thing he encounters — woodchucks, trees, grasshoppers, flowers, flies, squirrels, and bees.

Like that of Thoreau and Dickinson, Muir's ecological awareness leads him to find in nature evidence of divine purpose and language. Rather than intentionally developing a microscopic vision, as Thoreau and Dickinson at times attempt to do, Muir first discovers the intentions of God inscribed upon the landscape, etched into mountains and carried on the wind to the trees. His embracing of what Michael P. Cohen has called a "God's eye view," which combines both macroscopic and microscopic angles of perception, allows him to understand that every particle of creation is necessary, a letter in God's divine text, including some of the very smallest citizens of nature, insects.[43] Swarms of bees and other insects instruct Muir, as they do Thoreau, that the "condition" of life is spontaneous, pure "joy" [NH 4]. Like Thoreau and Dickinson, Muir begins to regard insects as evidence of God's plan for universal order and harmony, even considering them to be family, brothers and sisters united with mankind in the common experience of being. Muir most consciously adopts an insect's point of view when he describes the vast flowering plains of California from the perspective of the bees that inhabit it, and he directly addresses and converses with several insects throughout his journals. Muir's fascination with the art of beekeeping and bee culture allows him to believe that a beneficial, reciprocal relationship between humanity and other members of creation might be possible.

Thoreau, Dickinson, and Muir approach insects from several distinct angles and perspectives, observing the world from the obscure angle of the insect on a leaf as Thoreau believes Nature invites us to do and using those images, experiences, and viewpoints to get closer to a more inclusive ecological understanding of nature, to support their belief in a creation divinely ordered and maintained, and to redefine their own position in and relationship with nature. As they explore the function and position of insects in nature, Thoreau, Dickinson, and Muir learn how to read the processes of and the patterns within nature, how to recognize the divine purpose inherent in every speck of creation, and how to translate the language of God that is transcribed in the songs of crickets, the ripples of water-skaters on a pond's surface, the flight of the bees, and the metamorphosis of the butterflies. In addition to acknowledging and discussing insects from an ecocritical perspective and adding to the developing field of literary entomology, an examination of how Thoreau, Dickinson, and Muir portray insects using the lenses of natural history, science, observation, and imagination in order to reevaluate and reflect upon ecology, spirituality, and human culture will contribute to a more comprehensive understanding of how they related to nature and defined their positions within it.

I

Insects and the Nineteenth Century

Cultural Entomology and the Nineteenth Century

Insects have had more influence on the development of human culture than most people realize. In "Cultural Entomology," C. L. Hogue notes that "entomology has long been concerned with survival (economic or applied entomology) and scientific study (academic entomology)"; for example, American entomologists initially focused on expanding and improving European classification systems and exploring emerging discoveries in agricultural entomology. Cultural entomology, "the branch of investigation that addresses the influence of insects (and other terrestrial Arthropoda, including arachnids, myriapods, etc.) in literature, language, music, the arts, interpretive history, religion, and recreation has only recently been recognized as a distinct field."[1] Entomology is no longer the exclusive realm of the scientific community, and many scholars, influenced by an increasing concern about ecological issues, are rediscovering that insects play a vital role in the humanities as well as in the sciences.

Literary entomological studies have been largely ignored despite the prominent appearance of insects in literature. Even though critical ecological issues have inspired critics to explore more widely the natural world, utilizing methods that invite natural perspectives and topics, very few scholars have elected to explore literary entomology. The absence of entomology as a focus in nineteenth-century American literary research is even more surprising, considering the primary importance nature has during that time period. *Insect Lives: Stories of Mystery and Romance from a Hidden World*, edited by Erich Hoyt and Ted Schultz, an anthology of entomological literature, includes brief excerpts from classic nature writers, poets, and scientists, such as Henry David Thoreau, Aristotle, William Wordsworth,

William Cowper, Edward O. Wilson, Charles Darwin, and Jean-Henri Fabre, but the overall purpose of the text is not to be a definitive collection of insects in literature; rather, the editors hope their book will "give enlightening pause to the steppers, swatters, and screamers who live in fear or dread of six legs" and "bring insects entertainingly to light."[2] Another book, *The Poetics of the Hive: The Insect Metaphor in Literature*, by Christopher Hollingsworth, focuses on the hive as a literary metaphor, but, while it extends discussion at times to literary insects other than the bee, it only briefly addresses nineteenth-century nature writers. Eric C. Brown's *Insect Poetics*, the first anthology of critical literary entomology, includes only one essay devoted to the insects in nineteenth-century literature: "Imperfect States: Thoreau, Melville, and the 'Insectivorous Fate'" by Tony McGowan.

Multiple influences helped shape Thoreau, Dickinson, and Muir's understanding, treatment, and depiction of insects in their work. The science of entomology and American nature writing evolved simultaneously and, though Hogue claims that a "narrative history of the science of entomology is not part of cultural entomology," an examination of entomology as a science and profession is relevant to any discussion of insects and the nature writing of the period. While Thoreau and Dickinson shared an academic interest in entomological discoveries and all three writers were actively interested in gardening and horticulture, scientific and practical knowledge comprised only a small portion of what they would have known about insects. In order to paint a cultural portrait of insects in the nineteenth century in relation to what entomological knowledge and interests Thoreau, Dickinson, and Muir may have had individually or collectively, both as members of the general population and as experienced observers and recorders of nature, I will focus on several areas of cultural entomology that I believe both to have important relevance to each of them as well a significant societal impact: the development of entomology as a science, such as innovations in apiculture and agriculture, especially in connection to controlling and preventing insect infestations; the medical applications of insects, both folkloric and scientific; the role of insects in folklore and superstition; the use of insects in fashion and art; the interest in insects as food; the presence of insects in the Bible; and the representation of insects in literature.

In a discussion about the possible influences and attitudes toward insects shared by Thoreau, Dickinson, and Muir, an overview of the growth of entomology from an often-belittled hobby to a legitimate science and profession is particularly important. As a student, friend, and frequent correspondent of Thaddeus William Harris and an accomplished specimen hunter, Thoreau was directly involved in the efforts of early entomologists to discover and classify new species, and the observations of his scientifically-oriented eyes, trained to notice and record the smallest details of a butterfly wing or ants' nest, are often the focus of passages in the *Journals* and in *Walden*. Like Thoreau, Dickinson would have had passing knowledge about entomological developments and discoveries because of her academic interests in botany and horticulture; she certainly gleaned additional information from the multiple journals and magazines to which her family subscribed as well as from her relationship with Thomas Wentworth Higginson, a prominent entomologist in his own right. Several of her poems rely on imagery connected to the practice of mounting, or pinning, specimens or are informed by her knowledge of the process of metamorphosis. While Muir cannot be said to have a strong interest in the development of entomology as a science, except in relation to bees, he was a student of botany and natural history and would have been curious about the applications of entomological knowledge to geographical development and agriculture, two subjects that passionately interested him.

Apiculture is a branch of entomology that would have appealed to all three writers, especially to Dickinson and Muir. Thoreau only makes passing mention of bees in his *Journal* and *Walden*, but he has been shown to have some basic knowledge of beekeeping practices. Similarly, it is possible to conjecture, as Tammy Horn does, that Dickinson would have been familiar with advances in beekeeping because of her reading material and the knowledge she had about gardening and pollination.[3] Muir had a lifelong interest in bees and apiculture and was fascinated by the idea that bees could represent a facet of agriculture that worked in harmony with the patterns of nature rather than against them, thanks to the advances of modern beekeeping that allowed the preservation of bees as well as the efficient extraction of large quantities of honey.

The constant possibility of the eradication of essential crops because of insect infestations was a very real fear for most Americans throughout the century, and Thoreau, Dickinson, and Muir certainly would have at least read about incidents of widespread crop destruction in newspapers even if they never were affected directly by them. Dickinson and Muir especially would have been likely to keep current with discoveries and advances connected to agricultural insect control because of their personal investments in gardening and farming. Farmers and laypeople may have had little regard for the laborious classification and collection efforts undertaken by early entomologists, but they were greatly interested in learning how to identify and eliminate pests that could destroy months of work in moments. By mid-century, professional entomologists were conveying information on pest control to farmers in agricultural publications, often in an effort to combat "folk wisdom" and other inaccurate information, and the introduction of Paris green in 1867 marked the beginning of effective and widespread pesticide use, the safety of which was initially debated by farmers and researchers but quickly accepted.[4] In contrast, Muir expresses more interest in and distress over the demise of thousands of bee colonies during a California drought [MC 352], unnecessary deaths that easily could have been prevented, than he ever does for human victims of insect plagues or drought.

While Thoreau, Dickinson, and Muir never directly express interest in the medicinal applications of insects, I believe that their mutual interests in cultural history and scientific developments would have exposed them to many of the historical and contemporary uses of insects in the pursuit of healing. The medical entomological knowledge of the nineteenth century would have been a mishmash of old wives' tales, native wisdom, and documented scientific treatments derived from that knowledge. Just as Thoreau, Dickinson, and Muir would have been familiar with the various folkloric beliefs regarding the healing properties of insects, they would have known about the popular practice of bloodletting using leeches for various disorders. Given their avid and varied reading habits, it is also plausible that they had heard of the healing attributes of maggots while reading accounts of the Civil War.

The superstitions and folkloric beliefs about insects so scorned and ridiculed by scientists and entomologists nevertheless played a very significant role in how many Americans regarded insects. While most of these customs seem ludicrous today, especially in light of the advances and discoveries of modern science, even some twenty-first century Americans playfully believe in superstitions and folk wisdom, especially in relation to agriculture. Novice gardeners are still advised to plant corn when oak leaves are the size of squirrels' ears, and to consult the *Farmers' Almanac* to determine when during the lunar cycle to plant seeds and clippings, prune rosebushes and fruit trees, and harvest and store crops. Every fall, children in southwestern Pennsylvania and surrounding areas point to the stripes on woolly bear caterpillars to predict the length and severity of the upcoming winter, and in many households across the country, killing a spider is believed to bring as much bad luck as does breaking a mirror.[5] Even if Thoreau, Dickinson, and Muir disregarded these beliefs, they were more than likely familiar with them, hearing them at the knees of parents or grandparents or in conversations with other gardeners and farmers. Thoreau, for example, refers to the practice of beating pans to summon the bees from the fields in *Walden* [W 133], Dickinson once alludes to the custom of informing bees of their owner's death so they won't abandon the hive [J50/F40], and Muir studies and refutes the common belief that bees fly in a "bee-line," a straight line leading directly to the hive [B 114].

As well as providing boundless inspiration for many artists, insects were instrumental in several industries related to fashion and art. The mysteries of the silkworm were revealed to the West, several dyes were produced from insects, and shellac, a product made from the secretion of the lac insect, was used by jewelers, carpenters, and other crafters. In addition to supplying essential ingredients for many valuable and essential products utilized by many industries, in the latter half of the century even the preserved bodies of insects and other small critters were incorporated into fashion trends popular in both Europe and America. The role insects played in fashion was probably most familiar to Dickinson, but it is unlikely that Thoreau and Muir would have been unaware of the fads involving insects. Thoreau could not have failed to notice hats embellished with the bodies of small birds, bugs, and mammals, stuffed or otherwise preserved; even though he never discusses this specifically, his criticism of the world of fashion and its subscribers presented in the "Economy" chapter of *Walden* reveals that he is knowledgeable about the trends around him. Dickinson refers to this practice in one of her poems, describing a butterfly attached to her hat [J70/F117], and she later uses the image of the fashionable butterfly struggling to survive in a society that will ultimately attempt to pin her as if she is merely another specimen [J354/F610]. Muir might not have noticed specific examples of insects in fashion, but in newspapers and magazines he likely would have come across descriptions of iridescent insect jewelry made from Brazilian beetles or of scarab jewelry unearthed in archeological digs.

In many cultures, insects are an abundant and nutritional food source, an idea that is most likely repulsive to modern appetites. While most nineteenth-century Americans would have likely agreed with this opinion, as the work of those venturing into the unexplored wilds of the world became available, interested readers would have been exposed to the idea that other cultures did rely on insects as food. In fact, in 1885, Vincent M. Hold, "fully conscious of the difficulty of battling against a long-existing and deep-rooted public prejudice," published *Why Not Eat Insects*, a book that praises the benefits of insect consumption and even provides recipes.[6] While this book was published after the deaths of Thoreau and Dickinson and there is no reason to believe that Muir ever read it, it is evident that the concept of insects as food was a topic of discussion within their culture even though it was not widely accepted or practiced.

The insect imagery presented in the Bible would have been very familiar to Thoreau, Dickinson, and Muir. Thoreau and Dickinson often allude to Biblical passages, and Muir was said to have memorized the Bible by age twelve. They would have understood that insect swarms could serve as the armies of God, as William Carpenter describes in *Scripture Natural History*, an idea reinforced in the minds of many Americans by the insect plagues, especially those of locusts that methodically ravished farm after farm. The admiration of the delicate beauty of insects that inspires Carpenter to explore his subject was shared by all three writers, who found in the simple perfection of insects evidence of God's design and power. Each writer comes to regard insects as important members in God's society, rejecting conventional beliefs in a chain of being that believes man to be superior in favor of a world view that recognizes that insects were deliberately and carefully created to fulfill a purpose ordained by God.

Thoreau, Dickinson, and Muir also would have been familiar with some of the many insects that appear in literature. Thoreau makes several classical references in *Walden*, two of which revolve around insects. The first appears in his depiction of his heroic, "Homeric" mosquito, which brings celestial music to him in the morning, and the second appears in his extended description of the battle of the ants, in which he refers to the myth of the Myrmidons. Dickinson received an extensive literary education and was known to have read many classical authors as well as Shakespeare, Donne, Milton, and even Thoreau. Like Thoreau and Dickinson, Muir was well-read; he would have been at least somewhat familiar with many literary classics as well as the work of his contemporaries, including Thoreau. All three authors were likely familiar with the literary history of the bees that Christopher Hollingsworth narrates in *The Poetics of the Hive*, and almost certainly they were familiar with most of the insect references in Shakespeare and Milton. While these writers might not have read all of the texts discussed in this section, the selections offered represent the variety with which insects were treated in canonical literature.

The Growth of American Entomology

An invaluable resource to any entomological scholar, W. Connor Sorenson's *Brethren of the Net: American Entomology, 1840–1880* offers an extensive overview of the development of entomology as both a science and a cultural interest. Sorenson observes that the origin of modern entomology begins in the seventeenth century, when microscopes were first used to assist in the daunting task of dissecting and classifying insects. Some scientists were already attempting to improve crop pollination and eradicate insect pests. By the mid-eighteenth century, many branches of natural study, including botany, ornithology, and entomology, "enjoyed an exciting period of discovery, expansion, and analysis." The "first self-conscious community of entomologists" revolved around Rene Antoine Reaumur, who "insisted that insects deserved to be studied for their own sake, ... rather than because of their importance to agriculture or their relevance to anatomical questions." By the late eighteenth century, Carl Linnæus' *Systema Naturæ* introduced a system of insect classification, seven insect orders based on "wing structure," that "greatly simplified" the study of entomology; later generations of entomologists modeled their classification system on his, relying on several characteristics, not only wings, to identify and classify specimens.[7]

By the early nineteenth century, American entomologists were actively engaged in collecting and classifying uniquely American insects. Several scientists felt that they needed to "defend" native American specimens against views that they were merely "degenerate Old World species," while others lamented the unavailability of printed material from Europe, the lack of publishing opportunities in America, and the impossibility of accessing the extensive specimen collections in Europe. While there was certainly interest in new entomological discoveries, there was very little financial incentive for entomological research that was not associated with agriculture. Entomology initially was "regarded at best as a harmless diversion and at worst as an indication of serious mental imbalance," a hobby pursued by "the idle, the effete, or foppish" or an exercise to amuse women or children; by mid-century, however, as interest in other areas of natural history grew and the practical agricultural applications of entomological research became more widely available, entomology became more accepted as a legitimate science or profession.[8]

Despite the difficulties involved in entomological research in America, however, several American naturalists were able to focus exclusively on entomology as their primary field of study. John Abbot, one of the first important American entomologists, produced a collection of over three thousand drawings depicting insects in various stages of maturity, personally raising generations of insects and keeping accurate records of their growth and development. A two-volume collection of his butterfly illustrations was published in 1797, and his images were also featured in Alexander Wilson's *American Ornithology* from 1808 to 1814. Another American naturalist, William D. Peck, published several articles about destructive insects before he became "the first professor of natural history and keeper of the botanical garden at Harvard" in 1805; in preparation for this position, he formed many contacts with prominent European natural historians, and even sent several insect specimens to William Kirby. The earliest work about insects published in America was written by Frederick Valentine Melsheimer, who presented a *Catalogue of the Insects of Pennsylvania* in 1806. Thomas Say, a founder of Philadelphia's Academy of Natural Sciences, published the three-volume *American Entomology; or, Descriptions of the Insects of North America* in 1824, 1825, and 1828, texts that described over a thousand species that had never before been recorded. John Eaton LeConte, interested especially in butterflies, co-authored two books with influential French lepidopterists between 1825 and 1839. One of America's most influential agricultural entomologists, Thaddeus William Harris, a medical doctor and Harvard librarian, had an extensive insect collection; he focused on listing native Massachusetts species and their influences, positive and negative, on agriculture, publishing his *Report on the Insects of Massachusetts, Injurious to Vegetation*, the first American text to emphasize agricultural entomology rather than classification, in 1841. Harris was a regular correspondent of Henry David Thoreau, who often sent him specimens that he could not identify, and a scientist much admired and respected by Higginson, especially because of his entomological interests.[9]

By the 1840s, this first generation of American entomologists began to recognize that the successful study of entomology required the establishment of formal organizations and institutes devoted exclusively to its study. Sorenson identifies three distinct circumstances that more than likely prompted scientists across the nation to join together professionally. First, just as entomology as a science was gaining legitimacy as a field of study in America, several prominent entomologists "were no longer active": Thomas Say had died in 1834, LeConte never recovered from a "physical collapse," and Harris lost the Chair of Natural History at Harvard to botanist Asa Gray, denying him a critical and influential position in the development of natural history as a field. It became evident that if American entomology were to survive, the remaining American entomologists must work together. Second, "rapid improvement[s] in transportation and communication" allowed scientists to share observations and specimens more easily than ever before, thereby prompting both new discoveries and new jealousies. Entomologists who previously sought to identify new species were learning that several other scientists had also "discovered" those species, thus making more obvious than ever before the need to develop national entomological journals for checking, establishing, and sharing known data. Third, the nationwide attempt to separate American cultural identity from its European roots touched even entomological pursuits, as American naturalists struggled to surpass European scientists and establish American scientific and cultural independence.[10]

While entomologists in the first half of the nineteenth century emphasized the importance of classifying and identifying American specimens and legitimizing American entomological discoveries and methods, entomologists in the second half of the century focused on expanding exiting personal collections and establishing institutions to support and finance entomological research. As the exploration of America increased, so did the exploration of America's insects, especially as agricultural interest in entomology grew. By the 1860s, the stereotypical image of the "eccentric 'bug-hunter'" brandishing a large net was commonplace as more natural historians became professional insect collectors, lured by the high prices both private collectors and institutions paid for unique specimens; by 1870, there were approximately 800 self-described entomologists practicing and collecting in the United States, supported by collectors, institutions, government expeditions, private benefactors, and agriculturalists. As collections grew, collectors perfected methods of storing and preserving specimens, and large collections required several curators to maintain them. By the 1880s, the Smithsonian Institution housed what was believed to be the "largest general collection [of insect specimens] in the country." The teaching of entomology as a profession also flourished in the latter half of the nineteenth century, beginning with W. D. Peck's classes at Harvard; as the need for entomological education and research became more evident to farmers and educators alike, funding became more available, and other colleges began to incorporate entomology into their curricula, including the Michigan Agricultural College, the University of Illinois, and the Kansas State Agricultural College. The first formal entomology textbook, *An Introduction to Entomology*, written by John Henry Comstock, an informal protégé of

Harris, was published in 1876, further evidence of the growing interest in and importance of entomology as an academic subject.[11]

The development of institutions to support entomological study and house collections was certainly important to the evolution of entomology as a science, but the financial investment of agriculturalists was perhaps even more critical. By the latter half of the century, agricultural research dominated the field of entomology. One explanation for the attention given to agricultural entomology is that it was dominated by American discoveries and innovations, emerging "primarily as a North American institution rather than as an extension of European science." Another reason for the popularity of agricultural entomology is that it was considered to be more useful than entomology for classification and identification purposes because of its importance to crop production and protection, and consequently it received more funding than other areas of entomological research. As agriculturalists attempted to increase production through "expansion" and "mechanization" while reducing production costs, it became evident that counteracting the damage insects inflicted on crops and profits might be possible if more entomological research focused on insect pests and methods of preventing or destroying infestations.[12]

By the latter half of the century, there was a clear separation between agricultural and nonagricultural entomologists, as seen by the creation of the American Association of Agricultural Entomologists in 1889, although earlier entomologists, including Harris, certainly explored agricultural applications of entomology. Rather than focusing on classification as a primary goal, agricultural entomologists defined their mission as "assisting farmers and horticulturists," which they attempted to do by refining classification methods for known insect pests. Instead of focusing only on adult insects, agricultural entomologists detailed the entire life cycle of injurious insects and explored creative new solutions to insect problems. As farms grew too large to employ traditional methods of protecting crops against insects, which often involved plucking insects by hand or constructing barriers around individual plants, entomologists were charged with finding other ways of eradicating insects. With the growth of agricultural entomology as an independent field of study, American farmers began to expect that entomologists could provide the answers to their ever-growing insect problems.[13]

Agricultural entomologists were never able to offer any absolute control over insect pests, and their advice generally fell into four categories. First, entomologists were quick to point out that natural methods of control, such as predator insects and birds, should not be interfered with and, if possible, should be introduced into environments that required insect control, not foreseeing the struggle for survival that many native species would face when competing with introduced species. Second, traditional cultivation methods, such as field and crop rotation, the burning of infested crops, and various fertilization techniques, were also studied and recommended by entomologists. Third, because mechanical means were often impossible or impractical for the average farmer to implement, hand picking of pests was recommended whenever possible. Finally, entomologists began to explore methods of chemically controlling insect populations, eventually leading to modern dependence on pesticides.[14]

American Apiculture

Although the study of entomology was limited to a handful of natural scientists, the art of keeping bees appealed to the general population. Honeybees were introduced into the American landscape as early as 1620 and by the nineteenth century a wealth of information was available about the raising and maintaining of beehives, practices which had remained relatively unchanged for centuries. The pervasive use of figurative language revolving around bee and beekeeping imagery, such as metaphors linking beehives to order, discipline, and industry, drones to perpetual laziness, and swarming to the colonization of America, further testifies to their cultural significance. As Tammy Horn observes in *Bees in America: How the Honey Bee Shaped a Nation*, the leaders in Jamestown and Plymouth colonies "used the beehive metaphor to rally colonists' spirits" after devastating losses, "realizing that men needed structure and activity if they were going to survive." During the Revolutionary period, Hector St. John Crèvecoeur envisioned America as "an industrious hive," images of bee skeps appeared on currency, and Pennsylvania "adopted the bee as its symbol of thrift and industry." Honeybees spread across the country rapidly, either by swarming or being transported by settlers, who designed small carts to pull hives behind their wagons.[15]

Like many other branches of natural science, beekeeping benefited greatly from new scientific discoveries based on refined observational techniques. Before 1851, skep beehives woven from straw and shaped like bells were common and those skilled in their construction were highly valued, if not highly paid; others kept bees in logs or "bee gums." Some beekeepers had to resort to killing their bees with sulfur to harvest honey, and had to develop extreme methods of treating American foulbrood (a spore which destroys bee larvae) and wax moths (which eat through wax cells), burning infected hives to control the spread of these and other problems that threatened collective hive health. Beekeeping had the potential to be profitable but wasn't very reliable; for example, by 1771, Philadelphia had produced almost 30,000 pounds of beeswax, but by the early nineteenth century, a majority of hives had been ravaged by wax moths, and eighty percent of the hives in Boston were destroyed by 1808 because of these threats. Beekeeping, like every other agricultural pursuit in the new world, was entirely dependent upon environmental conditions in order to flourish, and hive vulnerability to predator insects and disease was one of the leading causes of honey crop failure.[16]

Beekeeping was forever changed in 1851, when Lorenzo Langstroth, a skilled observer of his bees, designed a revolutionary "box hive" that featured movable frames and incorporated what is now known as "bee space" into the design so that bees would not anchor the frames to the outer hive box with wax. His design very quickly replaced the traditional skep hiving method, as it allowed access to the hive to control disease and insect pests and easy removal of the frames to extract the honey.[17] Three other inventions quickly followed Langstroth's moveable frame hive that made beekeeping even more simple and appealing. Wax comb foundation, invented in 1857 by Johannes Mehring and refined by A. I. Root in 1876, is still an invaluable product for all beekeepers. A thin sheet of wax embossed with hexagons is placed in the center of a wooden frame, providing a uniform foundation for the construction of honeycomb that reduced the time it took for a hive to become productive; in addition, once built, the honeycomb within the frames could be cleaned and refilled by the bees season after season, allowing them to devote even more time to honey production. The invention of the centrifugal extractor by Fransesco de Hruschka in 1865 allowed beekeepers to extract honey faster than ever before; prior to the invention of the extractor, the most effective method of retrieving honey involved "'cutting the comb from the frames, crushing it, and straining the honey from the wax,'" a process that must have been agonizingly and unprofitably slow. The bellows smoker, invented in 1873 by Moses Quimby, was a vast improvement over other smoking techniques, as it was easy to handle and allowed control over the direction and intensity of the smoke. These innovations revolutionized the art of beekeeping, allowing beekeepers to easily observe and maintain their hives, remove honey from hives without killing a thriving bee colony or wasting valuable honeycomb, and dramatically increase their honey production.[18]

Like other branches of natural science, apiculture inspired the publication of several journals, two of which are still published today. The first edition of Langstroth's *The Hive and the Honeybee* appeared in 1853, and subsequent editions and translations were published by the Dadant family. The *American Bee Journal* first appeared in 1861; although publication stopped during the Civil War, Charles Dadant, father of a bee supply company still in business, became editor shortly after the war ended and the journal flourished. A. I. Root, author of *The ABC and XYZ of Bee Culture*, another standard text in apiculture which appeared in 1891, began publishing a magazine now known as *Bee Culture* shortly after the war ended. Both journals invited submissions from anyone knowledgeable about bees and beekeeping, and often published advice submitted by women.[19]

In fact, by the 1880s, beekeeping had become a very respectable pastime for women, evidenced by the number of published submissions to bee journals and private diaries and letters written by women about their beekeeping experiences. In her forthcoming book, *Piping Up: A History of Women and Bees*, Tammy Horn discusses the importance of beekeeping to nineteenth- and twentieth-century women as a hobby and profession, introducing prominent and influential female beekeepers such as Anna Botsford Comstock, wife of prominent entomologist, John Henry Comstock, Lucinda Harrison, a frequent contributor to journals, Cassandra Robbins, President of the Indiana State Beekeepers Society in 1884, Jane Cole, who worked closely with A. I. Root, and Margaret James Murray Washington, founder of the Tuskegee Beekeeping Ladies, memorialized in Booker T. Washington's *Tuskegee and Its People: Their Ideals and Achievements*. Even the *Ladies' Home Journal* promoted beekeeping as a realistic and lucrative profession for women, because they "'have, usually, a gentler, finer touch than men.'" Although Horn says that Emily Dickinson "never touch[ed] a Langstroth hive," she believes the poet "represents a consciousness of bees in the American feminine mindset," an awareness that drew many women to beekeeping as an additional means of supporting their families.[20]

Insect Infestations

Perhaps the most significant factor in the development of American attitudes toward insects was the increasing threat of crop devastation.

Despite the application of predator insects as a form of pest control and the more recent discoveries that insects are beneficial in many ways, "including ... weed control, nutrient circulation and soil quality, waste decomposition, pollination and seed dispersal, human food, industrial and medicinal products, monitoring environmental quality and fashion and decorative applications," the human attitude toward insects continues to be one of fear or repugnance. In "Values and Perceptions," Steve Kellert explains that human aversion to insects is linked to multiple factors. The vast number of insects, for example, threatens our sense of individuality, and only adds to our "alienation from creatures so different and unlike our own species." Developing knowledge that insects play an important and sometimes deadly part in disease transmission also contributes to negative attitudes about insects. Even honeybees, despite their role in crop pollination and honey production, inspire more fear than gratitude. In the nineteenth century, this almost instinctive hatred of insects, the belief that they will always be in some way the enemy of mankind, was certainly amplified by the inevitable feelings of helplessness and rage following the destruction of precious fields. Several particularly ruinous insect species, including "the curculio, the Hessian fly, the chinch bug, the Colorado potato beetle, and the Rocky Mountain locust," dominated attention in the battles between agriculture and insects. Most nineteenth-century Americans would have been very familiar with the devastating effects of those insects as well as many others, such as armyworms, scale insects, cotton boll weevils, and mosquitoes, both on crops and the families and businesses that relied upon those crops for survival.[21]

The curculio, a weevil that attacks soft fruited trees such as plums, peaches, and cherries, "elicited the most extensive discussion of any insect pest in America" until the 1850s. Both farmers and entomologists explored every trick they could contrive to abolish the curculio, including spraying trees with tobacco juice or soap, rubbing manure on tree trunks, constructing tall fences around orchards, and smoking the insects out of the trees; but the most effective method of curculio control remained placing a sheet under infested trees, shaking the weevils out of them, and destroying the creatures after they fell. Even though the simplest methods of control were often the most effective, the large size of most American orchards made hand destruction of the weevils a daunting task.[22]

The Hessian fly, the "first insect to plague American farm crops on a massive scale," attacked the very lifeblood of American farming: wheat. The Hessian fly first destroyed a significant American wheat crop in 1778 on Staten Island, New York. By 1788, the spread of the fly was so extensive that Britain "prohibited the importation of American wheat," fearing for its own crops. Early entomologists recommended various cultivation and harvesting techniques, including smashing young wheat plants in an effort to destroy fly larvae. By the 1880s, however, American entomologists, supported by the knowledge compiled in state pest and agricultural surveys, recommended planting wheat during "fly-free periods," a strategy established in many states, and selectively growing fly-resistant wheat varieties. Previous methods of controlling fly populations, such as field burning and planting and destroying decoy crops were dismissed as ineffective by entomological research, as burning also destroyed the fly's natural predators.[23] To farmers desperate to successfully plant and harvest their wheat crops, the advice of the entomologists was invaluable.

Like the Hessian fly, the chinch bug attacks wheat crops but is also attracted to corn, oats, barley, hay, and rye, staple crops for American farmers. First appearing as a threat to American agriculture in 1783, the chinch bug quickly became one of the most destructive insects in American history; its level of crop destruction is comparable only to that of the Rocky Mountain locust. In 1864, the chinch bug was responsible for the destruction of half the corn crop and three-quarters of the wheat crop in the western states. Because the life stages of the insect were difficult to distinguish, it wasn't until 1875 that Charles Valentine Riley successfully described its life cycle. Entomologists recommended the usual preventative cultivation techniques, but they quickly became interested in the impact of disease on chinch bug population. Erecting barriers coated with tar or trenches filled with water designed to trap migrating swarms as they moved from one field to the next reduced but did not eliminate the chinch bug population.[24]

The Colorado potato beetle maintained a low profile in American agriculture until 1861, when its population increased enough to almost eradicate potato crops in Iowa and Nebraska, and crops in Missouri, Illinois, and Kansas were soon threatened as well by this voracious pest. Natural control methods, such as relying on natural predators, seemed to have little effect on an insect that multiplied so rapidly, as did preventative cultivation techniques and handpicking of pests. By 1867, even traditional chemicals useful in insect control, including "ashes, lime, hellebore, quassia, and tobacco," had failed to control the beetle, and researchers turned to the newest development in entomological control, an arsenic compound called Paris green. Even though some farmers initially were reluctant to spray their crops with a poison that they feared would be absorbed by the plants, Paris green was remarkably effective and farmers eventually forgot their fears. For the most part, American entomologists and medical doctors ignored concerns that the widespread application of pesticides was harmful to human health, and the use of pesticides to control injurious insects was "viewed as a triumph for American applied entomology."[25]

The Rocky Mountain locust plagues were most likely the most dramatic and frightening insect encounters nineteenth-century Americans endured. During the height of the plagues (1874–1877), locusts consumed over $200 million in American crops west of the Mississippi. Described as "a living wildfire," a locust outbreak was a terrifying event: a black cloud, briefly preceded by a distant "whirring buzz," descended from the heavens, and legions of locusts, devouring "fifty tons of vegetation per day" as well as clothing hanging on lines and wooden tool handles, marched across miles of farmland like an invading army. Entomologists struggled to find a way to halt the plagues, but were largely unsuccessful, and why the locust plagues suddenly ended in 1902 was an entomological mystery until recently.[26]

As Jeffrey A. Lockwood correctly observes, Laura Ingalls Wilder's account of her personal experiences during a locust plague in *On the Banks of Plum Creek* is "eeri[e]" and "terr[ifying]" and epitomizes what the settlers' experience must have been during a locust attack. Ingalls describes a cloud that without warning blocks the sun, a cloud that "hail[ed] grasshoppers" that clung to her hair, skin, and clothing and "filled the whole air" with the "rasping whirring of their wings" [207] and "one big sound made of tiny nips and snips and gnawings ... [, of] millions of jaws biting and chewing" [208]. After her family's wheat crops are destroyed and her father leaves home to search for work, she learns about the locust plagues in Egypt from her mother, acknowledging that she personally "knew how true" [230] the Biblical account was. For Lockwood, Ingalls' recognition of the parallels between the locust plague in Egypt and her experience of the grasshoppers that ate their way "'through all the land of Minnesota'" [230] is an example of how "the tale of the pioneers became interwoven with Western culture's most deep and abiding literary account of locusts." Many of the pioneers believed that the locusts were sent by God "as punishment for some moral shortcoming or evildoing" while others thought the infestation to be the work of demons. The locust, either a tool for divine justice or a minion of the devil, was much more terrifying than a mere garden pest and was a crucial element in the agricultural and psychological development of the frontier mindset.[27]

The final decades of the century were particularly important to the public image of entomology, according to L. O. Howard, who describes several critical entomological discoveries and the social impact they created. The identification by Mrs. C. H. Fernald of Amherst of the "armyworm" as the British gipsy moth, which had been imported from Europe in an effort to breed a disease-resistant silkworm to rescue a devastated French silk industry, accidentally released in Massachusetts in 1869, and not recognized as a threat until a massive outbreak in 1889, marked the beginning of this series of nationally noticed entomological events. As a result of efforts to eradicate these destructive caterpillars rapidly eating their way across the eastern states, Howard notes both a significant interest in and development of new and improved pesticides, as Paris green and arsenic were powerless against them, and an "enormous improvement of spraying machinery." The pernicious scale, or San Jose scale, identified by Comstock in California in 1880, was originally brought to the States on imported trees from China, transported to the east, where it thrived, by California nurseries, and eventually exported to Japan and Chile as passengers on shipped nursery stock. Eventually, as the insect swept through orchards around the globe, Germany, Canada, and Austria-Hungary established quarantines against importing American fruit, and other countries sent representatives to the States to further study the insect. The cotton boll weevil was first brought to American entomologists' attention in 1880, when it devastated a cotton crop in Mexico, but it was scientifically ignored until it migrated to Texas in 1894. Within three decades, despite Federal intervention and eradication attempts, the weevil "had invaded practically all of the more than 600,000 square miles included in the so-called cotton belt," ravaging the cotton industry and the Southern economy and spirit: "Mortgages on old plantations were foreclosed; negro labor fled before the weevil's advance; wealthy families were reduced to comparative poverty; banks failed; planters and speculators suicide." Farmers soon learned the value of crop rotation and variety, and the eradication of the boll weevil because such a subject of national concern that more colleges and universities across the nation began offering entomology as a topic of study in an effort to find an effective method off dealing with the voracious pest.[28]

Insects in Medicine

Insects and diseases are intimately connected, as insects are transmitters of some diseases and panaceas for others. While some medicinal uses of insects are rooted in folk wisdom and were viewed even in the nineteenth century as nothing more than the superstitions of the uneducated masses, a topic addressed in the next section, as scientists began to explore the efficacy of insect related cures and the connections between insects and disease transference, the study and practical applications of insect-related medicine became more popular and accepted. Perhaps the most important insect-related discovery of the nineteenth century, as Howard asserted, was the transmission of the malaria virus by mosquitoes, which ushered in yet another generation of bug-hunters, medical entomologists[29] — a profession that continues to expand as researchers discover the possible applications of insects as sources of new and innovative drugs, therapies, treatments, and materials, medical entomology marks the beginning of a new understanding of the importance of both insect research and preservation.

One of the earliest applications of medicinal entomology that was also extremely effective, described by Gilbert Waldbauer in *Fireflies, Honey, and Silk*, was the "use of ants as sutures to close wounds[, which] began in India before 2000 B.C.E." Because large ants such as leaf-cutters have such strong and nearly indestructible jaws, which lock in place like a pit bull's or weasel's might, ancient physicians recognized their practical value in holding serious wounds closed; they would apply a living ant to the edges of a gash, force the ant to clamp down on the edges of skin to secure it, and remove the body, leaving the head in place to secure the injury like a modern staple. According to accounts in the Sanskrit Vedas, this practice was used successfully even in operations for obstructed intestines more than three thousand years ago. As recounted by Waldbauer, the practice of using ant heads as primitive stitches moved from India to Arabia, Spain, Africa, France, and England. By "late medieval and early Renaissance times in Europe, ants were widely used to close wounds," but by the end of the seventeenth century the technique's popularity waned and it was considered to be a "long outmoded" method of treatment. However, one report by E. W. Gudger recounted by Waldbauer indicates that ants were used to secure a "gentleman's" head injury while in Asian Turkey in 1890, indicating that despite unpopularity in Europe, ant sutures were still regarded as a safe, effective, and surprisingly easy method of treatment for injuries in other parts of the world. Gudger also later translates the account of a French surgeon in Algeria who, in 1945, witnessed the similar use of a ground beetle. As Waldbauer explains, "using ant sutures is surely faster and more convenient than sewing up a wound and tying numerous knots,"[30] which offers a realistic explanation for why the practice never completely disappeared; it is likely that similar methods are still used today in places where modern medical practitioners and facilities are scarce or absent.

The use of leeches by physicians, according to Terry Devitt, was "so intrinsic ... to the practice of the medical arts in antiquity and the medieval world ... that the very name 'leech' was at times synonymous with the title 'physician.'" Thinking about ancient practices involving leeches conjures horrifying images of nearly fatal or even deadly bloodlettings for all types of common ailments, ranging from hysteria and depression to headaches and fevers. Not just a practice of the Middle Ages and Renaissance, by the nineteenth century, "leeches were enjoying a golden age. Millions were raised for medical use as their fame as a cure-all ensued.... Leeches were applied to the mouth and inside of the throat using a leech-glass, although patients frequently swallowed them." Thankfully, modern use of leeches has a much more solid foundation in medical fact. Today, leeches are applied to transplant and reattachment sites in order to prevent clotting and to promote increased circulation due to the natural anticoagulants they secrete as they feed, making them invaluable to patients needing skin grafts, such as burn or severe frostbite victims, limb reattachment, or other surgeries and conditions that compromise blood flow.[31]

Another effective and long-standing medical entomological practice that has been used through the ages, "maggot therapy," is enjoying a very successful resurgence in popularity today. Also known as "larval therapy" and "biodebridement," perhaps in an effort to disguise the true nature of the treatment, the use of maggots to clean infected tissue "was used by the ancient Mayan people of Mexico and Guatemala, in Australia by the Ngemba tribe of New South Wales, and by the hill people of Burma (now Myanmar)" with great success. The first mention of maggot therapy in Europe was in the sixteenth century by a French surgeon, Ambroise Paré, who realized that maggots seemed to speed the healing of "battlefield wounds." In America, the first account of maggot therapy was written during the Civil War by a Confederate surgeon, who noticed that wounds infested with maggots healed faster and cleaner and were more likely to result in the retention of an infected limb. William Baer, a surgeon during World War I, also recognized that soldiers whose wounds were filled with maggots were less likely to succumb to fever, blood poisoning, and sepsis, and that the wounds themselves showed more evidence of healing and healthy tissue than those that had not been exposed to maggots. In fact, over three hundred hospitals were using maggot therapy by 1933, either purchasing sterile maggots from enterprising companies such as the Lederle Corporation or raising them under controlled and sterile conditions on site. As antibiotics and other methods of fighting infection became more readily available and acceptable, larval therapy decreased in popularity, but was always remembered as a "last resort" treatment. Today, biodebridement is once again a booming business as many germs become more and more resistant to even the strongest antibiotics and as medical research confirms the importance and benefits of the treatment itself. Much more precise than any surgery could be, maggots remove only dead tissue, leaving the healthy intact; in addition, they secrete a natural antibiotic, allantoin, which both stimulates the growth of new tissue and destroys bacteria, assisting in the prevention of infection. As scientists and physicians become more afraid of the emergence of newly mutated super germs, such as MRSA or the dreaded necrotizing fasciitis, or flesh eating bacteria, maggot therapy may soon replace antibiotics as the standard treatment for moderate and severe infections, ulcers, and other conditions.[32]

The history of using honey as a healing agent parallels that of using ant heads as sutures; the first written account, found on an ancient Sumerian clay tablet which includes a poultice recipe and instructions for its application, dates back over four thousand years. Anthropological reports of Egyptian uses of honey vary, according to Waldbauer, but it is evident that honey was a critical ingredient in anywhere from 147 to over 500 prescriptions and remedies. Interestingly, honey was even used as a contraceptive; an Egyptian birth control recipe includes "a mixture of crocodile feces, honey, and saltpeter" and as recently as 1993 one writer reports that "cotton soaked in honey and lemon juice was then still used as a contraceptive." The beneficial applications of honey have been noted in Greek, Roman, Muslim, Irish, and Finnish sacred texts, folklore, and mythology. It is perhaps the most common and universal medicine known to man. Its popularity as a natural antibiotic is reinforced by modern research and it is a popular homeopathic remedy for allergies, burns, and other ailments. In fact, honey is so effective in the treatment of burns that some doctors believe "Medihoney," a product based on the highly regarded manuka honey of New Zealand, to be superior to conventional treatment of first and secondary burns. It is also still highly popular as a homeopathic remedy and cure for seasonal allergies, cuts, scrapes, and burns, coughs, sore throats, colds, chest congestion, and conjunctivitis, and some homeopathic practitioners believe that it may also be an effective treatment for cholesterol, gastrointestinal disorders like ulcers or GERD, arthritis, bladder infections, heart disease, weakened immune systems, influenza, hearing loss, and even cancer, especially when taken with cinnamon.[33]

The old-fashioned customs and beliefs surrounding insects have evolved into one of the fastest growing fields of modern medicine, medical entomology and related industries. A comprehensive list of the most recent advances in the field is beyond the scope of this study and is deserving of a book in its own right, but some advances are too fascinating to ignore here. Researchers are developing mechanical leeches with insatiable appetites, building mechanical cockroaches to assist in the discovery of earthquake victims, and monitoring lice to track pollution levels. Because of their short life span, among other reasons, fruit flies are critical to genetic research and are the most frequently used experiment subject in laboratories. A French company, Entomed, focuses exclusively on researching the insect world in a quest to develop new medications to treat everything from cancer to fungal infections,[34] and the Medical Entomology Centre, offering specialized insect-related medical services including efficacy testing, longevity studies, formulation development, and field and clinical trials, has been operating in Cambridgeshire, England, since 1984.[35] Researchers at the University of Nottingham have been experimenting on cockroaches and locust brains to find the next super-antibiotic in an effort to stay one step ahead of mutating super germs.[36] Medical entomology has become such an accepted field of research that it even surfaces in Hollywood; the elusive cancer cure in Sean Connery's 1992 movie *Medicine Man* was created by ant secretions in sugar, and the currently popular criminal anthropology television hit series *Bones* showcases almost weekly the benefits and uses of insects in criminal investigations. In fact, insects are often used in forensic investigations; forensic entomologists use insect evidence, such as the presence of certain flies and the ages of their larva, to determine time of death or point to environmental factors that may prove whether a victim was moved or killed at the crime scene.[37] Current research in developing innovative, new cancer therapies and drugs is also highly dependent on medical entomology; promising research on the cytotoxic effects of many insects, including "the Chinese gall, the Cicada slough, the hornet nest, and the batryticated silkworm," all of which are used prominently in traditional homeopathic, alternative, and folkloric Chinese medicines, the jewel wasp, and the Calliphoridae fly.[38] For every patient who may be frightened or disgusted by the use of insects in their treatments and medicines, there are as many families and patients who are certainly exceedingly thankful to and grateful for the seemingly insignificant creatures that have helped secure a conviction or cure a dangerously infected wound, and it is clear that insects are only going to become more important to many aspects of medical technology and treatment in the future.

Insects in Folklore

An interesting element of the collage of imagery and meaning surrounding the insect in the nineteenth century is the reliance on and faith in entomological folk wisdom and superstition. While agricultural contact with insects only reinforced ideas that insects are the enemy, folkloric entomological beliefs are rooted in a more intimate relationship with nature. Often held for countless generations, folk customs originated in pre-industrial communities that depended on nature to provide food, heat, shelter, and medicine. American folklore evolved from contributions from many cultures, each adding their distinctive beliefs to the ever-growing catalog of entomologically oriented superstitions and practices. Insects can predict the weather or an imminent death, cure a headache or toothache, and attract or repel a lover. *Insect Fact and Folklore*, by Lucy W. Clausen, presents both scientific and folkloric information about insects in order to "instill a sympathetic understanding through which people will overcome their natural (but unreasonable) aversion to insects." Clausen first presents a general insect primer, then goes on to discuss insect families and the superstitions and facts associated with them. Her brief descriptions of insect-oriented superstitions are particularly insightful, as many of those traditional beliefs have been held for generations and certainly would have been well known, at least regionally, in the nineteenth century.[39]

The unquestionable beauty of butterflies and moths has figured prominently in American folklore. Butterfly flight patterns have long been used to determine directions, as butterflies are known to migrate in specific and predictable directions. A white butterfly in a house in Louisiana brings good luck, while that same butterfly's entrance into a home in Maryland would predict an upcoming death; a butterfly of any other color often signifies marriage. A butterfly that flies into your face can signify an upcoming cold spell, and "in western Pennsylvania, when chrysalides are found suspended from the underside of rails and heavy branches," a wet season is predicted. While it is bad luck to pull off a butterfly's wings, an old English superstition advises that the first butterfly seen each year should be killed in order to guarantee good luck. A moth that lands on a new mother might foretell the death of her baby, and Irish superstition maintains that moths are the "souls of the dead waiting to pass through Purgatory."[40]

Beetles, cockroaches, grasshoppers, crickets, and mantids are other important insects in American folklore. The clicking of the death tick or death-watch beetle foretells the imminent death of a loved one, a belief that, even today, is widely held. Ladybugs were long believed to cure a toothache if crushed and applied to the tooth, and were also beneficial in cases of measles and colic; it is generally unlucky to kill one, perhaps because of both its healing properties and the belief that it brings wealth to a home. The number of spots on a gold beetle's wings can predict the corn harvest, a lightning bug in the house means that company will soon visit, and the blood resulting from the decapitation of a certain wood boring beetle, the bess bug, or *Passalus cornutus*, will cure an earache. To rid a house of cockroaches in Massachusetts, someone should pass one of them along with a small amount of money to a member of another household, and the rest will follow it home. The tobacco spit of grasshoppers is believed to cure warts. In Maine, trapped crickets are commonly rescued because it is bad luck to leave them stranded, and in Virginia and Maryland, they are believed to be "old folks"; in general, crickets across the country enjoy the reputation of being an "omen of prosperity" and accurate temperature gauges. The egg sacs of praying mantids were thought to have great medicinal value when carried by an afflicted person or sliced open and rubbed on affected areas, and were at times jealously hoarded, especially when out of season.[41]

Superstitions about spiders, flies, and dragonflies abound. It is bad luck to kill a spider, a superstition that Mark Twain's Huckleberry Finn vehemently believes; early in the novel, while hiding from Miss Watson, Huck flicks a spider off his shoulder into a candle, but is immediately repentant and afraid when he realizes he has killed it: "I didn't need anyone to tell me that that was an awful bad sign and would fetch me some bad luck, so I was scared and most shook the clothes off of me" [13]. No matter how many charms he tried to ward off his impending doom, he can think of nothing he has heard that "was any way to keep off bad luck when you'd killed a spider" [13]. Clausen explains that swarms of biting flies can signify an upcoming rainstorm, while a swarm in the house foretells sickness, as does dreaming about them. In Kentucky and Louisiana, if a fly incessantly hovers about anyone, it means that someone wants to meet that person; the death of the fly guarantees the meeting. Flies have even been used in mankind's never ending battle against baldness. In Pennsylvania, a certain dragonfly known as the "'snake doctor'" is said to warn snakes of danger, and it is bad luck to kill them because it might anger the snake. Dragonflies also have the ability to sew ears, lips, eyelids, nostrils, and even fingers and toes together, sting, and prevent fish from biting a line.

Bees, wasps, and hornets feature prominently in folklore and superstition. Bees will sting guilty people if they approach a hive, and beehives should never be sold, only traded, or they will die or become unproductive. A beehive must be told if its keeper departs or dies, and some recommend turning the hive or draping it with black ribbon after a death, else the bees will abandon their hives or die themselves. Some traditions also recommend informing bees of upcoming marriages and offering the hive samples of wedding and funeral cakes and portions of other dishes brought to the household. When bees store a large amount of honey, a heavy winter can be expected, and it is a common belief that they can sense rain. A yellow bee hovering around a person brings good news, while a black bee brings bad. Dreaming of bees is usually considered to bring good luck, but killing them in a dream is unlucky. Hornets and wasps, like honeybees, predict harsh winter weather by building their nests in low locations; nests found in high locations indicate a warmer winter. An empty wasp's nest is considered good luck, and in the Ozarks, girls hide small wasp's nests under their dresses to attract a husband.[42]

Obviously, folk wisdom and superstitions relating to insects vary from region to region; while Clausen's study is by no means comprehensive, her brief descriptions of the insect's prominence in American folk history help to create a more accurate image of what Americans have believed and to be true about insects. While they may have accepted the entomological community's efforts to widen their knowledge about the relationship between insects and apiculture, many Americans still kept mantid egg sacs in their medicine kits, covered beehives after the death of a beekeeper in order to inform and retain the hive, spared spiders in garrets when spring cleaning, and fell asleep praying that they would not be awakened by the tick-tick-tick of the death-watch beetle.

Insects in Fashion and Art

It is not easy to believe that the realms of fashion and art are at all reliant on insects, but insects have provided many integral materials to the creative endeavors of humans, most notably silk, red dye, ink, and lac, the primary ingredient in the finish known as shellac. Beeswax is used both in lost wax casting and in batiking, artistic techniques that have survived for centuries. The form of insects has been used as inspiration for jewelry design, as seen both in ancient Egyptian jewelry and its many incarnations to follow, insect body parts have been utilized as beads, and even whole insects have been incorporated into jewelry and other fashion accessories, such as hats and brooches, both dead and alive. More than just elegant and beautiful creatures that enthrall artists and inspire multiple forms of creativity, insects are essential ingredients in the production of clothing, jewelry, furniture, and more.

For thousands of years, the secret behind the production of luxurious Chinese silk was carefully guarded, until the sixth century, when "two Persian monks smuggled silkworm eggs to Constantinople in their hollow canes," but Waldbauer reports that silk production may have actually begun in the Stone Age, as evidenced by shrouds found in various archeological sites. In many countries and cultures throughout the ages, including China, Japan, the Middle East, England, Switzerland, Middle America, and Germany, the wearing of silk was allowed only for those in the highest social classes and the extremely affluent. Efforts to create silk industries in Europe and China continued through the nineteenth century, but the difficult process of silk production itself combined with the finicky appetites of silkworms, who will dine only on mulberry plants, the labor required to raise them, the prevalence of disease, and the competition from cheaper and easier fabrics like cotton and rayon prevented the silk industry from ever taking hold in the States. Silkworms no longer exist in the wild, and their lives in captivity have changed little over the centuries. Waldbauer says that the process has remained constant since 1903, when the U.S.D.A. bulletin establishing the guidelines for raising silkworms and making silk, or sericulture, was first released. It takes approximately four to six weeks for a newly hatched silkworm to grow into a worm mature enough to weave a cocoon. The U.S.D.A. bulletin says that the larva produced from one ounce of silkworm eggs, approximately 40,000, will consume over a ton of fresh mulberry leaves, or a little over nine ounces per worm, during their larval state and will, under ideal conditions, produce around 170 pounds of silk. Once the worms spin their cocoons, they are heated in water until they die and the silk cocoon is softened, because if they are allowed to hatch, the enzyme they use to make an exit hole from the cocoon breaks the desired long singular strand of silk fiber into unusable pieces.

Often, the caterpillars are consumed by the workers engaged in the delicate process of unraveling the silken strands and weaving them together to form thread. In another form of silk production common in Japan, the silken bags of the female bagworm are "slit open along one side, soaked in water to soften them, pressed flat, dried, and sewn together" to make small bags, coin purses, and other adornments.[43]

The production of red dye from tiny cochineal insects was first discovered by the Aztecs, who prized the brilliant red color produced by the powerful dye. Spanish invaders were also impressed by the brilliance and endurance of cochineal dye, and by 1523 it was already a valuable commodity in Spain. Waldbauer states that the dye was so precious that "dried cochineal insects became, per weight, second in value only to the precious metals." A small scale insect that prefers to feed on prickly pear cactus, cochineal insects are as particular as silkworms in their culinary habits, although their care in domesticity is not as labor intensive as that of the silkworm. Only pregnant females are used to make the coveted dye, and they are plucked from the cacti one by one, dried, either in the sun or in heated rooms (a quicker technique that results in an inferior dye), and packaged for use. Methods of using the dye to produce different color effects vary from artist to artist, but traditionally the dried and crushed insects are mixed with lime juice and other ingredients to produce a dye that is proven to be colorfast and resistant to fading for centuries.[44]

The secretions of the lac insect, yet another indispensable scale insect, have also been used with some success to produce a red dye, but it is as a producer of the valuable resin lac that it is most important. The sturdy resin exuded by a colony of lac insects as they feed can build up around a "twig to a thickness of as much as half an inch and for a length of 4 to 5 inches."[45] After it is collected, the resin is ground, soaked (and the water retained for the aforementioned red dye), melted, and stretched into thin sheets. These sheets can be processed to make beads, abrasives, and many other products, the most famous of which are phonograph records made prior to World War II and the wood finish known as shellac.

The printing industry also owes a debt to insects, as many inks are created from insects and their byproducts. Some believe that the first Chinese makers of paper itself were inspired by watching wasps make their nests by chewing wood into pulp and forming it into cells. Wasps are also instrumental in the creation of one of the most indelible black dyes known to man; the galls of certain wasps are boiled to extract the tannin, and the resulting ink darkens rather than fades as it ages. Ink made from gallnuts is still used today, most notably by "the U.S. Treasury, the Bank of England, the German Chancellory, and the Danish government."[46]

Jewelry featuring insect designs was very common throughout the nineteenth century, both in Europe and America. Late Georgian and early Victorian jewelry often featured delicately detailed images of bees, dragonflies, butterflies, and flies, as well as animals and flowers. One style that was particularly suited to insect jewelry entailed attaching a brooch or hairpin to a small spring, a technique referred to as "en tremblant," so that the featured butterfly or dragonfly trembled and quivered realistically. In the complex symbolic language of the Victorian era, flies represented humility and butterflies the soul, and these insects appear frequently in jewelry designs. By the 1840s, "beetle-embroidered fabric from India imported by England" to America was available, though it never became a true fashion trend.[47]

In the second half of the century, archeological excavations in Egypt prompted interest in insect imagery in jewelry and souvenirs. The scarab, or dung, beetle, sacred to the Egyptians because they believed the rolling ball of dung to be "symbolic of the sun moving across the sky," was, after 1800 B.C., a popular image on document seals, amulets, and sepulchers, and its image was even reproduced in hieroglyphics. Other beetles, including tenebrionid, buprestid, and elaterid beetles, were also reproduced in jewelry and funereal ornaments. Grasshoppers, representing "large numbers of individuals;" butterflies, representing beauty; honeybees, "linked with the solar cult of Re;" and two types of flies, large golden flies that symbolized "valor and tenacity in battle" and smaller flies that represented the "spirit of the deceased," were also immortalized in seals, hieroglyphs, and jewelry. As these treasures were rediscovered, the scarab beetle and other insects became popular motifs for jewelers.[48]

The mid- and late Victorian period, remembered most for mourning and remembrance jewelry elaborately woven from the loved one's hair, also relished pins, necklaces, and earrings made from dried insect specimens, such as butterflies or beetles, or perfectly preserved hummingbird bodies: "That which was deemed charming from the early 1860s through the 1890s included millinery creations featuring whole, stuffed birds in addition to fanciful creations such as hummingbird earrings and clothing embroidered with iridescent beetle casings." Even more bizarre to modern sensibilities, some "Victorian ladies took up the fashion of wearing live jewel beetles tethered by tiny golden chains." Kirby and Spence describe the use of fireflies trapped in gauze as hair scarves worn by Indian women, and an account by Frank Cowan describes women who would pin living fireflies to their hats and dresses.[49] Other women would adorn themselves with live jewel beetles secured by a minuscule harness and leash or trapped in an small yet ornate cage.

Jewel beetle is actually a catch-all term that can refer to many different beetles, all of which share the characteristic exhibiting spectacularly vivid iridescent colors. A popular display of such beetles at the Brazilian court at the 1876 Centennial Exhibition featured "brooches, ear-rings, and pins, which are set with insects.... Unseen, they cannot be imagined. The opal, the amethyst, and the emerald have been endowed with life ... and when we think of trees studded with them, it is like a dream of the Taj Mahal or a passing glimpse of the crown jewels in the London Tower." Another reviewer of the Exhibition also noted the vast collection of unusual Brazilian insects specimens, ranging from beetles "bright as gems" and moths larger than any before seen. Critic Jan Thomas attributes this interest in incorporating genuine natural specimens into human decoration to a growing interest in the natural world because of Darwin's discoveries and a fascination with freshly unearthed Egyptological wonders, which marked the beginning of yet another Egyptian revival movement. Michele Tolini, in "'Beetle Abominations' and Birds on Bonnets: Zoological Fantasy in Late-Nineteenth-Century Dress," agrees that women may have adorned themselves with insects and small animals to grow closer to the natural world, but admits that the fad quickly fell out of fashion by the end of the century, when attitudes toward ecological issues and species preservation began to change.[50]

Even today, the elytra, or wing covers, and thoraxes, what we would think of as an insect's chest, of jewel beetles are used in jewelry construction. Thoraxes have a natural hole that makes them wonderful beads, and the elytra can be used singly or in groups to create earrings, pendants, and headdresses. Artist Jan Fabre has incorporated nacreous beetle shells into much of his artwork, the most famous of which is undoubtedly the magnificent mural "Heaven of Delight" on the ceiling of the Royal Palace of Brussels. Jewelers Kathy Stout and Marilyn Kale cultivate caddisfly larvae, providing them with fragments of "'opals, garnets, tiger's eye, jasper, lapis, gold nuggets, emeralds, rubies, sapphires, and even diamonds'" with which to build their delicate and "portable, tubelike shelters"; once these caddisfly larvae mature and fly off, they collect these "shells," secure them with glue, and fashion jewelry uniquely sculpted by insects that sparkle with rainbows of precious and semiprecious stones, gems, and metals.[51]

Insects as Food

To modern American tastes, accidentally eating a bug is probably one of the most nauseating and unappetizing culinary events that could ever happen, and the concept of deliberately eating insects, savoring them, is difficult if not impossible to grasp. Most Americans would be shocked to discover the Food and Drug Administration's acceptable levels of insect contamination in food. To meet F.D.A. standards, apple butter must contain less than an "average of 5 or more whole or equivalent insects (not counting mites, aphids, thrips, or scale insects per 100 grams"; chocolate samples are rejected only if they average "60 or more insect fragments per 100 grams"; an "average of 225 insect fragments or more per 225 grams in 6 or more subsamples" is the threshold in macaroni; and golden raisins are acceptable as long as they do not contain "10 or more whole or equivalent insects and 35 Drosophilia eggs per 8 oz." Obviously, Americans, even those attempting to follow vegetarian diets, consume more insects than most of us ever suspected, and it does no harm. In fact, insects are a fundamental and traditional food source in many countries, providing readily available nutrition in areas where food is scarce. Sadly, as Waldbauer explains, our prejudice against insects as a legitimate food source has caused some people to depart from their insect menus, and they are "reluctant, if not altogether unwilling, to continue the tradition of eating insects, because they are influenced by *our* prejudices, communicated to them by Westerners such as missionaries and administrative officers."[52]

Nineteenth-century Americans had a similarly negative attitude toward insects as food. Many of those facing starvation during the locust plagues, for example, could have feasted heartily on the locusts, feeding themselves while curtailing the plague. As exploration of the third world continued, more and more people became exposed to the idea of insect food, often dismissing it as a practice of "uncivilized races," as Vincent M. Holt accounts in *Why Not Eat Insects*, published in 1885. Holt writes the book "fully conscious of the difficulty of battling against a long-existing and deep-rooted public prejudice," asking "of [his] readers a fair hearing, an impartial consideration of [his] arguments, and an unbiased judgment." He begins his discussion by explaining that many of our usual sources of meat, such as pigs and lobsters, feed on filth and decaying flesh, while edible insects such as slugs and locusts subside on cleaner, vegetarian diets. He also asserts that insects are nutritionally comparable if not superior to Western dietary staples, a fact with which current analysis concurs, and suggests that the farmers should encourage the poor to pick pests off their crops or food, their labor benefiting them both. Rather than allowing the appearance of an unexpected caterpillar in a cooked cabbage spoil our appetites, he "see[s] every reason why cabbages should be served up, surrounded with a delicately flavored fringe of the caterpillars which feed upon them." While the rich "can afford to be dainty," the poor, "in these days of agricultural depression," would benefit greatly if this "neglected food supply" was legitimized and explained.[53]

Holt then goes on to relate a brief history of the consumption of insects, beginning with biblical approval of and encouragement toward eating locusts, beetles, and grasshoppers and refuting the popular idea that John the Baptist did not eat locust insects but the pods of a species of podcassia. Locusts and beetles were popular across the globe, often served fried, boiled, and even curried. Moving on to the delicacies of grubs and caterpillars, Holt reminds us that the wise Pliny recounts a dish favored by the highest citizens of Rome that features a fattened larva of what was most likely the grub of a staghorn beetle. Another Greek historian describes a dessert dish of roasted grubs, probably palm weevil larvae, which were still "eaten with great relish" in the West Indies. Darwin himself tried a similar dish and "says that a white earth grub and the larvae of the sphinx moth are also eaten, which [he] ... found to be delicious." Caterpillars were eaten "both cooked and raw" by the Hottentots, and one traveler describes a recipe featuring caterpillars as "delicate, nourishing, and wholesome, resembling in taste sugared cream or sweet almond paste."[54]

In the third section of his book, Holt provides several recipes he believes will delight and amaze his readers, hoping to offer dishes that will be "a godsend to house-keepers," the possibility of "a new *entrée* to vary the monotony" of traditional cooking, unusual and delicate treats for hostesses who "thirst to place new and dainty dishes before [their] guests." He offers for consideration a sauce recipe whose main ingredient is the common wood-louse, the flavor of which he believes "equal, if not distinctly superior to, shrimp." The recipe is as follows: "collect a quantity of the finest woodlice to be found (no difficult task, as they swarm under the bark of every rotten tree), and drop them in boiling water, which will kill them instantly.... At the same time put into a saucepan a quarter of a pound of fresh butter, a teaspoon of flour, a small glass of water, a little milk, some pepper and salt, and place it on the stove. As soon as the sauce is thick, take it off and put it in the wood-lice. This is an excellent sauce for fish.

Try it." What enlightened and poverty stricken hostess could resist? Other culinary suggestions include sandwiches of baked trout with wasp grubs, and moths and caterpillars, which, as they commit suicide in our lamps and fires, "fry and grill themselves before our eyes, saying 'Does not the sweet scent of our cooked bodies tempt you? Fry us with butter; we are delicious. Boil us, grill us, stew us, we are good all ways!'" Snails and slugs should be regarded as a delicacy, as the French have long known, and should be repeatedly rinsed and boiled, then fried with butter and accompanied with piquante sauce.[55] At the very end of the book, Holt provides two complete menus in which every dish has an insect component, pointing out that presenting them in French makes them appear more elegant and palatable than when in English.

The most universally accepted insect related food product is without a doubt honey, the history and uses of which I have already discussed. While honey is the most well known insect-based sweetener in the West, other cultures have discovered another readily available and easily accessible source of sweetness: honeypot ants. Honeypot ants are found "in the southwestern United States, Mexico, Australia, New Guinea, and New Caledonia," and accounts of their use appeared in print by 1832. Unlike honeybees, who store their honey in constructed cells in the hive, honeypot ants have an interior storage system for their honey in their bodies. Worker ants "regurgitate their bounty" to the female workers that serve as living honeypots hanging from the ceiling of the hive like dried herbs in a food cellar. They are able to distribute the food as needed. The process of collecting them is quite simple; the colony is dug up, and the thousands of swollen honeypot ants, some of them distended to the point of bursting, are either carefully placed on a plate and processed for later use, or eaten directly from the hive, their contents slurped down or squeezed out, and their bodies tossed aside.[56] I imagine the gathering of honeypot ants to be rather like the experience of berry-picking: only half of what is picked ends up in the bucket, while the rest of the irresistible treats are enthusiastically enjoyed on the spot without guilt.

Insects in the Bible

A very strong influence on the American cultural identity of the insect was, of course, the Bible. The King James Bible contains 120 references to insects, including worms, caterpillars, snails, and leeches.[57] Scorpions, ants, spiders, fleas, lice, flies, hornets, moths, bees, and especially locusts are particularly important symbols, usually relating to God's ultimate control over the natural world. William Carpenter's *Scripture Natural History*, the third edition of which was published in 1833, contains a chapter that offers a detailed commentary on the insects that appear in the Bible. As much a natural historian as a biblical scholar, Carpenter is fascinated by the apparent perfection insects represent: "we certainly behold in the structure of insects abundant evidence of the most exquisite skill." Even microscopic examination of "invisible animalcules" reveals that "the same evidences of wisdom and design present themselves, ... and all ideas of imperfection cease." Carpenter's admiration and respect for the sophisticated design of these small, "inconceivable wonders" is obvious; for him, as for other natural scientists and scholars, insects offer evidence of the intricate beauty and perfection of the universe created and ordered by "the Artist": "How difficult to conceive the extreme minuteness of the muscles necessary to the motion of the heart, the glands for the secretion of the fluids, the stomach and bowels for the digestion of the food, the fineness of the tubes, nerves, arteries, veins; and, above all, of the blood, the lymph, and animal spirits which must be infinitely more so than any of these!" Carpenter's presentation of scriptural insects is informed not only by his knowledge of entomology but also by his belief, one shared by Thoreau and Muir, that "every thing that creepeth upon the earth" [Gen. 1:26] is part of the design of creation.[58]

Biblical laws regarding the cleanliness of insects are clearly outlined: "All fowls that creep, going upon all four, shall be an abomination to you. Yet these may ye eat of every flying creeping thing that goeth upon all four, which have legs above their feet, to leap withal upon the earth; even of these may ye eat; the locust after his kind, and the bald locust after his kind, and the beetle after his kind, and the grasshopper after his kind. But all other flying creeping things, which have four feet, shall be an abomination unto you" [Lev. 11:20–23]. John the Baptist survived in the desert by eating locusts, and manna is the edible secretion of a scale insect.[59] Modern sensibilities may balk at the idea of consuming hulking grasshoppers or insect secretions, but to the Israelites, locusts, manna, and honey were dietary delicacies and were truly gifts from the Lord.

Carpenter opens his discussion of biblical insects with scorpions, which appear frequently throughout the Bible. Known to cannibalize each other or even sting themselves to death if escape seems impossible, scorpions are dangerous, deadly, and "irascible." Moses describes Egypt as "a terrible wilderness, wherein were fiery serpents, and scorpions" [Deut. 8: 15], and Ezekiel "dwell[s] among scorpions" [2:6]. The Gospel of Luke has a passage devoted to proving the constancy of God's love: Jesus asks, if a son "shall ask [his father] for an egg, will he offer him a scorpion?" [11:12]; later, the Lord gives his followers the "power to tread on serpents and scorpions" [10:19]. In Revelation, the legions of locusts arising from the "bottomless pit" were "given power, as the scorpions of the earth have power" [9:3].[60]

Even in the Bible, ants are regarded as symbols of industry, labor, and organization, but they only appear twice. Proverbs 6:6 advises the "sluggard" to "go to the ant ... consider her ways, and be wise." In Proverbs 30:24–25, it is said that "there are four things which are little on the earth, but they are exceedingly wise: The ants are a people not strong, yet they prepare their meat in the summer." The forethought and planning of the ants, their willingness to work to ensure their survival, is one of the reasons they are among the select insects to be seen in a positive light.[61]

Rather than being praised for the beauty and intricacy of the design of its web, biblically, the spider is a weaver of false securities which trap and "deceive." In Job, Bildad states that a man who has left the path of God, is a man "whose hope shall be cut off, and whose trust shall be a spider's web" [8:14]. Isaiah says that the wicked "hatch cockatrice eggs, and weave the spider's web.... Their webs shall not become garments, neither shall they cover themselves with their work" [59: 5–6]. The web of the spider, a loathsome creature, is fragile, almost intangible, no protection against the wrath of an angry god, an image Jonathan Edwards utilizes in his famous sermon. In Proverbs, however, spiders are named among the small wise creatures: "The spider taketh hold with her hands, and is in kings' palaces" [30: 28]; in this passage, the spider's creativity, industry, and resourcefulness are admired.[62]

Fleas and lice also surface in scripture. The king of Israel is twice told that he is "seek[ing] a flea" [1 Sam. 26: 20] and "pursu[ing] ... after a flea" [1 Sam. 24: 14]. According to Carpenter, "the idea seemed to be, that while it would cost Saul much to catch the object of his pursuit, his success would afford him little advantage." One of the plagues reported in Exodus began when Aaron "smote the dust of the earth, and it became lice in men, and in beast; all the dust in the land became lice throughout all the land of Egypt" [8:17–18], which even the magicians couldn't abolish; some scholars, however, believe the true insect featured in this passage to be gnats. Individually, fleas and lice are minor nuisances, but they rarely travel independently; biblically, they represent both insignificance and intolerable suffering.[63]

Following the plague of lice came the plague of flies, insects which usually carry connotations of disease and destruction. Carpenter's respect for all insects shines through in his section devoted to flies, in which he cites at length a descriptive passage about the physical attributes, life habits, and superior design of the fly written by Mr. Bruce, a "distinguished traveller." Bruce's description of the effectiveness of a fly's "pointed proboscis" when stinging through camel skin reinforces the horror of a "grievous swarm of flies" sent to the Pharaoh in Exodus 8:22. In Isaiah, the Lord "hiss[es] for the fly that is in the uttermost part of the rivers of Egypt, and for the bee that is in the land of Assyria. And they shall come and shall rest all of them in the desolate valleys, and in the holes of the rocks, and upon all thorns, and upon all bushes" [7:18–19]. While a terrible pestilence for humanity, flies are one of the armies of the Lord.[64]

Like flies, hornets are used by the Lord to emphasize His divine power. The Lord promises Moses to "send hornets before thee, which shall drive out the Hivite, the Canaanite, and the Hittite, from before thee" [Exo. 23:28] and in Deuteronomy, he is assured that "God will send the hornet among [his enemies] until they that are left, and hide themselves from thee, be destroyed" [7:20]. Joshua is told that God "sent the hornet before you, which drave them out from before you" [24:12]. Carpenter reports that the hornet is "exceedingly strong for its size" and its ability to sting multiple times makes it a formidable and fearsome opponent, a worthy symbol of an enraged God.[65]

According to Carpenter, the moth represents either a destructive force or "an emblem of the fleetness and frailty of human life." Matthew explains that men should "lay up for [them]selves treasures in heaven, where neither rust nor moth doth corrupt" [6:20] rather than hoarding earthly wealth, which is subject to decay. Isaiah reports that those who deny the Lord "the moth shall eat them up like a garment, and the worm shall eat them like wool" [51:8]; earlier, he declares that disbelievers "all shall wax old as a garment; the moth shall eat them up" [50:9]. In Hosea, the Lord declares that he "will ... be unto Ephraim as a moth, and to the house of Judah as rottenness" [5:12]. Eliphaz states that those who believe themselves "more pure than his maker ... dwell in houses of clay, whose foundation is in the dust, which are crushed before the moth" [Job 4:17–19]. Similarly, in Psalm 39, David tells God, "when thou with rebukes dost correct man for iniquity, thou makest his beauty to consume away like a moth." Carpenter believes that "as the moth crumbles into dust under the slightest pressure ... so the man dissolves with equal ease, and vanishes into darkness, under the fingers of" either a wrathful or sorrowful and disappointed Lord.[66]

Swarms of bees figure prominently in the Bible, primarily appearing, as do most scriptural insects, as agents of destruction or of God's displeasure; honey, on the other hand, is one of the few positive symbols associated with insects. "[T]he fierce hostility and fury of the enemies of Israel," the Amorites, who attacked and "chased [them], as bees do, and destroyed" them, are described in Deuteronomy 1:44; likewise, in Psalm 118:12, threatening nations "compassed ... about like bees," consuming Israel; and in Isaiah 7:18 "the bee that is in the land of Assyria" is prophesied to protect the house of David. Honey always appears as evidence of the good favor of the Lord; the Promised Land, for example, is repeatedly described as "a land flowing with milk and honey" [Exo. 3:8]. Samson discovers a swarm of bees and honeycomb in a lion's carcass, as described in Judges 14:8; the bees do not attack and he brings the honey to his family. Honey makes survival in the desert possible: in Deuteronomy, God made man "to suck honey out of the rock" [32:13]; in Psalms, "the haters of the Lord" would have been nourished "with honey out of the rock" [81:16] if they had repented; and Matthew relates that John the Baptist is sustained by "locusts and wild honey" [3:4]. Proverbs 25 cautions against gluttony and overindulgence, especially when partaking of such a delicacy: "Hast thou found honey? Eat so much as is sufficient for thee, lest thou be filled therewith, and vomit it" [16]. David believes that the laws of God "are more to be desired ... than much fine gold; sweeter also than honey and the honeycomb" [Psalms 19:10]. Isaiah is told that Immanuel will be fed "butter and honey ... that he may know to refuse the evil, and choose the good" [7:15], echoing other cultural traditions that a bee alighting on a child's lips will inspire eloquence and that a taste of honey will bring sweetness to a child's life.[67]

Locusts are by far the most important insects that appear in scripture. The locust plague God sent to Egypt that Moses relates in Exodus was environmentally devastating: "for they covered the face of the whole earth, so that the land was darkened and they did eat every herb of the land, and all the fruit of the trees which the hail had left: and there remained not any green thing in the trees, or in the herbs of the field, through all the land of Egypt" [10:15]. While hornets and other winged creatures can turn back invading nations, the devastation of the locust is unique because it has such long-term environmental ramifications. In Jeremiah, it is prophesied that the invaders of Egypt will be "more than the grasshoppers, and are innumerable" [46:23]; the unimaginable number of locusts and the tremendous force of a locust plague are also referred to in Judges 6:5 and 7:12, Psalm 105:34, and Joel 2:3–10. Like ants and spiders, locusts are small and wise: "the locusts have no king, yet go they forth all of them by bands" [Proverbs 30:27]. In Revelation, locusts are compared "unto horses prepared unto battle" [9:7], "furious and impatient for war" as they pour out of the bottomless, smoky pit.[68] In most biblical references, the locust, or sometimes grasshopper, is described as an invading army, consuming and destroying everything in its wake. One notable exception to this image is the importance of the locust as a food source; a swarm of locusts can annihilate every green living thing for miles, while individual locusts can ensure survival. Another apparent contradiction to the image of the invading locust swarm occurs in Numbers, where those exploring Canaan report that when they "saw the giants, the sons of Anak, ... we were in our own sight as grasshoppers, and so we were in their sight" [13:33]. This passage points to the insignificance, the "weakness and timidity," of the "individual insect"; Moses' people perceive themselves to be as powerless and weak as a single grasshopper rather than as the catastrophic invading army locusts usually symbolize.[69]

Insects in Literature

The role of insects in literature would also have been familiar to American readers in the nineteenth century. Many canonical writers, including Homer, Virgil, Dante, Shakespeare, Milton, Donne, and Blake, relied on insect imagery to enrich their works. Compiling a complete catalogue of literary insect imagery that would have been well known in the nineteenth century is beyond the scope of this study because of the sheer volume of insects that have appeared; however, briefly discussing of a select handful of literary insects as portrayed by classic writers with whom Thoreau, Dickinson, and Muir would have been familiar, surveying entomological texts written for general audiences rather than scientists, farmers, and other professionals, and examining how modern critics address the presence of bugs in literature will help define the cultural identity of insects in the nineteenth century.

Shakespeare's works teem with insect life.[70] Mercutio's description of Queen Mab in *Romeo and Juliet* relies heavily on insect imagery to emphasize the minute size and ethereal nature of the "Fairies Midwife" and her accoutrement:

> Her Waggon-spokes made of long Spinners' legs,
> the cover of the wings of grasshoppers,
> Her traces of the smallest spider web,
> ... Her whip of cricket's bone ...
> Her waggoner a small grey-coated gnat,
> not half so big as a round little worm
> Prick'd from the lazy finger of a [maid.] [I.iv.62–69]

Shakespeare often uses the gnat as a symbol for a supreme irritation or annoyance or as an indication of insignificance, or as a reduction in character. In Act IV, Scene I of *The Life and Death of King John*, when Edward discovers that he is condemned to be blinded by a hot poker, he cries out "O heaven! that there were but a mote in yours,/ A grain, a dust, a gnat, a wandering hair,/ Any annoyance in that precious sense" [IV.i.92–94] in an attempt to evoke sympathy from de Burgh. In *Love's Labor's Lost*, the image of a "King transformed to a Gnat" [IV.iii.164] describes the foolish behavior of lovelorn men. Fleas often serve the same purpose, as in *Taming of the Shrew* when Petruchio, while arguing with Kate about her gown, calls the tailor "[a] flea, [a] nit, [a] winter cricket" [IV.iii.109]. Petruchio refers to Kate as a wasp when he first meets her, alluding to her shrewish personality. Shakespeare also uses the wasp in "The Rape of Lucrece" to represent an invader that has "suck'd the honey" [840] from the "weak hive" [839] of Lucrece's chastity. Moths usually represent of fragility or beauty, as in *Othello*, when Desdemona describes herself as "[a] moth of peace" [I.iii.256], in *The Merchant of Venice* when Portia compares herself to a moth "singed" by a candle [II.ix.79], and in *A Midsummer Night's Dream* in the character of Moth, one of Queen Titania's attendants. In *The Life of Henry the Fifth*, bees are described as "Creatures that by a rule in nature teach/ The act of order to a peopled kingdom," [I.ii.188–89], an image that echoes the classical representation of the beehive as a model for a perfectly ordered society.

John Donne's flea is perhaps one of the best-known examples of a literary insect, and several of his other poems include insect references as well. In "The Flea," the insect "swells with one blood made of two" [8], uniting two would-be lovers in a "marriage temple" [13] before it is "cruel[ly] and sudden[ly]" [19] squashed by the woman, her nail "purpled" by the "blood of innocence" [20]. In another poem, "On A Flea on His Mistress' Bosom," the flea is "envyde" [2] by the narrator as it creeps across the body of his love, a freedom he has been denied, and he promises the flea it "sholdst not dye,/ If [it] couldst suck from her her crueltie" [13–14]. In "The Canonization," Donne compares the lovers to a fly or moth attracted to and destroyed by a candle flame: "Call her one, me another fly,/ We're tapers too, and at our own cost die" [20–21]. Rather than relying on insect imagery to describe the insignificant or repugnant, Donne often turns to insects in order to evoke feelings of sympathy for thwarted lovers or to describe the overwhelming sensation of being consumed by love.

William Blake also turns to insects to enrich his poetry. In "The Human Abstract," the "Catterpiller and Fly" [15], which represent the potential of man, "Feed on the Mystery" [16] of human experience. In "Milton, A Poem in Two Books," the Wine-presses of Los, or War, to humanity, are surrounded by earth worms, grasshoppers, maggots, fleas, tapeworms, slugs, wasps, and hornets "rejoic[ing] with loud jubilee/ ... naked & drunk with wine" [23–24]. The insects in "Augeries of Innocence" are valuable assets to the natural world order and are protected, both by their own abilities and divine will: Blake warns that "The wanton Boy that kills the Fly/ Shall feel the Spiders enmity" [33–34] and entreats the reader to "Kill not the Moth nor Butterfly/ For the Last Judgement draweth nigh" [39–40]. Similarly, in "The Fly," musing over a fly "brush'd away" [4] by his own "thoughtless hand" [3], Blake finds little difference between the fly and mankind: "Am not I/ a fly like thee?/ Or art not thou/ A man like me?" [5–6]. Even though Blake uses insects to represent decay and corruption, he also recognizes their fragile place in the chain of being, an existence ultimately very similar to our own.

Jonathan Edwards, as both a theologian and a natural scientist, was very interested in insects. His close observations of spiders sailing through the air, anchored by a flimsy string of web, reflected in his earliest essay, "Of Insects," which served as the foundation for his later "'Spider' Letter," led him to "admire at the wisdom" ["'Spider' Letter" 168] and to consider "the exuberant goodness of the Creator, who hath not only provided for all the necessities, but also for the pleasure and recreation of all sorts of creatures, even the insects" [167]. His most famous use of insects is in his sermon, "Sinners in the Hands of an Angry God," in which he describes how God holds humanity "over the pit of hell, much as one holds a spider, or some loathsome insect over the fire." Edwards' God is not a loving, forgiving, welcoming God to the unregenerate, but one that "abhors" the sins of mankind and is "dreadfully provoked." Humanity, dangled by a thin thread over the fire, is weighed down by so much sin that a "healthy constitution, and ... care and prudence, and best contrivance, and ... righteousness, would have no more influence to uphold [it] and keep [it] out of hell, than a spider's web would have to stop a falling rock," and only God's "pleasure" prevents the thread from snapping. For Edwards, all men, "before God, are as grasshoppers; they are nothing, and less than nothing, ... feeble, despicable worms of the dust, in comparison of the great and almighty Creator and King." While Edwards uses the image of the insect to convey the insignificance and fragility of men in the face of God's wrath, he believes that insects themselves, like all of "God's creatures are good, and were made for men to serve God with, and do not willingly subserve to any other purpose."[71]

While Edwards's spider is certainly the most well known insect to appear in a sermon, other preachers have also used the insect to deliver their messages of salvation. Charles Haddon Spurgeon once warned his congregation to beware "a preacher making the gospel of the Cross small by degrees, and miserably less until there is not enough of it left to make soup for a sick grasshopper"; in "Everybody's Sermon," he uses the image of a gnat drawn toward a flame, "dazzled and intoxicated," to teach a lesson to sinners similarly lured by the "light of sin": "And while thou seest perhaps with little sorrow the death of the foolish insect, might that not forewarn thee of thine awful doom, when, after having been dazzled with the giddy round of this world's joys, thou shalt at last plunge into the eternal burning and lose thy soul, so madly, for nothing but the enjoyments of an hour?" In "Good News," Dwight Lyman Moody uses insect imagery to explain how faith in the Son of God has removed his fear of death: "Take a Hornet and Pluck the sting out; you are not afraid of it after that any more than of a fly. So death has lost its sting." Both Frederick William Robertson, in "The Three Crosses on Calvary," and Horace Bushnell, in "The Power of an Endless Life," use the worm to represent the uncertainty, pain, sorrow, and "regret[...]" that gnaw at the soul, dividing us from the divine. God's command over nature and the critical importance of insects as God's army is discussed by Reverend Samuel Davies in "Sermon IX: The Connection Between Present Holiness and Future Felicity," who asserts that even insects are "volunteers under the Captain of our salvation," who can "can commission a gnat, or a fly, or the meanest insect to be the executioner of his enemies."[72]

Quite a number of texts would have been widely available to a reader with a general interest in entomology, and an examination of a few representative authors displays their overall tone and approach. In general, books about entomology can be classified as technical manuals, field guides, or informational books designed to entertain and educate a nonscientific audience. A text written for juveniles, *Dialogues on Entomology, in Which the Forms and Habits of Insects are Familiarly Explained*, which was printed for R. Hunter in 1819, was written to "stimulate th[e] spirit of inquiry" which children naturally have. The study of entomology, like all branches of natural history, is an ideal topic of study because "it is easily kept down to the capacity of any age; and it presents a number of intelligible and striking facts, which amuse the senses, without fatiguing the mind, and which lead to observation, industry, and arrangement. That branch of it, which relates to Insects, possesses these qualities in an eminent degree: the great diversity of tribes, their brilliant colours, the ingenuity with which their habitations are constructed, the variety of stratagems to entice and catch their prey, and, above all, their wonderful transformations, captivate and fix the attention of the young observer."[73] Written as a dialogue between young Lucy (judging from her questions, she is most likely between six and eight years of age) and her Mother, the book begins with Lucy discovering a moth freeing itself from its chrysalis and asking her mother what was happening. The book explores moths and butterflies, beetles, earwigs, crickets, mantids, flies, bees, ants, and almost every other insect a young child could think of. Filled with interesting and curious facts, reasonable explanations children could understand, and beautiful illustrations to entice their curiosity, this book indeed serves as a stimulating and informative introduction to the mysterious world of insects for adolescents.

Maria E. Catlow begins her book, *Popular British Entomology; Containing A Familiar and Technical Description of the Insects Most Common to the Various Localities of the British Isles*, printed in 1848, by proclaiming that entomology "cannot fail to prove attractive to those who engage in its pursuit; not only from the extreme beauty and variety of colour and form displayed by the insect world, (though in these respects almost unrivalled,) but also from the unbounded proofs of the Divine goodness and wisdom evinced, in the adaptation of each member in its numerous families to the purposes of creation; and in the instincts bestowed upon them, by which these purposes are fulfilled." Designed to be a general introduction to the study of insects, Catlow hopes it will "prepare the student for the profitable reading" of more sophisticated and technological entomological texts.[74] Like most introductory texts designed to stimulate novice learners, it focuses on basic knowledge, but to add interest, she titles her chapters according to the calendar: she covers entomological terminology and classification information in January and February, and the rest of the months address the insect behavior that actually occurs in each month, creatively describing the metamorphic life cycles of insects. Accompanied by accurately and boldly colored plates of various insects, this text is indeed a beautiful introduction to the amateur pursuit of entomology.

John George Wood's book, *Insects at Home*, published in 1873, seeks to provide, unlike a textbook or field guide, which often "repel the intending student by the array of strange words with which the treasures of knowledge are surrounded," a layman's introduction to entomology unhindered by scientific language and concerns, as its title suggests. Wood asserts "that many have been deterred from pursuing a study hedged about with such difficulties is not a matter of wonder, and it is much to be regretted that writers on science too often increase rather than lessen the difficulties by their purely technical mode of handling the subject" and is determined not to alienate or deter his reader.[75] The book focuses on many aspects of entomology, discussing the definition of an insect, anatomy, life cycles, reproduction, classification, and identification and providing extremely detailed and informative illustrations throughout the text. In the sections on individual insects, he explains how they can be identified in all stages of their life cycles, discusses their natural habitats, explains how to construct artificial habitats to contain them for study, describes their diets and how to feed them in captivity, and offers facts about them he believes to be interesting and compelling. His goal is not to educate future entomologists but to entertain and enlighten an average audience.

The popularity of ecocriticism and the emergence of literary entomology as a new approach to be explored have prompted the publication of several recent texts crucial to the understanding of the position of the insect in literature, although that position has received some critical attention in the past. Colonel Thomas Wentworth Higginson, Dickinson's correspondent, mentor, and close friend, explores the importance and significance of butterflies in his own life and in literature, "Butterflies and Poetry," which appeared in *Part of a Man's Life* in 1905. He begins by asserting that their importance does not lie in their "beauty" or "transformations," appearing most interested in the idea that butterflies "represent an absolutely silent existence" and are thus susceptible to many interpretations, as "each observer makes his own interpretation, or his own sympathetic response, varying, as it may be, from any other." The bulk of this essay focuses on the multitude of poetic representations of butterflies, at times contradictory, with butterflies appearing as both "indolent" and laborious, as both carefree creatures and victims of abuse. Higginson's discussion of his own treatment of butterflies in his personal observations exposes both his interest in the physical experiences and life stages of butterflies and his reverence and regard for the butterfly as a natural work of art, superior to anything mankind could ever produce: "I find that to me works of art do not last like those of nature. I grow tired of pictures — never of a butterfly."[76]

Pearl Faulkner Eddy's 1931 essay, "Insects in English Poetry," another early excursion into literary entomology, begins by describing her initial delight at discovering the myriad insects present in poetry and, "imbued with the spirit of the collector," forming a literary "collection" of insects. She has unearthed beetles, gnats, and butterflies in Chaucer, lice and fleas in Pepys, midges and flies in Shakespeare, gadflies, ants, and flies in Shelley, and bees in Dickinson and Wordsworth. Like the early American entomologists, Eddy struggles to establish academic legitimacy for her insect interests, believing that her "requests for assistance for [her] enterprise were usually answered by a doubtful shake of the professional head or ill-concealed ridicule from [her] fellows." Wishing to convey "some idea of the great variety of insects and their amazing adaptability to any environment in the infinitely varied regions of the great Land of Literature," Eddy, a self-declared literary entomologist, emphasizes the variety of insect-related themes present in literature, including metamorphosis, minuteness, and color.[77]

May Berenbaum's essay, "On the Lives of Insects in Literature," included in Brown's *Insect Poetics*, is another text that offers a brief catalogue of literary insects. Berenbaum explains that "the most frequent use of insect imagery is for metaphorical or figurative purposes" and agrees with Hollingsworth that, for a poet, "precise life history details or species descriptions are irrelevant." She briefly notes insect appearances in literary history, including caterpillars in Rossetti, beetles in Gray and Tennyson, and flies in Keats, and discusses how "insects have inspired and enthralled the human spirit for centuries."[78]

Christopher Hollingworth's *Poetics of the Hive*, a wonderful example of the emerging field of literary entomology, is the first significant study of the evolution of a single insect image: the hive. Hollingsworth begins his rich discussion of over two thousand years of hive imagery with Homer's comparison of an army to a swarm of bees, observing that Homer's bee simile "treats the crowd as the natural unit of human cooperation and uses the view-from-above to decisively link the human social order with the image of the social insect." Virgil "domesticates" Homer's swarm, using hive imagery in four instances in *Georgic 4* to create an image of "cooperation" and "public virtue," a "perfect social order," a society "purif[ied] ... [of] the root of war." The image of city-as-hive is most likely one of the more familiar insect similes; Hollingsworth observes that "with no significant exceptions, from Virgil through the Renaissance, the beehive is used to picture the city." Hive imagery allows Dante to "knit together his hierarchical, visual order with ... his belief that Nature reflects the Mind of God"; in *Paradise Lost*, Milton's Hive of Pandemonium "repaganiz[es] the Hive" and returns to Homer's militaristic model, "a symbol for an oppressive and alien sociality that is firmly seated in our imagination as the (evil) twin to Dante's angelic formation." Classical hive imagery more often than not depicts "a collective figural and psychological orientation."[79]

Hollingsworth argues that "pre-twentieth-century writers knew the Hive as an artistic and therefore artificial analogy, a construct with a specific history and clearly delineated meanings and limits,"[80] untainted by scientific discovery. It is certainly true that nineteenth-century nature writers would have known the bee, as well as other insects, as artificial literary devices, and perhaps Hollingsworth fails to address insect imagery during that time period because he believes that their work is just an adaptation or extension of those common constructs. Nature writers of the nineteenth century, however, familiar as they were with classical constructs of insect imagery, hive or otherwise, were also very interested in and influenced by new discoveries in science and natural history. Their emphasis on fieldwork and observation added a new dimension and awareness to their use of insect imagery, allowing them to incorporate both scientific discoveries and personal experience into their entomological creations. Accordingly, as many writers were interested in moving away from classical imagery in order to create a new American literature apart from European influence and history, it is important to explore how nature writers perceived the world of insects in a distinctly American landscape. Unlike scientists and other researchers interested in examining insects for agricultural and classification purposes, attempting to control and/or eradicate destructive species or collect unusual and unique specimens, Thoreau, Dickinson, and Muir were inspired by the cultural information and scientific discoveries involving insects and began to regard them not as pests to be exterminated or exploited but as essential members of a intricately interconnected natural system or society, discovering in their curious and extraordinary beauty, flawless design, and harmonious relationship with and essential function in nature evidence of the perfection of God's creation.

11

"With Microscopic Eye": Thoreau's Insect Perspective

"Bear[ing] the Closest Inspection": Thoreau's Scientist-Saunterer

Henry David Thoreau often turned to the position or point of view of the insect in order to observe and understand his environment accurately and completely. Several critics, including Nina Baym and David Spooner, have acknowledged the passage in "Natural History of Massachusetts" that inspired this book: "Nature will bear the closest inspection; she inspires us to lay our eye level with the smallest leaf, and take an insect view of its plain" [4]. Very few of them, however, have recognized Thoreau's conscious and deliberate attempts to envision and imagine the world as he believes nature intended, a viewpoint influenced by his contemplation and understanding of the vantage point of the insignificant, the minute, the insect. His consideration of insects, comprised of and informed by his detailed and intensive observations of their ecosystems, life cycles, and behavior, his knowledge of their cultural importance and significance, and his imaginary excursions into what he imagines their world, their experience, to be like, leads him to believe that insects occupy a privileged place in the order and design of creation. While Thoreau seldom literally attempts to imagine himself *as* an insect, he frequently endeavors to interpret what it might be like to be one, imagining what meaning potentially exists in the evening chorus of the crickets, the war of the ants, the circles inscribed on the surface of Walden by the water-skaters, and the processes of growth and metamorphosis in order to explore the divine intent behind both the purpose and place of insects in creation and his own evolving understanding of his position in and relationship with nature.

II. "With Microscopic Eye"

This chapter begins with a discussion of Thoreau's commitment to close and accurate observation, a skill influenced by his interest in and knowledge of natural sciences, including entomology, and his attempt to adopt what he describes as "an insect view of its plain" [NH 4]. His efforts to remove himself as the center of his observations in order to better understand the processes of nature reveal to him the possibility for companionship and inspiration that nature offers. The song of crickets and the hum of mosquitoes, the focus of the second section of this chapter, teach Thoreau that all life except humanity participates in and reverberates with the harmony and pulse of creation, joyously celebrating existence, an awareness enhanced by his ecologically informed appreciation of the fragile interconnectedness of nature. The third section of this chapter explains how Thoreau manipulates his vision to acknowledge the multiple points of view nature presents and to explore the position and experience of water-skaters as they glide across the sacred surface of Walden. Finally, the fourth section of this chapter explores Thoreau's use of the process of metamorphosis to represent his belief that mankind has the potential to transform or evolve from a mindless, social insect into a new creature awakened to and aware of the harmonious equality shared by all members of creation.

On 22 October 1839, Thoreau first wrote the words: "Nature will bear the closest inspection. She invites us to lay our eye level with her smallest leaf, and take an insect view of its plain." This was his only entry that day. Such a brief statement is easy to overlook in a text as extensive as Thoreau's *Journal*, especially as Thoreau does not directly address this idea again until nearly four years later, in "Natural History of Massachusetts." Even though critics including Robert Sattelmeyer believe this essay "is patently an apprentice work which [never] finds a structure of its own,"[1] it is also evident that in several ways "Natural History of Massachusetts" provides a tentative sketch of several themes that Thoreau will playfully explore and manipulate in *Walden*, his *Journal*, and other essays for years to come.

Actually, "Natural History of Massachusetts" serves as ideal introductory text to Thoreau. His descriptions of the "crystalline botany" [NH 24], the "innumerable jewels" of ice that "jingled merrily" [NH 25] as he passes by on "a still and frosty morning" [NH 24] introduce ideas he later develops in *Walden*. The icy "ghost leaves ... were creatures of but one law; that in obedience to the same law the vegetable juices swell gradually into the perfect leaf, ... [a]s if the material were indifferent, but the law one and invariable" [NH 25]. Entranced by evidence of Godly design in nature,

Thoreau repeatedly returns to this idea in his *Journal* and in *Walden*, culminating with the celebrated passage in "Spring" that begins with the living sand foliage erupting from the thawing earth and ends with the exultant conviction that "the Maker of this earth but patented a leaf" [W 207]. Thoreau's fascination with this "crystalline botany," this "ice-foliage" [NH 24] which blooms across the landscape, is continued in *Walden* in his detailed portrayal of the honeycomb pattern he finds in layers of ice [W 202]. His attempts at accurate, scientific observation are evident in his accounts of the appearances, life histories, and habits of various creatures he encounters, including ducks, snapping turtles, crows, muskrats, phoebes, bitterns, and foxes, techniques he continues to refine and adapt as he matures as both a natural historian and nature writer.

One of the most significant themes that Thoreau introduces in this essay involves entomology, the perspective and experience of insects. His first reference to insects displays his budding awareness of the possibility of finding the voice of nature, of the earth, of men themselves, in the songs of insects: "What is any man's discourse to me, if I am not sensible of something in it as steady and cheery as the creak of crickets? ... Men tire me when I am not constantly greeting and refreshed by the flux of sparkling streams" [NH 3–4]. The conversations, even the voices, of men lack the vitality and exuberance of the crickets' "quire"; indeed, Thoreau appears to find verbal interaction with other men more exhausting and dull than anything else. Man has forgotten that "joy is the condition of life," and Thoreau entreats his reader to remember by "think[ing] of the young fry that leap in ponds, the myriads of insects ushered into being on a summer evening, the incessant note of the hyla with which the woods rise in the spring, the nonchalance of the butterfly carrying accident and change painted in a thousand hues upon its wings, or the brook minnow stoutly stemming the current, the lustre of whose scales, worn bright by the attrition, is reflected upon the bank!" [NH 4].

It is no accident that Thoreau includes insects in this brief list of joyous life; insects occupy a position in the natural world that he eagerly wants to explore and understand: "Entomology extends the limits of being in a new direction, so that I walk in nature with a sense of greater space and freedom" [NH 5]. By developing an awareness of the experiences of insects, by deliberately approaching and envisioning his world from their unique perspective, Thoreau "extends" his vision beyond the usual "limits" of human perspective. As he shrinks and hones his angle of vision, as he attempts to "lay [his] eye level with the smallest leaf," he discovers "that the universe is not rough-hewn, but perfect in its details" [NH 5]. Entomology suggests to Thoreau, as it does earlier to William Carpenter, that creation was no accident, that God's plan of design is evident even in the details previously believed insignificant and irrelevant.

Thoreau's interest in natural science and entomology was certainly influenced by his personal and professional relationship with Thaddeus William Harris. Thoreau enrolled in Harris' natural history class at Harvard the first term it was offered, and the subsequent relationship between the two naturalists endured until Harris' death in January 1856, giving Harris ample opportunity to observe and interact with Thoreau. Harris was once noted to have said to Bronsen Alcott, "Thoreau would be a splendid entomologist if he had not been spoiled by Emerson." J. S. Wade supposes that those "words were spoken whimsically or in jest" but prefers to believe that "it is probable that they contain a germ of truthfulness regarding the estimate of Dr. Harris of his friend." David Spooner correctly notes in *Thoreau's Vision of Insects and the Origins of American Entomology* that Thoreau's "vision," his intensive scrutiny of and reflection upon insects, reveals an ability that Harris much admired and respected, a skill absolutely necessary in the pursuit of entomology.[2] Neither Wade nor Spooner appears to recognize the subtle regret and perhaps even twinge of bitterness behind Harris' words. Thoreau, in truth, would have made a splendid entomologist, and Harris must have at least entertained the hope that Thoreau would have followed in his professional footsteps and actively pursued entomology as a career.

Harris shared with Thoreau an intimate respect and love for the natural world and the insects that inhabit it. According to a former student, Dr. Samuel H. Scudder, Harris was "so simple and eager, his tall, spare form and thin face took on such a glow and freshness as he dwelt so lovingly on antennae and tarsi, and as he so fondly handled his little insect-martyrs, that it was enough to make one love the study for life!"[3] It would have been impossible for Harris not to have recognized in Thoreau the passion for and fascination with the insect world that they both shared, and very natural for Harris to consider him as a possible successor. Entomology was only beginning to grow as a respected science, as noted in chapter one; to discover a student who had extensive experience in collecting, describing, identifying, and preserving specimens, a student who had a natural affinity for a science long regarded as foolish and useless, a student who shared his admiration and fondness for as well as his delicacy and tenderness toward insects, must have been tremendously exciting for Harris, both as a scientist and as a teacher. One can only imagine his disappointment when it became evident that Thoreau, who once successfully identified a new species of moth, *Schinia thoreaui*, or Thoreau's Flower Moth, had no interest in pursuing a career in entomology despite his affinity for it. It is also difficult to believe that his statement that Thoreau had been "spoiled by Emerson" was said entirely "in jest." Had Emerson not encouraged his literary attempts, Thoreau very well may have settled into the life of a research entomologist, scouring his beloved landscape for familiar species and new discoveries, examining their relationship with their world and ours, observing their habits and life cycles, and recording every detail with "a sympathy, an insight, a fidelity to detail," with "zest and delight."[4]

Thoreau's commitment to conscious observation, his attempts to manipulate and hone his perspective and vision, and how that alteration influenced his relationship with nature have been discussed at length by many scholars. Daniel H. Peck, in *Thoreau's Morning Work: Memory and Perception in "A Week on the Merrimack Rivers," the "Journal," and "Walden,"* focuses on Thoreau's intimate knowledge of his environment, knowledge he gained through "very little work," by observing.[5] Yet, even in a study devoted to Thoreau's perception of his environment, Peck, like critics before him who characterized Thoreau as "an eccentric loafer or an impractical dreamer," seems to dismiss the effort Thoreau made to observe actively, precisely, and compassionately: "Walden is that axial point from which, by simply watching and waiting, one may 'behold' the full kaleidoscope of nature's phenomena." For Peck, the "observer-scientist" point of view that Thoreau often adopts centers Thoreau in a world view in which the "subject-viewer [is] totally in control of his perceptions," perhaps because the expectations behind those perceptions are already clearly defined, a control that implies that only the observer's perspective will be recognized.[6]

In *Thoreau's Alternative History: Changing Perspectives on Nature, Culture, and Language*, Joan Burbick asserts the similar point that "Thoreau believed that both the perceiving subject and the perceived object were essential for an understanding of natural history," and insists that for Thoreau as well as other emerging nature historians, "nature became the foreground from which all human action must be perceived, justified and understood." Landscape and the environment, nature, serve only as a measure and guide for human experience, as a vehicle through which God's intent for humanity is made clear, and does not exist for its own sake. Eventually, Burbick concludes, it becomes more evident that "perception, rather than presenting a synthesis of the real and ideal, or of natural history and human consciousness, often evokes a sense of separation between the world and the human mind."⁷ It is this separation, however, that Thoreau continually tries to bridge through his detailed observations.

Frederick Garber's *Thoreau's Redemptive Imagination* also addresses perception and observation, and Garber claims that, for Thoreau, "the most successful seeing requires a withdrawal from entanglement in the intricacies ('the maze') of phenomenal activity" and that "all Thoreauvian perception begins from his awareness of the point of self shooting out radii."⁸ The central point of the Thoreauvian experience is to discover where we are, how humanity situates itself within the landscape. For Garber, Thoreau, as a surveyor, was a civilized man performing the civilizing act of reclaiming nature for man's use and consumption; as a man at the edge of civilization and wilderness, Thoreau "mapped" the relationship between his identity and the world surrounding him.

As these critics have observed, Thoreau himself is obviously at the center, the heart, of these observations, but what they often fail to note is that the true foundation of Thoreau's attempts to observe, record, and analyze nature is his attempt to remove himself as that focal point, that center of being, and perceive his world from a perspective separate from his own. As Sharon Cameron explains in *Writing Nature: Henry Thoreau's Journal*, for Thoreau, "man is in the natural world as its witness or beholder, not as its explicator"; the *Journal* especially is Thoreau's attempt "to write about nature that is divorced from the mind's symbolizing procedures," to compose "an entire book predicated on such analogies in which the terms of the ordinary hierarchy that subordinates nature to human nature ... are suspended and transposed." In the *Journal*, "[c]onsciousness does not just mediate or mirror natural phenomena; ... consciousness is displaced by them." Thoreau does not, as Garber claims, want to withdraw from the intricacies he discovers while observing nature; instead, he wants to absorb them, to lose himself in the experience of being not-human, to "displace[... the] human perspective" and allow "nature [to] replace[...] the self which is given up."⁹

Thoreau does not create for himself a solitary experience in nature; in fact, part of the purpose of the Walden experiment was to immerse himself in the community of nature, to regain an intimacy with his environment, to earn the privilege of becoming a newly initiated member of the family of nature itself. As Annie Russell Marble notes, "at Walden, the mice and the squirrel, the loons, the ants, the phoebe in his shed, the robin in his nearest pine tree, became the friends from whom he learned many lessons and upon whom he bestowed all honor and love." Desperately trying to forge a connection to and comprehend the language of the community of nature, "one of his acknowledged purposes was to note the actual awakening of spring in the subtle, secretive phases of soil, woodland, sap, and insect. Eagerly he saw and compared the primal signs of release from hibernation of all vegetable and animal life; with the exultant thrill he heard the first note of the bird, the earliest buzz of the bee, and the faintest chirps of the frog."[10] Just as Thoreau advocated being present at "dawn" in anticipation of spiritual enlightenment, so he anticipates the arrival of the birds, bees, and frogs as he would that of a friend sorely missed, aspiring to listen to and translate their voices, to acknowledge and appreciate their presences, in an effort to remove himself from the assumptions of a perspective centered only on human concerns.

The companionship, not solitude, he finds in Nature allows Thoreau to "foresee [his] recovery" from the "slight insanity" brought on by his separation from and his apparently unbreakable connection to society: "I was suddenly sensible of such sweet and beneficent society in Nature, in the very pattering of the drops, and in every sound and sight around my house, an infinite and unaccountable friendliness all at once like an atmosphere sustaining me, as made the fancied advantages of human neighborhood insignificant, and I have never thought of them since. Every little pine needle expanded and swelled with sympathy and befriended me. I was so distinctly made aware of the presence of something kindred to me, even in scenes which we are accustomed to call wild and dreary, and also that the nearest of blood to me and humanest was not a person nor a villager, that I thought no place could ever be strange to me again" [W 92]. He believes himself to be "no more lonely than a single mullein or dandelion in a pasture, or a bean leaf, or sorrel, or a horse-fly, or a humble-bee. I am no more lonely than the Mill Brook, or a weathercock, or the north star, or the south wind, or an April shower, or a January thaw, or the first spider in a new home" [W 96]. As he begins to understand the structure of the universe and his place in it, as he finally manages to initiate and maintain contact with something, anything, other than himself, he no longer feels like a stranger to nature, but a brother. Even the pine needles and the wind befriend him, revealing themselves to be better company than anyone he finds in human society.

Thoreau repeatedly attempts to allow nature to speak for itself, to exist for itself, in order to avoid the belief that "the purpose of the perceived object is exactly the perception of it by man." Cameron explains that Thoreau attempts to change his point of view, to confront and understand the alien and Other, "by also imagining he could impersonate the alienness — that he could voice nature or be nature's voice.... He says he can abandon the human, can make himself into the alienness he was forced to confront."[11] Bradford Torrey, in the Introduction to the *Journal*, asserts that Thoreau's "craving was for a friendship more than human, friendship such as it was beyond anyone about him to furnish, if it were not, as may fairly be suspected, beyond his own capacity to receive," a friendship that Torrey and Charles R. Anderson both describe as "unattainable."[12] These critics recognize Thoreau's need to create a connection with individual members of creation and his belief that through immersion and observation he could both relate to the nonhuman and forge a meaningful relationship with it.

For John Dolis, author of *Tracking Thoreau: Double-Crossing Nature and Technology*, a critical component of Thoreau's experience at Walden is his effort to translate it: "[T]he subject (matter) of *Walden* will be its very work, will be about narration's own returns, the way it turns itSelf." Narration leads to redemption; "the subject rights itself ... [by] writ[ing] itSelf." Seeking to separate himself from the consuming economy of culture, to "save" himself from the deadly trap of "saving for the future," Thoreau embraces simplicity rather than "accumulation[, which] depletes the subject's 'space.'" and "shuns the grand, the ornate, as unimaginable, unmanageable, unwieldy." To find transcendence, rather than attempting to expand and extend his perspective, "Thoreau's imagination ... moves toward compression and intimacy." Nesting in his hut, "making the earth say beans" [W 108] by day and reading by firelight at night, Thoreau begins a project of "self-cultivation" through language. While one of Thoreau's goals at Walden may have been to reduce himself to find himSelf, Dolis recognizes that this "compress[ed]" experience and perspective leads to an unencumbered "appreciation" and understanding, beyond Reason, of more than self: "Appreciation lets things in, allows them to be, to (co)exist.... It stands to reason that the highest appreciation permits the greatest number of things to enter the picture; it sees how things belong, their different fit, in maximum complexity." Rediscovery of himself allows Thoreau to perceive and translate "a world of possibility, a fabric of compossible worlds."[13]

Thoreau's devotion to the idea that he could somehow erase the human perspective from his angle of vision and replace it, however temporarily or imaginatively, with another, his "appreciation" for and "awareness" of the possible worlds that surround him, is perhaps one reason he never committed to entomology or any other science. The sterile and clinical detachment of scientific observation and data collection, however useful and insightful such information was, could never fully acknowledge the presence of divinity inherent in nature or escape the assumption that humanity's requirements and ambitions and expectations were far more important than the natural world's. This is not to say that he abandons an objective, scientifically oriented approach; as Cameron explains, Thoreau's simultaneous "suspicion of science and his passion for it" cause him to reject the idea "that scientific descriptions of nature and perceptual descriptions of it (which the former are presumed to preempt) are incompatible." His scientific approach informs his attempts to understand the processes of nature, allowing him to recognize and celebrate the intricacies and wonders he believes to be evidence of a divinely ordered and planned creation. In "Thoreau's View of Science," Nina Baym proposes that Thoreau believed that a "complete scientist ... reacquired instincts" in order to hear the "universal rhythm" which all creation but humanity obeys; men must learn it, return to it, in order to "sharpen perception and make out finer patterns and precise regularities," to rediscover the order, the law, the divinity behind nature.[14] In the early years of his *Journal* and in *Walden*, Thoreau continually struggles over maintaining a balance between the clinical attention to detail employed by the scientific observer and the ecstatic wonder and intuition of the saunterer, the "sojourner in nature" [W 29]. Trying to maintain this balance between scientific fact, close observation, instinct, and imagination is how he attempts to redefine his relationship with nature, to gain the unattainable. Thoreau's ideal scientist-saunterer "will smell, taste, see, hear, feel better than other men" [NH 29], and will try to learn, through observation, intuition, and imagination, how to transcend human experience and self-centeredness, how to shift his human-oriented perspective in order to include and accommodate nature's.

Adopting "an insect view of [his] plain" is an observational and philosophical technique to which Thoreau repeatedly returns in order to reevaluate and redefine his own relationship with nature. Excited by the potential discoveries this new angle of vision might reveal, he begins to explore his world anew, invigorated by a heightened "sense of greater space and freedom"; ears sharply cocked, eyes freshly opened, fingers eagerly twitching (had he antennae, they would have quivered), Thoreau attunes himself to the delicate, fragile, almost crystalline beauty and harmony he unearths in the insect and botanical worlds. Less interested in the literal scientific value of his observations, which later will become more important to him as he widens the scope of his entomological explorations, Thoreau emphasizes the universal and spiritual messages of unity and purpose he discovers from attentive observations. The "insect view" allows him to move closer to becoming "the true man of science [who] will know nature better by his finer organization," the scientist-saunterer who learns about nature "by direct intercourse and sympathy" rather than solely "by inference and deduction," in order to participate in "a deeper and finer experience" [NH 29].

"The Interjections of God": Crickets in "Natural History of Massachusetts" and the *Journal*

As Thoreau begins to adopt "an insect view," the first voice he recognizes, one that will fascinate and inspire him throughout his literary entomological career, is that of the cricket. That Thoreau hears what he believes to be a universal rhythm in the "invisible, incessant quire" [29 Aug. 1938] of the crickets has been noted before, especially by James Hedges, who observes that Thoreau finds "the recurrent cycle of the universe" in the crickets' song.[15] Just as a "day is the epitome of the year" [W 202], the crickets' chant marks the cyclical passing of time: "in the autumn days, the creaking of crickets is heard at noon all over the land, and as in summer they are heard chiefly at nightfall, so then by their incessant chirp they usher in the evening of the year" [NH 6]. Thoreau not only finds the pattern of the year, of time, in the crickets' song but also discerns the voice of the "earth herself chanting for all time" [29 Aug. 1938], discovering in the perfection of the crickets' song evidence that creation was no accident, but deliberately designed and orchestrated by the will and hand of God. Crickets, mosquitoes, and the swarms of insects dancing above the surface of Walden, along with the rest of creation, participate in a universal chorus that humanity elects to ignore. The crickets' choir teaches Thoreau that the most insignificant elements of creation unite and work together to form a whole greater than anything mankind has ever achieved, a vital and living reminder that "joy[ous]" celebration and accord rather than human-oriented progress is the natural "condition of life."

As early as November 1837, Thoreau is already conscious of the "clock-and-bell jingling of the crickets" and finds it "very agreeable, penetrating, and not without a meaning" [15 Nov. 1837], and by the following August he pens another critical passage later inserted into "Natural History of Massachusetts": "Every pulse-beat is in exact time with the cricket's chant, and the tickings of the death-watch in the wall. Alternate with these if you can" [10 Aug. 1938; NH 4]. The text immediately preceding this, which Thoreau chooses not to include in "Natural History," reveals even further how crucial Thoreau believes it is to be aware of the "myriad sounds which crowd the summer noon": "the human soul is a silent harp in God's quire, whose strings need only to be swept by the divine breath to chime in with the harmonies of creation." The human perspective, as he has already observed, does not perceive nor participate in the "joy," the delight in creation, that "surely ... is the condition of life"; for the soul of humanity is silent, uninspired, unaware of the joy surrounding it. The song of the crickets, however, is the closest thing to "divine breath" that humanity will ever experience, and acknowledging it, truly listening to it, inspires a connection to the natural world that typically eludes human perception. The chant of the crickets and the tick of the death-watch beetle mark the beginning and end of human experience: the universal hum that ushers us into being and the gradually increasing awareness of our finite existence. Alternating between celebrating birth and anticipating death intensifies our experience of living, of participating in "God's quire."

Sensory immersion in the songs of the crickets, "which seem the very grain and stuff of which eternity is made" [NH 4], becomes for Thoreau a way to escape the worldly and trivial concerns of society, a way to perceive through the "din of religion, literature, and philosophy, which is heard in pulpits, lyceums, and parlors," the true pulse which "vibrates through the universe" [NH 4]. Like "the pure Walden water [that] is mingled with the sacred water of the Ganges" [W 200–201], transcending space and time, the crickets' choir links him to the sacred and timeless heartbeat of creation: "Of what manner of stuff is the web of time wove, when these consecutive sounds called a strain of music can be wafted down through the centuries from Homer to me, ... conversant with that same unfathomable mystery and charm which so newly tingles my ears? These single strains, these melodious cadences which plainly proceed out of a very deep meaning and a sustained soul, are the interjections of God. They are perhaps the expression of the perfect knowledge which the righteous at length attain to" [8 Jan. 1842]. Rather than finding salvation or knowledge in pulpits or parlors, the "righteous" should begin listening to the "unambitious" and melodic hum of insects for inspiration.

Revealing these "interjections of God" in the crickets' chanting, finding that "the very locusts and crickets of a summer day are but ... a continuation of the sacred code" [7 Aug. 1841], reinforces Thoreau's belief that until mankind is willing to change its perspective, to remove himself as focal point, in order to acknowledge and emulate that of the natural world, joy will remain elusive. Thoreau detects a note of sadness in the song, as if the universe itself is mourning humanity's lack of awareness, recognizing that mankind's "silent harp" is a necessary yet absent instrument in the universal song: "The clear liquid notes from the morning fields beyond seem to come through a vale of sadness to man, which gives all music a plaintive air" [8 Jan. 1842]. As Thoreau trains himself to be increasingly receptive to the voice of God in the insignificant chirping of the crickets, to the universal pulse that vibrates through all creation, he realizes that "it hath caught a higher pace than any virtue I know. It is the arch-reformer. It hastens the sun to his setting. It invites him to his rising" [8 Jan. 1842]. The song of crickets, as it marks the eternal rhythm of the passing days and years, inspires the setting and rising of the sun as it should inspire the transcendence and reformation of humanity's perception. The crickets' chanting "invites [man] to his rising" by requiring that he remove the blinders instilled by society, reducing his own position of primacy in favor of what he once regarded as insignificant and trivial, in order to truly behold the wonderful harmony and perfection of creation.

While discovering and listening to the sound of God's voice in the song of the crickets might appear to some to be a mark of insanity, Thoreau measures his personal sanity against his ability to perceive that voice: "I am sane only when I have risen above my common sense, when I do not take the foolish view of things which is commonly taken, when I do not live for the low ends for which men commonly live.... My pulse must beat with Nature.... [O]nly in the quiet of evening do I so far recover my senses as to hear the cricket, which in fact has been chirping all day. In my better hours I am conscious of the influx of a serene and unquestionable wisdom which partly unfits.... I feel my Maker blessing me. To the sane man the world is a musical instrument" [22 June 1851]. The common sense of society and the "low ends" to which humanity generally aspires deaden humanity's sense of the glorious voices of the crickets, preventing mankind from feeling the blessing of their Maker. When man retreats from the chaos and limited vision of society, he recognizes that "it is heaven where [the crickets] are, and their dwelling need not be heaved up.... Only in their saner moments do men hear the crickets. It is balm to the philosopher. It tempers his thoughts.... By listening to whom, all voices are tuned.... They are not concerned about the news. A quire has begun which pauses not for any news, for it knows only the eternal" [22 May 1854]. By abandoning a perspective that insists that the interests of culture, religion, and history are more important than those of nature, by recognizing that the root of the crickets' song and the insects' hum is "a glorifying of God and enjoying of him forever" [22 May 1854], Thoreau begins to develop a greater knowledge of both the interconnectedness of the natural world and his true place within it: "The mosquitoes hum about me.... I begin to distinguish myself, who I am and where; as my walls contract, I become more collected and composed, and sensible of my own existence.... With the coolness and the mild silvery light, I recover some sanity, my thoughts are more distinct, moderated, and tempered" [5 Aug. 1851]. Human culture, human preoccupation with current events and trivial pursuits, is a disruptive force, a negative energy that interferes with his ability to comprehend both himself and his world. As his vision narrows, as his "walls contract" and he hones his perspective to incorporate only that which an insect might perceive and celebrate, he regains that part of himself originally sacrificed to society. Ultimately, the universal chirping of crickets, locusts, grasshoppers, even mosquitoes, becomes for Thoreau "a sound from within, not without" [14 July 1851], external and internal evidence of a divine design, a cosmic dance, in which all life participates, even man, should he choose to join the choir.

Even though crickets do not frequently appear in *Walden*, Thoreau did not deafen his ears to their song. Another member in the cosmic choir, the mosquito, is the first insect discussed at length in *Walden*, and it plays a role very similar to that of the crickets in the *Journal*. While "sitting with door and windows open ... at earliest dawn" [W 63], a time of day especially sacred and productive to Thoreau, he suddenly becomes acutely aware of the presence of "a mosquito making its invisible and unimaginable tour through [his] apartment." The "faint hum" of the mosquito "as much affected" him as could "any trumpet that ever sang of fame" [W 63]. He begins his discussion of the mosquito by describing not only its buzz but its very existence in a distinctly human context, calling it "Homer's requiem; itself an Iliad and Odyssey in the air, singing its own wrath and wanderings" [W 63–64]. Rather than shrinking his perspective to imitate that of the insect, a technique he often turns to in the *Journal*, Thoreau elevates the mosquito to epic proportions, praising its heroic intentions in a way that on the surface resembles the usual interpretations of the ant battle. From a limited human perspective, the noble qualities of the mosquito, like the "satiric" heroism of the ants, cannot possibly exist in the animal kingdom, especially in insects; therefore, it would be easy and predictable for readers to assume that a comparison between such an insignificant creature and the glorified journeys and battles found in Homeric literature can only be in jest, another "mock epic" that points to the brutal and often hidden nature of war,[16] that rather than being truly moved and inspired by the mosquito's song, Thoreau is really commenting upon the tragic casualties memorialized in "any trumpet that ever sang of fame" [W 63]. From this vantage, the mosquito's voice is only important in terms of what it says about human experience and the false glory associated with war.

I believe it more likely, however, that Thoreau's depiction of the mosquito in this passage is more closely connected to his idea of the universal harmony, the divine music, he finds in the chanting of crickets than it is to his attempt to criticize human behavior. It seems quite likely that Thoreau is recalling those "consecutive sounds ... wafted down through the centuries from Homer to me" that he describes earlier in the *Journal* that lead him to discover the heartbeat of creation. In the morning, Thoreau professes, he is most aware, most awake, and "then there is least somnolence in [him]; and for an hour, at least, some part of [him] awakes which slumbers all the rest of the day and night" [W 64]; in the morning, which "brings back the heroic ages," before he becomes tainted by the din of industry and civilization, duty and disappointment, "some part of [him]" is able to recognize and accept the cosmic nature of the mosquito's experience. The inspiration and purity inspired by the prospect of a new beginning, a new cycle, opens his eyes to the "cheerful invitation" presented every morning by nature, the opportunity to reconnect with "Nature herself" [W 64]. The mosquito had "something cosmical about it; a standing advertisement ... of the everlasting vigor and fertility of the world" [W 64], of God's commitment to creation, of the promise of existence itself; it serves as a reminder that "Little is to be expected of that day ... to which we are not awakened by our genius, ... by our newly-acquired force and aspirations from within, accompanied by the undulations of celestial music, instead of factory bells, and a fragrance filling the air—to a higher life than we fell asleep from" [W 64]. Rather than rudely jarring him awake like "factory bells" or "the mechanical nudgings of some servitor" [W 64], which veils his sight and inhibits his true vision, the "celestial music" of the mosquito, the cricket, the all-encompassing hum of creation, allows him to visit, if only for a short time, an Edenic landscape where a faint, delicious perfume rather than the stench of civilization invigorates the air and all citizens of creation undulate and vibrate to the same rhythm.

Thoreau's belief that "To be awake is to be alive" [W 64] is ultimately connected to his understanding of the natural harmony of the universe. One of the ways he can "learn to reawaken and keep [himself] awake, not by mechanical means, but by an infinite expectation of the dawn" [W 64], is to heed the persistent whine of the mosquito. His attempt to "to drive life into a corner, and to reduce it to its lowest terms" in order to "be able to give a true account of" the sublime experience of nature, his effort "to live deliberately" [W 65] and participate in the "innocence" and savagery of nature, is inseparable from his awareness and appreciation of this cosmic droning.

Thoreau returns to the notion of the music of the universe, of creation's pulse and voice, several times in *Walden*. Later, he contracts his vision, refining his focus even further by reducing "all sound," not just the chirping and buzzing of insects when "heard at the greatest possible distance," to "one and the same effect, a vibration of the universal lyre.... There came to [him] ... a melody which the air had strained, and which had conversed with every leaf and needle of the wood, that portion of sound which the elements had taken up and modulated and echoed from vale to vale" [W 86–87]. The wind actively "converse[s]" with all aspects of the world, both the throbbing melody of creation and its discordant human counterpart, diffusing the din of society and incorporating even human voices into the "undulations" of the voice of nature. Even the joyous choral celebrations, the hymns, of God's most delicate creation are overwhelmed by, absorbed into, the melody of the "universal lyre," the delicate yet deafening roar of the wind, the subtle vibration that tingles simultaneously throughout the cosmos.

In this pulse, "the music of the harp which trembles round the world," Thoreau deciphers the message that "goodness is the only investment that never fails" [W 149]; believing that the universe "insists" on goodness "thrills" him, inspiring him to believe that "the harp is the traveling patterer for the Universe's Insurance company, recommending its laws, and our little goodness is all the assessment that we pay" [W 149]. If we can recognize the music of the universal harp, if we can succumb to the gentle caress of the wind and the echo of insect song, our souls are no longer "silent harps"; even though "we cannot touch a string or move a stop[,]" perhaps because we have no individual control or influence over the melody, "the charming moral transfixes us," enlightens us, so that the "irksome noise" of culture is distanced, then diminished, then finally "heard as music" [W 149]. Despite his effort to be good, to celebrate and appreciate the patterns and voices he finds in nature, Thoreau still detects an element of sadness, "a proud sweet satire on the meanness of our lives" [W 149] in the universal choir, perhaps in acknowledgement that humanity can only escape the narrowness of its perception for a limited time before dawn passes and the mosquito is drowned out, once again, by the desensitizing clamor and inharmonious yapping of men.

"Myriad Eyes Suitably Placed": The Water-Skaters of *Walden*

Thoreau's development of and reliance upon the insect perspective is most often an observational technique, a philosophical tool, rather than a conscious attempt to imitate or imagine the literal experiences or thoughts of an insect. Thoreau does not write about pretending to be an ant, a spider, a cricket; there are no passages in *Walden* or the *Journal* that are told using an insect's voice or that try to record the thoughts, the internal, psychological process, the self-conscious awareness of being a bug. Most often, his use of the insect view is just another attempt to reduce egotism and remove himself from the assumptions and preconceptions of his own vision, to appreciate and comprehend nature from another angle, to hear and attempt to respond to a voice other than mankind's. Other times, most often in *Walden*, he uses insects as symbols of metamorphosis and potential for both himself and society, which I will address later in this chapter. A significant exception to Thoreau's usual treatment of insects is his depiction of the water-skater in the *Journal* and *Walden*, an insect that plays a crucial yet critically unrecognized role in Thoreau's intimate relationship with Walden. As he begins to focus on the microscopic details of the miniature environments surrounding him in an effort to remove himself as the center of his observations, aware of the divine intent inscribed on the landscape and concealed in the eternal song and dance of insects, Thoreau recognizes the privileged position of the water-skater sailing across the surface of Walden, which comes to represent the convergence of earth and heaven, and the infinite perspectives that nature discloses to those willing to see.

Thoreau does not lose his interest in entomology and the unique perspective it offers after opening his ears and soul to the universal harmony of cricket song; attempting to imagine an insect's position and experience in nature is an effort he continues throughout the *Journal* and *Walden*. His awareness of the pulse of the earth evident in the crickets' chanting awakens a desire to immerse himself, lose himself, in a world more vast and uncharted than humanity's experience of it: "Would it not be a luxury to stand up to one's chin in some retired swamp for the whole summer's day, scenting the sweet-fern and bilberry blows, and lulled by the minstrelsy of gnats and mosquitoes.... To hear the evening chant of the mosquito from a thousand green chapels[?]" [16 June 1840]. Wallowing neck-deep in stagnant swamp-mud, or half-standing, half-floating, suspended between heaven and earth in the sacred waters of Walden, between water and sky, is an experience that Thoreau periodically reimagines and manipulates as he reduces his vision to accommodate and incorporate that of the insect.

Lawrence Buell notes that "Thoreau's works are designed to replicate a universe in miniature." As Dolis explains, "Thoreau's imagination wants nothing to do with the sublime;" he favors the small and seemingly inconsequential, the humble "huckleberries" instead of the vast expanse of "'all America,'" things "too small, ... too subtle to be seen by bigger things (transparent eyeballs, for one thing)."[17] Rather than becoming an Emersonian "transparent eye-ball" sweeping its majestic gaze across "the tranquil landscape" or "the distant line of the horizon" [E 10], Thoreau reduces his vision to what he calls his "microscopic eye" [23 Sept. 1838], more suited for the delicate and intricate world he wishes to observe; a central design in his attempt to turn this "microscopic eye" to previously unnoticed details of creation is his exploration of the insects' angle of vision. From this angle, "the pines are only larger grasses which rise to a chaffy head, and we the insects that crawl between them" [13 June 1851]. Rather than assert the primacy of humanity's position in the universe, Thoreau deliberately constructs microcosms, miniature universes that challenge that position, that reflect an awareness of the myriads of life surrounding him: "I am always struck by the centrality of the observer's position. He always stands fronting the middle of the arch, and does not suspect at first that a thousand observers on a thousand hills behold the sunset sky from equally favorable positions" [10 July 1851]. There is no reason to assume that those thousand other observers that Thoreau imagines are human. An indispensable part of Thoreau's experience at Walden is focused on re-visioning his beloved pond from as many angles as possible, scientifically, philosophically, imaginatively, in order to truly know it and all life that resided there: "First of all a man must see, before he can say.... Things are said with reference to certain conventions or existing institutions.... See not with the eye of science, which is barren, nor of youthful poetry, which is impotent. But taste the world and digest it. As you *see*, so at length will you *say*" [1 Nov. 1851]. As Walden becomes the central focus of his observations and he becomes intent upon getting to know his neighbors, the fox, the loon, the woodchuck, the eagle, the flying cat, the ever-present chanting of the crickets heightens his awareness of the potential to find the rhythm of the universe in the seemingly most insignificant of life forms. As he begins to realize that "Nature and human life are as various as our several constitutions," he naturally begins to wonder "who shall say what prospect life offers another? Could a greater miracle take place than for us to look through each other's eyes for an instant?" [W 10]. By altering his angle of vision, by celebrating the minute citizens of nature and trying to look through the alien eyes of insects and other life forms, Thoreau discovers that the world "is not a chamber of mirrors which reflect me. When I reflect, I find that there is other than me" [2 Apr. 1852]. Those thousand eyes on as many hilltops could easily be the sharp eyes of the eagle or fox or the multifaceted eyes of a fly or spider or the infinite reflection of the eyes of the water-skater in the gentle waves of the pond.

Thoreau's increasing respect for the inhabitants of Walden and his effort to acknowledge and understand what they experience, what they have to say, is reflected in his rejection of mankind's assumed superiority: "I do not value any view of the universe into which man and the institutions of man enter very largely and absorb much of the attention. Man is but the place where I stand, and the prospect hence is infinite" [2 Apr. 1852]. Recognizing that "man's eye is so placed as to look straight forward on a level best, or rather down than up" [2 Apr. 1852], a world envisioned only from the perspective of mankind is a hopeless and stifling prospect for Thoreau: "I love Nature partly because she is not man, but a retreat from him. If this world were all man, I could not stretch myself, I should lose all hope. He is constraint, she is freedom to me. He makes me wish for another world. She makes me content with this" [3 Jan. 1853]. In order to create microcosms that depict the infinitesimal and delicate citizens of Walden, to "stretch" his vision and escape the limited perspective of man, Thoreau shifts his stance, peers through myriad layers of his own vision, attempting to gain a "wider view of the universe" by looking up, aside, underneath, behind, around, askew. Nature offers more than a forward or downward glance can reveal, and was designed to be especially appreciated from the insect's point of view; even the "painted ... underside[s]" [7 May 1852] of leaves, God's penultimate, "patented" creation, upon which Thoreau "scrawl[s] to send heaven his prayers" [8 Feb. 1841], are "concealed from men's eye — only not from the insects" [7 May 1852]. Thus, to escape the limitations of human perspective and join the choir and transcend himself, man "must patiently study the method of nature ... in the establishment of all communication, both insect and human" [7 Mar. 1852]. Man, "in order to avoid delusions, [must] ... go by and behold a universe in which man is but as a grain of sand" [2 Apr. 1852], must try to experience the world as an insect experiences and perceives it, must recognize and be humbled by his own insignificance in the supreme creation, and learn to find peace in humility and community in nature.

A brief discussion of the ways in which Thoreau interacts with and relates to Walden Pond is necessary background for understanding the importance that is attached to the water-skater. The pond itself, as Thoreau perceives it, is a character, has a personality and presence that supports and sustains more life than even Thoreau thought imaginable and a voice that reverberates with the hum of all creation. Walden Pond actively participates in the innocent beatitude and "liquid joy" that envelops all the myriads of life flitting above, darting below, and gliding upon its surface. The pickerel of Walden, the water-skaters, the dragonflies and gnats and the wild loon, dance upon, or perhaps with, Walden's surface in unconscious harmony while an entranced and slightly envious Thoreau fumbles to create a gateway, or even a peephole, into that experience. Walden's surface, glistening, rippling with the birth of countless and eternal generations of unknowable and incomprehensible life, reflecting earth and heaven, becomes the focal point for Thoreau's attempt to begin true communication with nature and the divine hand that conducts her orchestra.

The critical importance of the pond's central position in *Walden* is widely recognized. Charles R. Anderson's portrayal of the pond as the center of a giant web of creation and text, "as a symbol of the purity and harmony yearned for by man,"[18] comes close to relating the importance of the pond for Thoreau. Longing to release himself from the influential voice of society, yearning to immerse himself in the drumming, incessant voice of nature, Thoreau attempts to reduce the centrality of his own position as observer, and defers to the pond. Walden becomes a living character, engages Thoreau in interactive dialogue, communicates with him, influencing him so deeply that its surface becomes "the earth's eye"; as he peers into it, behind his own reflection, beneath the reflection of dry land and liquid heaven, he notices the faint glimmer of consciousness and self-awareness, an unfathomable eye that unblinkingly stares back at him, "looking into which the beholder measures the depth of his own nature" [W 125], his own soul.

Walden is a sacred space for Thoreau, who professes that "[the Maker] rounded this water with his hand, deepened and clarified it in his thought, and in his will bequeathed it to Concord" [W 130]. Eager "to stand on the meeting of two eternities" [W 11], to forge a bridge between himself and nature, mankind and the prospect of heaven, he contemplates the surface of the pond, reveling in the dual reflection of earth and heaven it offers, a vision of the transcendent heights humanity could attain if only it would listen, would see: "the water, full of light and reflections, becomes a lower heaven itself so much the more important" [W 58]. The eye of Walden, like the eye of a young squall he meets in the forest, "suggest[s] not merely the purity of infancy, but a wisdom clarified by experience" [W 152], an eye "alternat[ing]" with the chirp of the crickets and the ticking of the death-watch, an eye firmly affixed on eternity: "Such an eye was not born when the bird was, but is coeval with the sky it reflects" [W 152]. Walden's eye, the squall's eye, Heaven's eye itself, reflect the timeless promise, the existence, of deliberate creation that all eyes of nature witness and celebrate, as does "the night-hawk circl[ing] overhead in the sunny afternoons ... like a mote in the eye, or in heaven's eye" [W 107]. As he gazes into Walden's surface, searching for some sign of recognition, of possible interaction, and asks, somewhat self-consciously and tentatively, "Walden, is it you?" [W 130], he recognizes that the earth's eye mirrors the eye of the Maker beholding his creation.

The surface of the pond, the face of Walden, the eye of earth and heaven, is a physical location to which Thoreau repeatedly returns in order to listen to the language and song of nature. Some of the most beautifully composed and acutely sensitive passages in both the *Journal* and *Walden* are reflections upon his experiences while floating upon the earth's eye, "sit[ting] in [his] boat, playing the flute[,] ... charm[ing]" [10 May 1841] the pickerel and perch. When he "go[es] forth [to] hear the crickets chirp at midnight[, ... to] feel the antiquity of the night" [9 Sept. 1851] in their universal chant, he turns to Walden. If Walden itself is a sacred site, its surface is liminal space, the stage upon which creation dances, the altar upon which Thoreau can construct a "solid foundation" for a true and pure interaction, communication, with nature. On warm evenings, lulled by the soft lapping of the waves against his boat, absorbed into the multitude of voices surrounding him, the mosquitoes, the crickets, the frogs, encompassed by their resounding chorus, he improvises his own tune and incorporates his own existence into the cosmic melody, playing his flute along with the music he finds in their song, finally participating in the ritual celebration of life. Just as morning is a time of heightened perception that allows Thoreau to be aware of and interpret the significance of a single buzzing mosquito, so evenings on the pond are times for him to actually participate in the choir, to transcend human limitations and communicate as directly as he can with the divine.

At other times, he almost becomes hypnotized by the light of the moon, or by a thousand gleaming eyes hidden in the shoreline and hilltops, endlessly reflected in the water as Walden, too, dances with creation. As Walden mirrors the promise of heaven, embodies the eye of the earth, during the day, Thoreau discovers "a certain glory [which] attends on water by night. By it the heavens are related to the earth, undistinguishable from a sky beneath you" [13 June 1851]. Watching the "reflection of the moon sliding down the watery concave" from the shoreline, he becomes fully conscious of those "myriad eyes suitably placed" that share his vision, and the "shimmering ... bright flamelike reflections of the moon's disk" [13 June 1851] appears in those eyes. As the "waves turn up their mirrors," as Walden pulses in harmony with nature and invites the gaze and gentle touch of its Maker, dazzling those who observe it, Thoreau imagines that "if there were as many eyes as angles presented in the waves, the whole surface would appear as bright as the moon" [13 June 1851]. The infinite number of tiny precise moons mirrored in each ripple, each undulation, of the water, overlaid by Thoreau's own reflection and vision, superimposed again by the unlimited eyes twinkling on land, eyes upon eyes upon eyes, merge into a multifaceted, kaleidoscopic image of universal awareness. The surface of the pond, reflecting all the eyes that observe it, becomes a prism as bright as the moon itself, continually displaying layers and layers of possible perspectives, potential glimpses into the eyes of the other, spontaneous opportunities to look into the eyes of nature.

In a later entry, Thoreau again reflects upon the presence of "the moon ... as bright as in the heavens [and] ... the stars ... dimly reflected in the water" [7 Sept. 1851]; echoing his previous awareness of the insect life surrounding him, he also notices "the path of water-bugs" darting across the pond, streaking like minuscule comets across the heavens reflected in Walden's surface, dancing "in the moon's rays ... like ripples of light" [7 Sept. 1851]. The water-skaters of Walden, skating on the eye of the earth, perpetually cruising on a sacred space, the union between heaven and earth; their eyes, their viewpoint, become the "myriad eyes suitably placed," not along the shoreline or in the trees, but on the water itself. Their eyes are reflected in the waves of Walden as they glide on the surface of heaven and frolic here on earth. Like the pickerel of Walden, "the pearls, the animalized nuclei or crystals of the Walden water," the water-skaters "are Walden all over and all through; are themselves small Waldens in the animal kingdom" [W 191]. Water-skaters exist in the perfect microcosm of the universe, straddling heaven and earth, "partak[ing] of the color of both" [W 121].

The section of *Walden* devoted to the water-skater offers an extended and unified example of how Thoreau attempts to depict an insect's experience that is matched only by Thoreau's treatment of the battling ants and the beautiful bug gnawing its path into existence in later chapters of the book. Thoreau begins to explore the water-skater's microcosm by narrowing his focus once again on the surface of Walden, noticing that "a slight haze makes the opposite shore line indistinct" [W 128], water and land melding together, blurring the margin between land and water. Cocking his head slightly, readjusting his angle of vision, squinting, he aligns his sight so that it parallels the pond's surface, mimicking the viewpoint of the water-skater: "it looks like a thread of finest gossamer stretched across the valley," a silken strand "separating one stratum of the atmosphere from another" [W 128]. The line, the division, that separates the earth and sky from this perspective is so indistinct, diffused, that even "the sparrows which skim over ... sometimes dive below the line ... by mistake" [W 128]. He then raises his gaze, looking "westward," finding himself "obliged to employ both ... hands to defend [his] eyes against the reflected as well as true sun, for they are equally bright" [W 128].

Squinting again to constrict his vision to include only the margin between the true and reflected sun, to "survey [the pond's] surface critically," he discovers that the seam between heaven and earth is "as smooth as glass, except where skater insects at equal intervals scatter over its whole extent, by their motions in the sun produc[ing] the finest imaginable sparkle on it" [W 128]. Effortlessly gliding along the gossamer web that links all creation, rustling along the ripples of light which flicker in response to the pulse of the earth, the water-skater dances along the tightrope that both separates and unites heaven and earth. Thoreau becomes so sensitive to the transcendent position of the water-skater that he claims that "not a pickerel or shiner picks an insect from this smooth surface but it manifestly disturbs the equilibrium of the whole lake" [W 129] and thus the entire universe; the absence of the subtle contributions of even a single water-skater disturbs the cosmic rhythm much more significantly than does the absence of any human influence. From his "distant perch," Thoreau expands his visual range once again to include the entire surface of the lake, and is able to "distinguish the circling undulations" of the path of the water-skater intersecting with the ripples in the water, endless concentric and intersecting circles "half a dozen rods in diameter" [W 129].

That such a small insect could cause such an extensive effect on the surface of the pond that represents the eye of the infinite staring back at creation must have been a very appealing idea to Thoreau. After emphasizing the skater's effect on the pond, Thoreau once again contracts his vision to "detect a water-bug (Gyrinus) ceaselessly progressing over the smooth surface a quarter of a mile off; for they furrow the water slightly, making a conspicuous ripple bounded by two diverging lines" [W 129]. The direct path of the water-bug intersects the delicate circles of the water-skater, weaving a pattern that fascinates Thoreau, causing him to widen his vision once more: "It is a soothing employment, on one of those fine days in the fall when all the warmth of the sun is fully appreciated, to sit on a stump on such a height as this, overlooking the pond, and study the dimpling circles which are incessantly inscribed on its otherwise invisible surface amid the reflected skies and trees.... Not a fish can leap or an insect fall on the pond but it is ... reported in circling" [W 129]. The spontaneous joy of the leaping perch, the bird swooping to pluck the dragonfly from flight, the magnificent choir of the crickets and mosquitoes, all the voices of Walden, are encircled, compassed, by the circles of the water-skater. These circles do indeed compose an inscription, a text writ large by nature's miniature scribes.

The lines inscribed on Walden's surface by the delicate dance of the water-skater, the "dimples" it creates, are "lines of beauty" [W 129]. Like the waves of Walden, eternally reflecting multiple perspectives as it pulses with life, the converging concentric circles of the skater echo "the constant welling up of [Walden's] fountain, the gentle pushing of its life, the heaving of its breast" [W 129]. In his reconstructed vision of the pond, through the eyes of the water-skater, Thoreau realizes that "the thrills of joy and thrills of pain are indistinguishable" [W 129] as all of nature alternates, teeters, between life and death. "Every motion of an oar or an insect produces a flash of light" [W 129], and every action, no matter how insignificant or trivial, is revealed in the tremors that run across Walden's surface.

Extending his field of vision to stretch beyond Walden, he sees that any "field of water betrays the spirit that is in the air. It is continually receiving new life and motion from above" [W 129]. All water is "sky water" and "needs no fence," surviving even the corruption of "nations [which] come and go without defiling it" [W 129]. Water "retains no breath that is breathed on it, but sends its own to float as clouds high above its surface, and be reflected in its bosom still" [W 129], breathing itself into creation just as God breathed life into humanity, giving birth to itself in the clouds, endlessly contemplating itself in its own reflection, continually regenerating.

Following the cycles of the seasons, Thoreau notes that "the skater and water-bugs finally disappear in the latter part of October, when the severe frosts have come; and then and in November, usually, in a calm day, there is absolutely nothing to ripple the surface" [W 130]. The surface of the pond is so glassy, so polished, that "it was difficult to distinguish its surface"; in the absence of the water-skaters, only the "undulations produced by [his] boat extended" [W 130] across it. He wistfully imagines that he can see "at the distance a faint glimmer, as if some skater insects which had escaped the frosts might be collected there" [W 130]; when he reaches "one of these places, [he] was surprised to find [him]self surrounded by myriads of small perch ... in such transparent and seemingly bottomless water, reflecting the clouds, [he] seemed to be floating through the air as in a balloon, and their swimming impressed [him] as a kind of flight or hovering, as if they were a compact flock of birds passing just beneath [his] level on the right or left, their fins, like sails, set all around them" [W 130]. Suspended between sky and water, creating his own ripples in the glossy surface, contemplating the "fish in the sky" [W 70], he attempts to double his vision, to conflate sky and water, blue/green, into a single image, a duality, a layering of imagery, a flash of "rainbow light" [W 138]. In another instance he describes a similar sensation, his experience of standing within a rainbow, which "dazzl[ed him] as if [he] looked through colored crystal" and allowed him to experience, "for a short while" [W 138] what it would be like to live like a dolphin.

Thoreau later returns to the image of the water-skater gliding across the pond and the unique perspective it affords during his discussion of the first ice that forms along the pond's shores. In the winter, there is no boat separating him from the surface of the pond, nothing preventing him from stretching his limbs across the solid surface of the lake, balanced "like a skater insect," to "study the bottom at [his] leisure, only two or three inches distant, like a picture behind a glass" [W 166], and he is finally able to see what the water-skaters see. Thoreau's later description of the "double shadow of [him]self, one standing on the head of the other, one on the ice, the other on the trees or hillside" [W 196] reflected in the "shallow puddles" of "beautifully blue," "greenish" [W 200] ice melting in the spring, another picture in the ice, echoes his earlier techniques of blending the perspectives of the crickets and water-bugs with his own to create a unified yet multifaceted image within the prism of Walden's surface, of fusing bird and fish, of blurring the distinction between earth and sky. Thoreau stands on his own reflection, coexisting between earth and sky, sauntering alongside the water-skater, balancing the tightrope between heaven and earth like a spider dangling between the margins and edges of creation.

"What Will Be Hatched Within Me?": *Walden* and Metamorphosis

One of the most widely recognized aspects of Thoreau's interest in and use of insects is his repeated return to images of transformation and metamorphosis. Thoreau's interest in regeneration and rebirth evolves into his fascination with metamorphosis, as he narrows his scientific and poetic focus from the "myriads of life" endlessly regenerating to individual cocoons and pupae. Walden becomes the stage for his own metamorphosis, and his "hut" in the woods has been described as "a cocoon, a self-manufactured chrysalis, an entomological space altogether set apart from society."[19] His solitary experiences allow him to "[weave] for [him]self a silken web or chrysalis, and, nymph-like, [he] shall ere long burst forth a more perfect creature," transformed from an "inorganic and lumpish" larval existence into a new life informed by his new relationship with nature [8 Feb. 1857]. Inspired by his close scrutiny of nature, he uses insect and metamorphosis imagery to reflect nature's limitless fecundity and to symbolize humanity's condition and potential, individually and socially, for positive regeneration.

Thoreau's deliberate attempt to listen to the voice of creation, the "breathing and panting of all nature," which he finds in the "universal crickets' creak" [7 Sept. 1851] and mosquitoes' hum, paired with his developing knowledge of the pond's surface and the insects that live there, lead him to fuller appreciation of the multitude of life begetting life around him. As he contemplates Walden, he notices that "the rushes over the water are white with the exuviae, the skeletons of insects—like blossoms,—which have deposited their eggs on their tops" [20 June 1850], death and rebirth alternating, displayed perfectly before him. Later, in November, after the crickets have ceased their song and the rest of nature has retired to await spring, confronted by the barrenness of fall and winter, Thoreau recognizes his own initial urges to create something, to participate in the cosmic anticipation of spring, as well as his uncertainty about how to proceed, perhaps frustrated by his attempts to revise his draft of *Walden*: "I feel ripe for something, yet do nothing, can't discover what that thing is. I feel fertile merely. It is seedtime with me. I have lain fallow long enough" [16 Nov. 1850]. Thoreau returns to the thrilling potential of creation and birth the following August, after immersing himself once again in the universal hum: "Each sound seems to come from out a greater thoughtfulness in nature, as if nature had acquired some character and mind. The cricket, the gurgling stream, the rushing wind amid the trees, all speak to me soberly yet encouragingly of the steady onward progress of the universe.... Ah, I would not tread on a cricket in whose song is such a revelation.... I mark that brook as if I had swallowed a water snake that would live in my stomach. I have swallowed something worth the while.... How many ova have I swallowed? Who knows what will be hatched within me?" [17 Aug. 1851]. Whimsically wondering what might hatch inside him as he recalls the thousand eyes from the hilltops, the myriad eyes reflected in the pond's waves, the infinite number of dragonflies and water-bugs and imps dancing with the water, he also feels the churning and rumbling of creation writhing within as he struggles to transcribe and translate his experiences at Walden, to render the relationship he has developed with nature into a language mankind can understand, and to redefine and redirect himself and humanity.

As he attempts to translate the language of nature into the text of *Walden*, to merge "impotent," "youthful poetry" with "barren" scientific observation in order to form a pulsating, living text, Thoreau turns to the "formative metamorphoses" of nature to describe his understanding of the human condition and the possibility, the necessity, of transcendence. In *Thoreau's Vision of Insects*, David Spooner asserts that "the long extended fourfold structure, related to insect metamorphosis, of individual evolution ... [is] ... the process that ... unifi[es] *Walden*": "the quadruple (philological) movement from ovum to larva, thence to pupa or chrysalis, and finally to psyche, or butterfly, is related to the spiral of (self-)education and maturation hypothesized as a universal plan of regeneration in *Walden*, and realized by the author." Thoreau "assum[es] humanity is more intimately related to the insect than the ape, and that society has to be defined in relation to the abstractions of the metamorphic process. This is the pragmatic outgrowth of the living relationship he set up with nature."[20] In *Walden*, Thoreau calls for the conscious and deliberate metamorphosis of the "human insect." Spooner's use of the four stages of insect metamorphosis provides a helpful framework for understanding Thoreau's conception of the development and maturation of the human insect. After experiencing the literary quickening of the countless ovum he has swallowed while forging his friendship with Walden, he reduces mankind to its most basic form, the fertile seed or ova of the creator implanted in the earth: "the plant, instead of going on to blossom and bear its normal fruit, devotes itself to the service of the insect and becomes its cradle and food. It suggests that Nature is a kind of gall, that the Creator stung her and man is the grub she is destined to house and feed" [30 July 1853]. Just as Thoreau imagines himself to be "ripe for something," to be implanted with the enormous potential of life by Nature, he imagines the original act of creation in insect terms. In this image, God resembles a giant cosmic botfly, inoculating the "grotesque vegetation" [W 205] of the unsuspecting earth with the eggs that will become humanity. In this stage, mankind is still pure, latent, existing in harmony with the pulse of the earth, mindlessly growing within but not yet disturbing without. For Thoreau, insect eggs come to represent not only the endless potential and possibility of life itself but also the condition of humanity as it was meant to be, coexisting simultaneously with nature without disrupting it, unified with creation: "The whole tree itself is but one leaf, and rivers are still vaster leaves whose pulp is intervening earth, and towns and cities are the ova of insects in their axils" [W 206].

The movement from ova to grub or larva to mature adult is inevitable, and Thoreau returns to this progression multiple times in order to explain his understanding of the human position in society and nature. Mankind is but a "lumpish grub in the earth" [W 206] a "gross feeder ... in the larva state" akin to the "voracious caterpillar" and the "gluttonous maggot" [W 146] and appears content to remain that way. Society acts as if no other possible conclusion to humanity's development exists, concentrating on endlessly swarming and replicating; "there are whole nations in that [larval] condition, nations without fancy or imagination, whose vast abdomens betray them" [W 146]. Society itself becomes the pinnacle of creation, consuming, like locusts, everything in its path to ensure its own survival. Town and cities, once harmless "ova of insects," isolated pockets of human potential, once hatched, multiply across the landscape, drowning out nature with the incessant false hum of industry and progress. Social insects such as bees and ants, usually praised for their structure and organization and viewed as positive symbols of society, represent for Thoreau the mindless self-involvement and self-absorption that ultimately separates mankind from the rest of creation.

As Hollingsworth explains, bees have always served as a useful symbol for the benefits of an industrious life, an affirmation that the individual busy bee contributes to the well-being and continuing survival of its hive, its society. Swanson declares "it is easy to see ... how the economy of the bee could provide the perfect paradigm for that of a human colony in terms of independence and self sufficiency. Bees produce everything for the maintenance and continuation of the colony — shelter, food, protection, even 'government' — with substances produced in their own bodies — wax, propolis, honey, venom, royal jelly." Thoreau, however, "reject[s] ... the 'virtuous-bee' paradigm" in *Walden*,[21] sympathizing with the unacknowledged fate of the unmourned individual drone or worker bee trapped in the self-perpetuating business of the hive, bred to be incapable of existing on its own.

Bees appear very briefly in *Walden*, and only metaphorically. Describing the faint echo of gunfire from town carried to him by the wind as he hoes his beloved beans, he says, "It seemed by the distant hum as if somebody's bees had swarmed, and that the neighbors, according to Virgil's advice, by a faint *tintinnabulum* upon the most sonorous of their domestic utensils, were endeavoring to call them down into the hive again. And when the sound died quite away, and the hum had ceased, and the most favorable breezes told no tale, I knew that they had got the last drone of them all safely into the Middlesex hive, and that their minds were bent on the honey with which it was smeared" [W 110]. Swanson acknowledges Stanley Cavell's interpretation of this passage, reiterating that "Thoreau simply means he hears the militia and thinks it sounds like the clatter that the villagers would make beating spoons and brass keys against cooking pots and warming pans, which was the traditional way of trying to frighten swarming bees into a new hive," but she believes that the metaphor functions on additional levels.[22]

Thoreau's allusion to Virgil extends beyond Cavell's idea of a simple evocation of "epic ambition" for *Walden*.[23] Swanson believes that Thoreau would have known that the practice of summoning a hive by banging on pots and pans was ineffective, as this method had been challenged many years earlier by Jerome V. C. Smith in 1831. Just as a swarm cannot be called to the hive by the "clanging noises" of housewives banging on pots, so the legions of soldiers trained to defend the hive during the revolutionary war could not be appeased or sustained by the ringing of bells, the popping of gunfire, or the "waifs of martial music" [W 110]. Old soldiers, like old drones, are now "stingless, ... useless and a drain on society." In a condition similar to the drone, a worker bee exists only to produce, nurture, and protect the next generation, "her first task in life being to clean the cells from which she has just emerged, in preparation for their next occupants. The insignificance of the individual worker bee is emphasized by this telling detail. Indeed, the single bee is meaningless, and not even viable." In the hive of the bee and the hive of society, the individual's potential is measured only by contributions to the hive: The "only 'viable' individual is the colony, and in order to reproduce, the colony must swarm, creating a new, second colony, exactly like the first." Mankind's slavish devotion to patriotism, to industry, to tradition, creates an individual unable, even unwilling, to exist outside of the hive. Swanson contends that Thoreau moves away from the traditional interpretations of hive society "as a model for human behavior," claiming that "what is virtuous among social insects Thoreau believes not to be so among men." In a hive, "the single bee is meaningless, and not even viable," and the only method of reproduction a hive has is to swarm. It is this image of swarming that Swanson believes to be so disturbing to Thoreau: the continual reproductions of culture endlessly repeated in the name of culture and tradition. Individual bees, portrayed as individual soldiers in the ant episode, are, like soldiers, "used by society ... and cast off afterwards as useless," truly "self-less, in fact, mindless."[24]

    Thoreau's extended parable of the ants also functions to illustrate his belief that in order to realize its full potential, humankind must separate itself from its hive mentality. Ants, like bees, exist in a highly structured society, whose only goal is to perpetuate itself. Thoreau uses the image of the ant twice in *Walden* to point to the controlled and stagnant existence of an individual controlled and defined by society. The first reference to ants is quite brief: "Still we live meanly, like ants; though the fable tells us that we were long ago changed into men; like pygmies we fight with cranes; it is error upon error, and clout upon clout, and our best virtue has for its occasion a superfluous and evitable wretchedness" [W 65]. In his article, "'The Battle of the Ants': Two Notes," Patrick O'Connell clearly establishes the connections between this short excerpt and the later, longer battle of the ants. O'Connell retells the story of King Aeacus of Aegia, whose subjects were destroyed by "a pestilence"; in response to his prayers, his father Jupiter "transform[ed] a colony of ants into men and thus repopulated the island kingdom."[25] Despite the transformation from insect into human, "still we live meanly," battling each other over trivial concerns, steadfastly praising industry and loyalty to the hive over individual accomplishments and deviations, achieving only a "superfluous and evitable wretchedness" for all our troubles.

Thoreau's second example of the ant-like existence of humanity, the battle of the ants, is enhanced by the earlier ant passage that appears in *Walden*. O'Connell is the first critic to note that Thoreau's reference to the ants as "legions of ... Myrmidons" is linked to the earlier excerpt. Achilles, the leader of the Myrmidons, is King Aeacus' grandson, and the allusion links both Thoreau's ants and Achilles' ants to the race of ants transformed into humans by Jupiter in the story of King Aeacus, perhaps "plac[ing] the battle of the ants firmly in the mythological context used earlier in *Walden* and elsewhere, as well as introduc[ing] the whole series of mock-heroic comparisons" that have become the focus for much of the critical exploration of this passage. Francis D. Ross is correct when he says that "the close-up view" of the ant battle "is essential ... for it reveals what Thoreau intends to say about war: when it comes right down to dirt reality, war is grotesque and horrible,"[26] but criticizing the atrocities of war is not Thoreau's only purpose in this section.

O'Connell comes closer to the mark when he realizes that "the point of the whole story" is explained later,[27] when Thoreau claims that he was "[him]self excited somewhat even as if they had been men. The more you think of it, the less the difference" [W 156]. There is nothing to distinguish the epic and proud battles of men from the presumably meaningless and instinctive battles of the ants; after witnessing the ant battle, Thoreau "felt for the rest of that day as if [he] had had [his] feelings excited and harrowed by witnessing the struggle, the ferocity and carnage, of a human battle before [his] door" [W 156]. As Ross observes, Thoreau "wants us to see the human side of the ant war," to learn not only the literal, destructive consequences of war but the lesson that even war is not a uniquely human institution and that our perspective is not as unique as we like to think.[28] The patriotic fever, the drive to sacrifice the individual to ensure the continuation of society, society's glorification of its sacrificed heroes, does not elevate humanity above the rest of creation; our epic wars are no different, no less inspiring or horrifying, from the battles of the ants and bees driven to protect their hives. Thoreau reports that, according to William Kirby and William Spence, "the battles of ants have long been celebrated and the date of them recorded" [W 157], perhaps in recognition of the blind devotion, the team spirit, displayed by both ants and men.

Swanson adds an interesting element to the critical dialogue on the battle of the ants when she explains that François Huber, "the only modern author who appears to have witnessed" those battles, actually witnessed a battle between bees, not ants. Observing six hives through a glass table, Huber actually sees the simultaneous "massacre" of the drones by the worker bees, who "seized them by the antennae, the wings, and limbs, and after having dragged them about, they killed the unfortunate victims by repeated stings directed between the rings of the belly"; in the fall, another generation of drones, its usefulness outlived, reduced to an unwanted mouth to feed, will be slaughtered, either stung to death, which involves the self-sacrifice of the worker bee, or, more often, simply forced out of the hive to eventually die of exposure. Swanson observes that even though Thoreau jests that his wounded ant is recuperating "in some Hotel de Invalides" [W 157] he understands that "the fate of both the wounded ant and idle drone" like "the fate of the wounded or idled soldier," both spurred on by their "brute natures," will always be to be "used by society ... and cast off afterwards as useless." The individual ant, bee, or human will invariably be expected to sacrifice itself in order to preserve the whole; the only difference is that man "let[s] himself be used by society," choosing to live "the mean lives of social insects, ruled by instinct...; their virtue is not virtue at all, but 'wretchedness.'"[29]

Convinced that humanity can escape the limitations and meaninglessness of living as a social insect, Thoreau turns to images of metamorphosis to describe his hopes for the eventual transcendence of humanity. The "lumpish grub [implanted] in the earth" by the creator must overcome its brute nature and experience yet another transformation, must shed the trivial trappings of society in order to become "the airy and fluttering butterfly" [W 206]. Just as the "snake casts its slough, and the caterpillar its wormy coat, by an internal industry and expansion" [W 19–20], mankind must experience a "moulting" that "must be a crisis in our lives" [W 19], a solitary experience like the moulting of the loon or cicada. The "'great deeds, and ... divine songs, which shall never die'—that is, as long as we can remember them," the "progress in art and science and literature" recalled by men "with satisfaction," must be forgotten, replaced by the simple understanding that "We know not where we are" [W 223]. Hopeful that man can expand his perspective and overcome his instinct to place himself at the summit of all creation, Thoreau still realizes that "we esteem ourselves wise" and are unlikely to disrupt the "established order on the surface" [W 223] we have created. However, Thoreau holds firm to the belief that "These may be but the spring months in the life of the race" [W 223], refusing to believe that humanity has already reached its full potential and understanding of the workings of the universe: "As I stand over the insect crawling amid the pine needles on the forest floor, and endeavoring to conceal itself from my sight, and ask myself why it will cherish those humble thoughts, and bide its head from me who might, perhaps, be its benefactor, and impart to its race some cheering information, I am reminded of the greater Benefactor and Intelligence that stands over me the human insect" [W 223]. The insect attempting to hide itself in the pine needles experiences the world in a way no different from Thoreau, who imagines himself to be a bug scurrying about under the tall pine trees that, from his altered perspective, could be tall blades of grass; both are insignificant residents of a world continually basking within the gaze of its creator, one no more important than the other.

Walden's dependence on the metaphor of metamorphosis culminates in "Conclusion," with Thoreau's description of the bug that gnaws its way out of an old apple-tree table. Spooner recognizes that this event, like the ant episodes in *Walden*, is "drawn not from the author's observations, but from other sources."[30] The true story of the apple-tree table began in 1786, when the eighty-year-old tree was cut down and manufactured into a table for Major General Putnam. The Major General's son later moved the table from Connecticut to Massachusetts; over the years, from 1806 to 1814, three "strong and beautiful" [W 224] insects chewed their way out of the table, perhaps stimulated by the heat of the fire, an iron, or, as Thoreau claims, an urn. The story first appeared in a little-known periodical, the *Literary and Philosophical Repertory*, in March 1816; another version surfaced in 1821, in Timothy Dwight's *Travels in New England and New York*. The story was reprinted, in edited form, in 1829 in D. D. Field's *History of Berkshire County, Massachusetts*, a book owned by Herman Melville. In 1839, the story again appeared, in an abridged form, in J. W. Barber's *Massachusetts Historical Collections*. As Thoreau refers to Dwight's book several times in the *Journal* and *Cape Cod*, Walter Harding concludes that Thoreau's source for this story was Dwight's version. Harding acknowledges that Melville also referred to the book, and supposes that Dwight's and Field's books were Melville's only sources for his version of events told in his story.[31] Frank Davidson, however, argues that the details present in Melville's story exist only in Thoreau's version told in *Walden*, and believes that Melville's inspiration to write "The Apple-Tree Table" is influenced by all four renditions.[32]

The paragraph that contains the reference to the "strong and beautiful" insect begins with "The life in us is like the water in the river" [W 223], recalling the countless ova the insects have deposited into the water which will eventually hatch within Thoreau as well as the grub of humanity originally planted into the earth by the creator. Similarly, the beautiful bug was hatched "from an egg deposited in the living tree many years earlier still, as appeared by counting the annual layers beyond it" [W 224], existing in a somnolent, latent state within the concentric circles of tree growth that are reminiscent of the concentric circles of the water-skaters gliding across the eye of heaven, secure in the gall of nature, which is "destined to house and feed" it [30 July 1853]. The soul of humanity, like that of this "beautiful and winged life," "has been buried for ages under many concentric layers of woodenness in the dead dry life of society, deposited at first in the alburnum of the green and living tree, which has been gradually converted into the semblance of its well-seasoned tomb" [W 224]. Human society, which once coexisted in harmony with the rest of creation, once hatched out of the "living poetry" [W 207] of the earth, a fleshy lobe, a quivering leaf, has constructed for itself a tomb rather than a cocoon and has emphasized the glorification of the past rather than the gift of existing within the present. As Thoreau says in the beginning of *Walden*, "God himself culminates in the present moment, and will never be more divine in the lapse of all the ages" [W 69]. As man awakens, as he becomes aware of the voices surrounding him, as he is "enabled to apprehend at all what is sublime and noble ... by the perpetual instilling and drenching of the reality that surrounds [him]" [W 69], he is inspired to "gnaw" his way through the dead shell of society into a new state of mind, a new morning. Even society's "most trivial and handselled furniture" may house such a hidden treasure, a perfect testament to the unbounded spirit of all life, emerging from its larval state, its spring, "to enjoy its perfect summer life at last!" [W 224].

Many critics have noted that Thoreau's approach to nature changed gradually but dramatically after the publication of *Walden* in 1854. Donald Worster notes that "After several decades of happy, innocent wandering through local orchards and woods, Thoreau ... began at the age of thirty-five to approach nature with more method and precision," and Spooner claims that, after years of seeking to identify and relate to the individual members of the natural world, "by 1855, [Thoreau] had garnered all he needed from taxonomy, especially in the spheres of plants and aquatic creatures, and was redefining himself along the lines of what would today be called an ecologist,"[33] widening his vision to include the vast, interconnected system of nature his intensive scrutiny has revealed. No longer content to rely on his "microscopic eye" to uncover the patterns of resurrection found in Nature, he realizes, as he expresses at the end of *Walden*, that "the universe is wider than our views of it" [W 214]. The narrowed perspective of insect vision that allowed him to experience the wideness of the universe now seems limiting to him, preventing him from seeing "views as wide as heaven's cope" [19 Aug. 1851]. In *Walden*, he manages to balance and merge the visions of both his scientific and poetic eyes. Later, as he moves farther away from Emerson's influence and develops a growing interest in Darwin's writing,[34] his insect vision becomes less poetic and symbolic and more scientific as he begins to focus less on the microscopic details of the natural world and more on the complete picture, the ways in which the individual parts make up the whole, perhaps influenced by the ecological interconnectedness he witnesses among the inhabitants of, his neighbors at, Walden Pond. Perhaps in unconscious tribute to his long-time kindred spirit, Dr. Thaddeus Harris, who died less than two years after *Walden* was published, Thoreau's observations of the insect world in the later years of the *Journal* emphasize the insect's position within its individual ecosystem rather than the symbolic and transcendent messages revealed by the scrutiny of that position, characterizing another stage in the metamorphosis of his literary and entomological interests.

III

"A Minor Nation": Emily Dickinson and the Insects' Society

"Whatsoever Insect pass —": Dickinson's Entomological Poetry

Emily Dickinson's relationship with and depiction of nature as reflected in her poetry is usually considered evidence of her connection to Romanticism; as Joanne Feit Diehl notes in *Dickinson and the Romantic Imagination*, Dickinson's poetic "preoccupations — the self's relation to nature, the power of the imagination as it confronts death, a heroic questing that leads to a trial of the limits of poetic power — are the primary concerns of Romanticism as well." More recently, ecocritics and others have begun to explore Dickinson's treatment of nature from other angles, emphasizing her awareness and understanding of science, including chemistry, physiology, botany and horticulture, geology, and entomology, and her exposure to "a whole number of proto-ecological discussions" offered in natural history essays, textbooks, and even field excursions. A self-described "Scientist of Faith" [J1241/ F1261], her scientific knowledge and expertise do not interfere with her quest for spiritual guidance, enlightenment, and certainty; rather, they enhance it: "her approach to the subjects of her poems typically blends close, nearly microscopic, empirical observations of phenomena with speculations about the significance of what she is seeing." Her developing knowledge of ecology, her understanding of the fragile connections between all members of the natural world, reinforced by the small, daily miracles and reminders of a greater power that she discovers in her observations of nature, primarily in her garden, lead her to consider

"The pretty people in the Woods" [J111/F113] as "Citizen[s]" [J1374/F1407] of a complex society, as her neighbors, companions, friends, and equals.¹

In many ways, it is impossible to separate Emily Dickinson's poems, her "italic Seed[s]" [J946/F1112], from the blossoms and insects she observes in her garden; silken and iridescent petals and feathers and wings are gently gathered from the air and offered and displayed in her poetry [J86/F98], sometimes accompanied by freshly picked or dried blossoms. In an early letter to her brother Austin, describing her desire to chase off the gloom of a graveyard with the song of crickets, she capriciously wonders, "will they grow if I transplant them?" [L 43], a jest that points both to her clever humor and her frequent synthesis of flower and insect, forever and intimately intertwined and interconnected in her mind and in nature. Judith Farr notes that when Dickinson chose to share her poems with others, they were "often enclosed in letters pinned together by flowers, or in bouquets that made the poem concealed at the flower's center and the flower themselves one message" and she "often spoke of the written word as a flower"; at times, Dickinson even included the corpse of an insect, a cricket or bee, with her poetic missives. Wendy Martin observes that "The word fascicle ... is ... a botanical term referring to a flower pattern in which the petals spring irregularly from the top of the main stem like a peony. In binding her poems into fascicular packets, Emily Dickinson chose an appropriate form for the blossoming of her poems; each poem was a petal, each packet a flower."² Clearly, in Dickinson's mind, her poems, her flowers, and in many respects even her insects are intertwined, discrete yet inseparable elements of an organic whole that can be seen to reflect her understanding of and appreciation for a multiform but unified and sacred nature.

This chapter investigates how Dickinson's familiarity with the ecological interconnectedness of all the citizens of her garden, plants and insects alike, encouraged her to incorporate into her poetry her own interpretations and translations of their societies and cultures, the symbiotic nature of the unacknowledged relationships between insect, flower, humanity, and the divine force that governs creation. The first section of this chapter explores how Dickinson's religious faith and uncertainty and her scientifically-based knowledge enhanced her experience in and observation of nature and her ability as a poet, allowing her, as Inder Nath Kher describes, to "comprehend[...] all the worlds from here to eternity" and to develop a "proto-ecological" awareness of nature.³ Dickinson's knowledge of science, especially natural history, botany, and entomology, as well as her appreciation and understanding of Nature as a possible vehicle to or as the voice of the divine allows her to meet and befriend a society of "Nature's People" [J986/F1096], "A Minor Nation celebrat[ing]/ It's unobtrusive Mass—" [J1068/F895]. In the second section of this chapter, I explore how Dickinson's observation of and interaction with her insect neighbors lets her perceive the equality of all members of creation, inspiring her to appreciate the value of all life, even insects, worms, and spiders, to question mankind's assumed superiority to nature, and to participate in the joy and exuberance that is, as Thoreau and Muir also observe, the "condition of life." Dickinson's use of cocoon and metamorphosis imagery is the central topic of the third section of this chapter. Unlike Thoreau, who uses the process of metamorphosis to support his belief in the possibility of growth for all humanity, Dickinson's interest in metamorphosis emphasizes the transformation of the individual within its self-constructed, solitary cocoon. In the process of metamorphosis, in insects' ability to transform and resurrect themselves, Dickinson finds evidence for the possibility of personal transformation and spiritual resurrection, strengthening her faith in immortality and Heaven.

Throughout her career, Dickinson frequently focused her poetic eye on the same subjects; her "poetry reaches its maturity almost immediately" and her failure or conscious refusal to deviate from those central topics of interest frequently has been noted. Both David Porter and Steven Winhusen have observed that "Dickinson's particular style ... remained largely without evolution during the thirty years of her writing career." Winhusen elaborates upon this idea by claiming that "the necessity of dating Dickinson's work by handwriting stands as a testament to its stability of grammar, style, and subject over the span of her career. While such subjects as love, faith, death, and eternity are certainly encompassing of human thought and experience, Dickinson's obsessive treatment of them over the years shows little development. They remain the stable material consumed in the singular flame of Dickinson's idiosyncratic style." It is so difficult to trace the development or growth of any particular idea in Dickinson's poetry partially because of her interest in examining philosophical dialectics, "the conflicting claims of two worlds," such as life and death, science and religion, and heaven and earth, and the ever-changing spectrum of ideas between those poles, her mind and faith ever vacillating, sometimes stumbling but never failing, never quite settling on an absolute truth or a perfect answer, in an effort to reconcile her conflicting ideas and uncertainties about those subjects. James McIntosh asserts that she was especially interested in exploring the mysterious, unknowable, and inexplicable in her poetry, explaining that "Dickinson accepts her vocation as a poet of intellect whose special province is the unknown — in God and God's creation, in the inner life of human beings, in the human experience of nature, and in the sorcery and chaos of death."[4] Dickinson repeatedly turns to nature to assuage her doubts about the character of God, the purpose of life in the face of the inevitability of death, and the possibility of salvation, discovering in its subtle and intricate processes and relationships, endless fecundity, and perpetual celebration evidence of a creation divinely ordered and maintained, a creation in which every member serves a unique and distinct purpose and is equally deserving of the attention and love of God.

Dickinson's doubts about the Calvinist tradition in which she was raised and about the certainty of her personal salvation as a sinner, one who "hardheartedly resisted the call of Christ," have long been of interest to scholars. Joan Burbick observes in "'One Unbroken Company': Religion and Emily Dickinson" that Dickinson's poems "are often interpreted against the background of either Puritanism or Transcendentalism" by critics who interpret her rejection of formal conversion as a "'rebellion' against the authoritarianism of religion" or "against an authoritarian father and a guilt-inducing mother." Burbick refutes this idea, explaining that "the feminized nineteenth-century religious persuasion of the evangelicals ... emphasi[zed] ... group continuity and familial love," not a "nightmare" of "humiliation" as some have suggested; and she asserts that Dickinson believes that "God is benevolent; [it is] her 'heart' [that] is unwilling." According to Burbick, Dickinson's interest in conversion and heaven "involved less individual salvation than group continuity before and after death," exemplified by her desire and hope that that life and death will come full circle and she will be reunited with those who have already passed on [J1743/F1784], thus situating Dickinson's desire to believe despite her doubts within her need to "avoid isolation and to cement the bonds of friendship."[5] Unlike Burbick, in "Queen of Calvary: Spirituality in Emily Dickinson," Nadean Bishop agrees that Dickinson's religious doubts center on her inability to accept "the autocratic God of patriarchy" and argues that "Dickinson's spirituality is ... marked by negation of the resisting dogmas and a decision based on Self-Reliance to remake God and to create her own Heaven." Despite their differing opinions about the root of Dickinson's religious doubts, both Burbick and Bishop agree that Dickinson explores the possibility of believing in a compassionate and kindly God, one which Bishop describes as "a God constantly in process, interacting lovingly with suffering humankind," one "who is not autocratic, who does not act arrogantly..., and who rewards collaborative effort over individualism."[6]

As Bishop says, "[t]oo often in the past, critics have taken Emily Dickinson's Mount Holyoke rejection of God as her final world on divinity." Dickinson may have rejected formal conversion to the Church despite pressure from her mother and friends, and she surely experienced periods of spiritual devastation and uncertainty when faced with personal illness or disappointment or the illness, absence, and death of her loved ones, but she never completely abandons her faith even though she frequently questions it. In her contemplations of the nature of and her relationship with God, "she alternately believed in, questioned, quarreled with, rebelled against, caricatured, even condemned, but never ceased to engage" divine authority. Dickinson's uncertain faith is reflected in McIntosh's description of her attitude toward the Bible: "her continuing engagement with it as a text she knew in intimate detail led her to both believe and disbelieve in it, painfully or nimbly"[7]; this doubt, accompanied by an intense desire to believe, almost certainly extended to other aspects of her religious and spiritual life. Dickinson's lack of faith often centers on her personal unworthiness and insignificance and her inability to accept her personal salvation with the confidence and innocence she felt as a child. The poem "The Child's faith is new—" [J637/F701], for example, describes the abandon with which children are free to believe in Heaven, a faith that is unwavering, steadfast, and confident, "Whole—like His Principle—/Wide—like the Sunrise," until adult experience taints innocence. As they mature, children learn to recognize the dangers hidden behind beauty, to fear the unexpected and sublime, and forget the exquisite yet at times terrifying perfection behind God's design.

In "I should have been too glad, I see—" [J313/F283], she realizes that she "should have been too saved—," should have excelled at attaining salvation, should have exceeded the expectations of her family and friends urging her to accept grace; instead, she admits that a "Fear too dim," too unsubstantial and seemingly inconsequential, to impel her toward that salvation, causes her to forget the lessons and "Prayer[s]/ [She] knew so perfect—yesterday," in a past when she needed them. She realizes that she "should have had the Joy/ Without the Fear" and dreams of a humanity that could be saved without Jesus' sacrifice even as she acknowledges the necessity of the Crucifixion, longing for an idealistic and Edenic existence even as she attempts to accept the imperfect. Her "'Faith' bleats — to understand" the contradictions that form existence, how life and death, ecstasy and agony, faith and fear are intertwined and inseparable, and she learns that true faith endures precisely because it is tested.

She pursues this idea again in "He strained my faith —" [J497/F366], describing a faith that is constant but unacknowledged and unrewarded. Her faith in Jesus was vibrant and resolute despite the trials to which she is subjected; even though she does not know why she is being punished, she accepts the suffering willingly, desiring only for her faith and loyalty to be acknowledged, not rewarded. She never questions, only pleads for attention and forgiveness, describing herself as his "little 'John'" in reference to her innocence reverence and lamenting that her constancy and her *self* have gone unnoticed: "Do'nt you know — me?" Even though her faith has been able to withstand the trials that life has delivered, she is still at times unable to believe that she is important enough for Jesus to "know."

Her desire to rekindle her relationship with God, to rebuild her faith after it has been shaken, is evident in the poem, "I prayed, at first, a little Girl" [J576/F546], which emphasizes the impossibility of preserving the blind faith of childhood after enduring the trials of adulthood. When Dickinson was a child, God was a constant presence, a gentle, parental figure focused on her almost exclusively, attentively listening "Each time [her] Childish eye/Fixed full, and steady, on his own" as she "told him what [she]'d like, today" and reassuring her about "parts of his far plan/ That baffled [her]." As she aged and became more aware of "The mingled side/ Of his Divinity —," the dark that must accompany the light, more "qualified to guess/ How prayer would feel — to [her] —," she still longed for the comfort she found as a child in a god in whom she had absolute faith and trust. The best she can manage is a tentative "Balance/ That tips so frequent, now" that, despite her efforts "to poise — [,] ... does'nt stay —." Praying because and as "they told [her] to" no longer sustained her faith that God was able or even willing to watch over her; but in nature, Dickinson rediscovers the "Balance" between Creator and creation that came so easily to her as a child.

Dickinson, perhaps "long[ing] for the gentle and generous ... female diety who exude[s a] loving spirit,"[8] at times describes God as a maternal force watching over her creation, an image in stark contrast to the stern, distant, judgmental God she was "told" was her Savior. The cold impartiality of her father's patriarchal God is reflected in five short lines:

> Of course — I prayed —
> And did God Care?
> He cared as much as on Air
> A Bird — had stamped her foot —
> And cried "Give Me" — [.] [J376/F581]

By contrast, in "'Mama' never forgets her birds" [J164/F130], a poem written on the occasion of the death of her Aunt Lavinia in 1860 and sent to her cousins Louise and Frances, she is once again able to envision and relate to God with the childlike wonder that she yearns for in "I prayed, at first, a little Girl." God is "Mama," a warm presence that loves her maturing creation just as much as she did when it was newborn, at the beginning of creation:

> She looks down just as often
> And just as tenderly
> As when her little mortal nest
> With cunning care she wove — [.]

Our world, a "little mortal nest," was lovingly created and actively tended and each member of creation is equally marked and loved by God; echoing Matthew 10:29, Dickinson declares that "If either of her 'sparrows fall,'/ She 'notices,' above," a reassurance of God's compassionate attendance that neither she nor her cousins would have received from her father's "authoritarian" and distant God.

In "Nature — the Gentlest Mother is" [J790/F741], a female figure that could represent God, especially when read in conjunction with "'Mama' never forgets her birds," is depicted as a gentle, nurturing parent who understands the weaknesses and limitations of her children. Even "The feeblest — or the waywardest —" of her children do not incite her annoyance or wrath. She exacts delicate control over the organic and elemental forces of nature, "Restraining Rampant Squirrel —/ Or too impetuous Bird —," and a beautiful summer day represents a "Conversation" with "Her Household," like a mother who subtly directs the creative energy of her children. In the evening, she listens to the prayers of all of her progeny before they retire, encouraging their devotions by her presence, recognizing the worth of even the smallest and unworthy, her presence

> Incit[ing] the timid prayer
> Of the minutest Cricket —
> The most unworthy Flower — [.]

At dusk, after her children are tucked in and tended as if by a doting and conscientious mother, she

> With infinite Affection —
> And infiniter Care —
> Her Golden finger on Her lip —
> Wills Silence — Everywhere —

and creation sleeps. Here, as in "'Mama' never forgets her birds," Dickinson is able to rest assured in the belief that when her small and "childish eye" searches for divine reassurance, God will at least "notice" and "Care."

Dickinson eventually comes to believe that faith is a constant negotiation, a balancing act, between absolute certainty and incapacitating doubt. She does not abandon her faith out of fear or lack of proof or religious passion; she knows that, as Patrick J. Keane says, "to wrestle with God, even at times to denounce him, is still to have a relationship, however stormy,"[9] and she balances her spirit, adrift on this stormy sea, through her poetry. As she says in a poem included in a letter to Samuel Bowles, there is still a "Balm," a healing power, in a "Religion/ That doubts — as fervently as it believes —" [J489/F1449]. Just as the rest of creation is built on contradictions and uncertainties, it is expected that "Faith slips — and laughs, and rallies —/ Blushes, if any see —"; even as she "Plucks at a twig of Evidence —," attempting to uncover the facts behind creation, she understands that finding proof is impossible, and faith must be blind even when doubt, like a rotten "Tooth[,]/ ... nibbles at the soul" [J501/F373]. In "Faith — is the Pierless Bridge" [J915/F978], it is faith that spans the gap between "what we see," the proof in the landscape, and "the Scene that we do not —," the Heaven beyond our scope, a link "Too slender for the eye" to see on its own. Uncertainty is part of God's design, as Dickinson describes in "How brittle are the Piers" [J1433/F1459]. The Bridge to Heaven "is as old as God —/ Indeed —'twas built by him —"; Jesus was "sent to ... test the Plank,/ And [God] pronounced it firm." Even though she may believe her faith to be "brittle" and frail, because of God's plan and Jesus' sacrifice, it will be enough. Indeed, it is faith that connects and unifies all elements and movements of creation, an idea explored in "My Faith is larger than the Hills" [J766/F489]. In this poem, just as the crickets have the power to set the sun, her faith will "show the Sun the way" across the sky. If the sun does not rise and morning never comes, "The Bird would not arise/The Flowers would slumber on their stems"; she "dare[s]" not

> stint a faith
> On which so vast depends —
> Lest Firmament should fail...[,]

refusing to risk the rest of a creation which pivots on her faith to indulge and wallow in her own doubts.

Dickinson's attempts to rediscover her faith in a benevolent and loving God based on the evidence she finds in nature are in many ways based on her advanced understanding of the interconnected ecological processes and relationships that govern creation, an insight that today would be described as an ecocritical perspective; in this way, her scientific knowledge and expertise clearly influences her understanding of and belief in God. In the essay "'Often seen — but seldom felt': Emily Dickinson's Reluctant Ecology of Place," Christine Gerhardt explains that "the growing recognition of Emily Dickinson's involvement with the world around her has sparked fresh interest in the links between her poetry and nineteenth-century views of nature." Gerhardt believes that "[t]he dawning of environmental discourses that reached across the U.S. in the mid-nineteenth century is of crucial importance to understanding Dickinson's poetry about the natural world" and discovers in her poems evidence of a finely tuned ecocritical perspective, only natural considering her era's budding "interest[...] in serious nature study" and development of a "heightened awareness of natural systems ... especially [for] white middle class women." Her extensive background in botany, a discipline that "encouraged students like Dickinson to pay detailed attention to their immediate natural surroundings, developed indispensable tools for cataloguing and systemizing plants, and dealt with topics later gathered together as the science of ecology" most likely contributed to her interest in natural history essays, which "combin[e] personal narratives of nature appreciation with new scientific insights," and transcripts of "public debates about the need to protect vanishing wilderness areas," which would have been included in many of the publications to which the Dickinson household subscribed. Dickinson's poetic focus, Gerhardt asserts, "intersects in subtle but crucial ways with these early environmental discourses. In writing about place, in particular, her poetry engages with a number of proto-ecological concerns of her day and also anticipates later positions about the possibilities and limitations of human interaction with the natural world."[10]

Dickinson's interest in "proto-ecological" issues certainly informs both her faith in a divinely designed and ordered creation and her perception of the natural world as a system comprised of indispensable individuals, no matter what their relative size or degree of importance to mankind; her scientific approach to nature allowed her to hone the vision necessary to perceive those minute truths. Several critics have addressed the way her scientific studies molded and transformed the way she perceived and imagined her environment and reflected it in her poetry. For example, in "'Sweet Skepticism of the Heart': Science in the Poetry of Emily Dickinson," Fred D. White asserts that "at Amherst Academy, Dickinson had almost certainly fallen under the spell of the naturalist and Christian mystic Edward Hitchcock, who taught geology at the college ... and who believed that close study of nature was a way of coming to know God." At school and at home, Dickinson often was exposed to both scientific and religious models of interpretation for the natural world, perspectives which often clash, each contradicting the core beliefs, the philosophical foundations, of the other, an inherent conflict to which Dickinson alludes in the succinct poem,

> "Faith" is a fine invention
> When Gentlemen can see —
> But Microscopes are prudent
> In an Emergency! [J185/F202].

According to White, Dickinson "uses poetry to perform, in effect, experiments in language, her counterpart to scientific experiments, which she accepted as equally valid efforts for apprehending Truth," and writes "poetic equations [that] ... work to counteract scientific reductionism, ... tempt[ing] us into thinking that science can present reality whole and undistorted." As she filters scientifically accurate data based on her intensive scrutiny and examination of nature through the creative, imaginative lens of her poetic eye, conducting "experiments" and calculating "equations" as she attempts to suffuse her poems with life (recall her request that Colonel Higginson determine whether her poems were "alive" and "breathed"), her "scientific angle of vision, complete with scientific and technical language, amplif[ies] rather than reduce[s] the mystery of what is being dwelt upon." Instead of sterilizing her vision, blinding her with raw data and empirical facts, White believes Dickinson had a scientifically informed gaze that is able to distinguish and interpret the fine nuances and minute details of her environment, allowing her more fully to appreciate nature and explore it in her poetry.[11]

Dickinson's description of herself as a "Scientist of Faith" is discussed by James Guthrie in *Emily Dickinson's Vision: Illness and Identity in her Poetry*. Conjecturing that Dickinson might have had exotropia, a deviation of the cornea that results in excruciating pain and extreme sensitivity to light, Guthrie believes that recognizing Dickinson's fear of possibly losing her sight is central to understanding both her religious uncertainty and her poetry. Guthrie asserts that "poetry functioned as an extension of herself, an alternate mode of perception that took the place of her injured eyes and which was equally as capable of revealing the truth to her" and that "illness was a formative experience as well, one which shaped her entire poetic methodology from perception to inscription and which very likely shook the foundations of her faith." Desperate to find divinity, yet doubtful of its existence, "Dickinson hoped that a measured combination of restrained vision and imaginative explorations ... might safely reveal the insights into divinity she sought." By "appropriating the tools and concepts of science" and using her enhanced vision to root out sacred truths in the landscape, Dickinson "hybridize[s] the scientist's intense observation with an amateur theologian's insights," finding faith in facts. Dickinson's use of scientific observation to reinforce her understanding of a sacred and meaningful natural order that is immediately and eternally available "contradict[s] both scientific dispassionateness as well as religion's insistence upon deferred gratification." Imagining her world through the seemingly opposed lenses of science, religion, and imagination and engaging in a conscious, deliberate "synthesis of faith and observation" permits her to "experience nature with her whole being, not with her intellect alone."[12] Although she sometimes worries that she, like other scientists "who know [nature]," will "know her less/ The nearer [she] get[s]" [J1400/F1433], the intricate design she unearths as she immerses herself in the natural sciences continually reinforces her belief in a divine plan.

Dickinson's dependence on science to help her reveal the divine intention behind creation was more than likely also influenced by her relationship with Colonel Thomas Wentworth Higginson, who, like Dickinson, practiced a "synthesis of faith and observation" to enhance his understanding of God's role in the natural world with his scientific eye. Dickinson recognizes the kindred soul embodied in Higginson, asking in an early letter, "I know the Butterfly — and the Lizard — and the Orchis — Are not those *your* Countrymen?" [L 268], fully confident that they were. While critics universally acknowledge Higginson's commanding influence on Dickinson and her poetry, they have only lately begun to emphasize how much of a factor his interest in natural history and entomology might have been in their relationship. Midori Asahina, author of "'Fascination' is absolute of Clime': Reading Dickinson's Correspondence with Higginson as Naturalist," believes that Higginson's nature essays, which offer evidence of "his detailed observation of natural phenomena and his and Dickinson's shared sense of wonder at the natural world," were of primary significance to Dickinson. Frank D. Rashid observes in "Higginson the Entomologist" that "Higginson's conventional nineteenth-century stance toward nature and his preachy evangelism on nature's behalf may have masked the extent of his involvement in the natural sciences, particularly entomology." Rashid reports that, like Thoreau, Higginson learned natural history at the knee of Thaddeus William Harris and was enough of a budding entomologist that he served as "student curator of entomology at Harvard." Harris even selected him "to report to the Harvard Natural History Society on Harris' own discovery of a species of tropical butterfly (*Laertias philenor*) new to the northern United States." Like Dickinson, he was fascinated by the insect life he discovered during his explorations of nature. Rashid admits that Higginson was much more concerned with the "literal, ... the science of Entomology," than Dickinson, whose "bees, butterflies, crickets, spiders, and flies are far more figurative and less scientific than his," but it is clear that he "was not opposed to reading insect poems, and Emily Dickinson knew it." It is impossible to measure how much of an influence Higginson's entomological knowledge and background may have had on Dickinson's inclusion of insects in her poetry, but it is certainly an interest they actively shared and discussed.[13]

Dickinson's interest in and relationship with the plants and blooms in her garden and conservatory is also closely connected to her efforts to allay her religious doubts through her scientific knowledge, and a discussion of that relationship is necessary to any discussion of Dickinson's portrayal of the insects that inhabit those spaces. Keane explains that "for Dickinson, a lifelong, expert gardener as well as a poet, the central issue of theodicy — what to make of suffering and death and possible rebirth in an ordered world presided over by a supposedly providential and loving God — was seasonally enacted year after year in her own beloved garden, over whose plants and flowers she doted as if she were the world's first gardener, Milton's 'Eve, alias Mrs. Adam.'" Domhnall Mitchell devotes significant attention to Dickinson's obsession with flowers and plants in "'A Little Taste, Time, and Means': Dickinson and Flowers," chapter four of *Emily Dickinson: Monarch of Perception*, situating Dickinson's horticultural interests within her family's socioeconomic position rather than acknowledging the remarkable achievement Dickinson's garden represented. The cultivation of flowers, especially the exotic bulbs Dickinson preferred, was an expensive pursuit, as bulbs and plants ranged from five to fifty cents each and became "a measure of refinement" which would have been unattainable in less affluent households. The addition of Franklin stoves to the Dickinson home in 1855, another costly luxury, afforded Dickinson the ability to privately practice both poetry and botany in her room, penning verses and forcing bulbs by firelight. In addition, her father, Edward Dickinson, built the conservatory in 1855, which allowed Dickinson to indulge in her gardening passion throughout the year. Rather than praising Dickinson's development of two distinctly difficult crafts, Mitchell emphasizes that her successes in both gardening and writing would have reflected very well on her father, enhancing his social "status, because it meant that he could afford to keep his daughter at home." Instead of interpreting Dickinson's success in these areas, the results of years of study and experience and countless hours of careful, observant, and skilled attention, as a "rejection" of her father's and her society's perceptions of the limited possibilities for women, Mitchell asserts that gardening and writing were both "historically preconditioned" activities for women and that "Dickinson's choice of poetry as a career, like her interest in flowers, ... [represented] a partial acceptance of those values."[14]

Farr more completely explores Dickinson's obsession with plants and flowers in *The Gardens of Emily Dickinson*. Disagreeing with Mitchell that her garden and conservatory were more symbolic of Edward Dickinson's social status and an acceptance of socially proscribed roles for women than they were of Dickinson's skill as an experienced horticulturist, Farr believes that her "passion for gardening was more intrinsic both to her personality and to a much larger movement in American culture." In a rich discussion of the various meanings assigned to the blossoms of both her garden and her brain, Farr explains that flowers come to represent for Dickinson her poetry, her self, her soul, her lover, her faith, and even her belief in "life itself," asserting that "it was [Dickinson's] garden that encouraged her to believe in eternal life and to hazard belief in the existence of God," discovering in the constancy and process of nature comforting evidence of God's design. Flowers become such an intrinsic part of Dickinson's identity that she often refers to herself as a blossom; for example, Dickinson twice represents herself as a cow lily, or simple orange daylily, once to her girlhood friends, as recounted by Emily Fowler, alluding to the "orange lights in her hair and eyes," and once to Higginson, upon their first meeting, when she extends to him two orange daylilies as her introduction, proffering, as Farr describes, "her thoughts, friendship, loyalty, and artistry for his pleasure and acknowledgment."[15]

If Dickinson finds comfort and renewed faith in the awe that nature inspires, it is perhaps because she hoped or even, at times, believed God intended her to find them there. In "The Bumble of a Bee" [J155/F217],

Dickinson describes her surrender to the harmony and beauty she finds in nature. She succumbs to the voice of the bee, "A Witchcraft" that stops her in her tracks and has the power to awaken Spring, although "'Twere easier to die — Than tell —" why she is affected that way. Sunset also leaves her breathless and helpless and "Taketh away [her] will," and Dawn "Addeth to [her] Degree," allowing her to transcend herself, although, again, she cannot explain why. She is only certain of God's presence, "for God is here," and only he, the "Artist — who drew [her] so" can fully understand or explain why nature transforms her, or why she is able to be transformed. In "I could suffice for Him, I knew —" [J643/F712], when she positions herself "face to face with Nature," indulging in the sensory experiences of listening to the buzz of a bee and witnessing a sunset or the unfolding of a blossom, she finds herself "face to face with God." She describes in "My period had come for Prayer —" [J564/F525], as she looks for evidence of God written in the horizon, how she is "awed beyond [her] errand —," seized by the wonder and beauty of nature. Instead of praying for forgiveness or asking for salvation, she again imagines how God must feel when constantly confronted with the troubles and requests of the penitent, and "[She] worshipped — did not 'pray,'" praising creation rather than questioning her position and purpose within it.

"They make me regret I am not a Bee —": Dickinson and Nature's People

Most of the critical discussion centering on the insects in Dickinson's poetry emphasizes their symbolic importance, concentrating, for example, on the spider as a representation of the artist, the butterfly as a symbol for beauty or human aspiration, or the bee as a sexual predator or divine fertilizer.[16] An ecocritically informed reading of Dickinson's treatment of insects, however, reveals her awareness, recognition, and celebration of their critical position in the complex web of creation. Instead of emphasizing how insects might represent human concerns or desires, an ecocritical perspective suggests that, at least on some level, insects might very well represent themselves. As she begins to understand the intricate processes of nature, its eternal cycle and delicate balance, a knowledge informed in part by her academic background, probable reading material, personal relationships with prominent natural historians, and, perhaps most importantly, maintenance of and interaction with her garden, her poetry begins to reflect a belief that nature, a deliberately designed organic system, a neighborhood or community comprised of eternally grateful and joyous residents, exists for itself. Awed and comforted by the harmony and delight she finds in the natural world, Dickinson rediscovers her faith in a divine presence and purpose behind creation and perceives the Eden, the Heaven, on earth. Ultimately, her observations of the interconnected processes of nature lead her to realize that all life has a right to exist and to fulfill its divinely ordained purpose, that "To be alive — is Power —" [J677/F876], and that the smallest and most insignificant life, even the life of a solitary insect, is an essential and unique strand in the tapestry of nature.

Gerhardt emphasizes three ecological traits of Dickinson's poetry especially relevant to a discussion of her treatment of insects that will form the critical foundation for this section of my discussion of Dickinson and insects. First, Gerhardt explains that Dickinson is very attentive to "the relationships among natural phenomena, betraying an eye for ecologically significant processes." Her scientifically trained eyes enable her to see that "the links among plants, soil, climate, and animal are not so much indeterminate as they are multiple, since each of the parts is connected with more than one unit, so that their relationships are surprisingly multidimensional." While planning, tending, and observing her garden and conservatory, actively applying her horticultural and ecological knowledge to the maintenance of her beloved plants, experimenting with light, fertilizer, temperature, new and exotic varieties, cuttings, bulb forcing, seed collection, storage, and propagation, soil and bed preparation, composting, companion planting, and insect control, Dickinson witnesses firsthand the delicate balance of multiple conditions necessary for most plant and animal life to survive. While it could be argued that her gardening techniques and experiments are nothing more than an attempt to manipulate the natural world for her own purposes, Dickinson likely imagined that her scrupulous study of botany and her daily plant-care rituals, her attempts to create a more stimulating, nurturing, and hospitable environment for her plants, were on some level an attempt to get to know them, to understand their physical and even emotional requirements, as any mother would, as nature did, so that they might thrive. Her awareness of this balance and her engaged participation in it reflects her development of what Gerhardt calls a "bioregional" perspective, an "organic connection" with her ecosystem that is described in the poem "The Robin's my Criterion for Tune —" [J285/FR256]. In this poem, Dickinson "describes herself as physically nourished by the region just as the plants and birds are, growing out of the soil together and linked to them through a collective 'we.'" Her recognition of her own place in the fragile ecosystem, one who tends and is tended, "resonates with her time's growing awareness of the unexpected *interrelatedness* of nature's small and large, past and present elements."[17]

Second, Dickinson's poetry often focuses on a "seemingly" insignificant and unremarkable plant, insect, flower, or "unspectacular landscape that exists on its own terms and has a right to continued existence," a perspective that Gerhardt believes to be "a crucial prerequisite for environmental awareness." In her analysis of "Four Trees — upon a solitary Acre" [J742/F778], a poem she describes as "one of Dickinson's most ecologically sensitive contemplations of human-nonhuman relationships," Gerhardt explains that, while customary readings of the poem emphasize the "speaker's spiritual, emotional, or intellectual disposition" and find only "isolation" and "the poet's inner chaos," an ecocritical stance reveals the primacy of "a place whose physical presence matters." Rather than being a symbol for the condition of the speaker, a reflection of human concern and preoccupation, "a stepping stone for transcendence," in this poem, this particular place itself is "a subject in its own right" and "participates in mapping its cultural *and* natural geographies." In general, "Dickinson's poetry fosters a non-utilitarian recognition of horizontal natural systems," reflecting her growing belief that the world existed for its own sake, not for the use of humanity.[18]

Third, Dickinson's poetry, "for all its elusiveness and supreme mastery of metaphor, also perceives human-nonhuman relationships as specific to particular locations"; indeed, her detailed descriptions of her garden neighbors and her desire to understand their world indicates that "her poetic interest in being 'aware/ Of Neighbors and the Sun' [J822/F817] might involve more than mere transcendence." Her recognition that all of nature is connected and that each element has a right to exist, to fulfill its own destiny, allows her to perceive and develop deeply intimate connections to the natural world; in "the little cosmos of her garden, its tenants and visitors," flitting between blossoms and singing praises from the grasses, capture much of her attention and appreciation, and she begins to believe that "The Gnat's supremacy," its position in creation, its right to exist, "is large as" [J583/F419] if not larger than her own. After all, "God made no act without a cause —/ Nor heart without an aim —" [F1192], and to make that presumption is sheer human arrogance. Just as Dickinson "loved flowers quite as much and as if they *were* human," "*were* people," the insects in her garden become distinct, individual characters, essential presences that in many ways help pollinate her "italic Seeds," the "Blossoms of [her] Brain" [J945/F1112].[19]

Dickinson's understanding of the complicated process that precedes and initiates any growth of life, the "Constancy [that] must be achieved/ Before [a Seed] see[s] the Sun" [J1255/F1298], is perhaps best expressed in the poem, "Bloom — is Result — to meet a Flower" [J1058/F1038]. In this poem, informed by her scientific observation and her attempts "to experience empathetically what it might be like ... to *be* a flower,"[20] she describes the complicated and unexpectedly dangerous process a plant must experience in order to produce a bud. Usually regarded as purely ornamental or decorative, a symbol of beauty or fragility, a flower is a deliberate creation, an effect of labor, evidence of a successful plan, a fruitful journey, a thriving experiment. To the uneducated passersby, a flower is a trivial thing, a pretty frippery, and its fine and delicate appearance provides no hint of the precise environmental conditions and the very real hazards a flower needs and endures. A careful and knowledgeable observer, a student of nature, in contrast, is well aware of and awed by the elaborate design and purpose flowers represent. In order to "pack the Bud," to initiate the thought of a bloom, the mature plant (some plants take years to reach blooming age) must first be rooted in appropriate soil and exposed to the proper level of light at the correct time of year. If all of these conditions are met and a bud does form, it must "oppose the Worm" and other insect predators, including bees, which are known to rip petals asunder in their frenzy to reach a flower's nectar, caterpillars, aphids, grasshoppers, and cutworms. A bud must grow strong enough to "Obtain its right of Dew," which can be heavy enough to snap off or wilt a petal, cause powdery mildew or other molds and fungi to flourish, burn a leaf if exposed to extremely strong sun, and turn into a deadly frost in the drop of a degree. A plant must learn to "Adjust the Heat," adapting to unexpected and extreme ranges of and fluctuations in temperature, and "elude the Wind," which can irreparably damage it. After it blooms, an event eagerly anticipated by "Great Nature," "Awaiting Her that Day —," the blossom's work truly begins: "To be a Flower, is profound/ Responsibility —." After its birth, it is a flower's "Responsibility" to somehow survive the destructive effects of wind, rain, frost, insects, animals, people, and even other plants long enough to be fertilized and produce sufficient seeds to contribute to the next generation, which it then surrenders to the wind or the grass, dying before it knows their fate. This respect for and understanding of a flower's nature, its soul, is not mere poetic whimsy; in a letter to the Norcross sisters, she proclaims, "the career of flowers differs from ours only in inaudibleness. I feel more reverence as I grow for these mute creatures whose suspense or transport may surpass my own" [L 388], a passage that clearly supports her ever-growing awareness of the identity, the essence, of all of Nature's citizens, even and most especially flowers and their consorts, insects.

As Dickinson imagines a deity that cares for and maintains its creation, relating to it personally and individually, just as she does the plants and insects in her garden and conservatory, she realizes that every life, including her own, is valued and planned by God. Life, rather than existing for the use and convenience of mankind, needs no other function or purpose than simply to exist as it was meant to:

> To be alive — is Power
> Existence — in itself —
> Without a further function —
> Omnipotence — Enough — [J677/F876][.]

In nature, all of creation has a purpose separate from human concerns. Throughout her career, Dickinson reflects on the role and function of some of the most disregarded and inconsequential members and forces of creation, including bees and blossoms, storms and tides, grass and worms, spiders and caterpillars, dewdrops and wind, and even stones and sand.

Dickinson's advanced "proto-ecological" interest in and awareness of nature is evident in the first poem she composed and recorded, "Awake ye muses nine, sing me a strain divine" [J1/F1]. Dickinson always seems to have recognized that love is the governing force behind creation, where "all things do go a courting" according to divine plan, on an "Earth ... *made* for lovers." The proof is in the very existence of life itself: "life doth prove the precept;" thus, "The bee doth court the flower, the flower his suit receives." In a later poem, "Spring comes on the World —" [J1042/F999], Dickinson alludes to this idea again, while expressing her longing for a distant companion; she is aware of spring on the horizon, but even the resurrection of color and light is dull without her love, as the flowers, heralding spring, "stand negative," sterile and dormant, until they are "Touched to Conditions/ By a Hum" of a bee or other insect, unable to reproduce themselves without external pollinators. Even the non-organic forces of creation are governed by this love:

> The storm doth walk the seashore humming a mournful tune,
> the wave with eye so pensive, looketh to see the moon,
> their spirits meet together, they make them solemn vows [J1/F1][.]

While this poem certainly relies on traditional romantic imagery and personification to reflect this universal harmony and design, it is also written with a respect and awareness for environmental processes. From an ecocritical perspective, the above passages acquire additional meaning: the bee pollinates the flower, the moon governs the tides, storms ravage the shores, perhaps with a touch of regret for the ecological necessity of the possible resulting destruction, and the winds from those storms "woo[s] the branches," spreading pollen and seed. This poem clearly reflects Dickinson's advanced understanding of the vast and subtle connections that unite all of creation.

Dickinson also explores the "use" or function of nature in the poem "The Grass so little has to do—" [J333/F379], in which she outlines the supposedly simple and meaningless tasks Grass must undertake and demonstrates her superior understanding of the individual components of an ecosystem. Easy to take for granted and generally unnoticed and unappreciated, at least until it dies, grass touches all of nature. Grass provides a playground and breeding ground for bees, butterflies, and multitudes of other insects, dances endlessly to the universal music carried on the wind, cradles "the Sunshine in it's lap," adorns itself with jewels of dew, and yet remains humble enough to "bow to everything." While these might appear to be trivial tasks, so "little ... to do" that Dickinson "wish[es she] were a Hay," grass is critical to an ecosystem: it creates a breeding ground and habitat for many species, assists in ground moisture control, prevents and controls erosion, shades seedlings until they outgrow its shadow, and provides food upon its death. In wishing to become "a Hay," Dickinson recognizes the cosmic truth that simple, under-appreciated grass is more useful, more necessary to creation, than she is. Eventually, she begins to view grass as an individual member of creation, a being with personality, capable of forming connections with other beings and experiencing emotions. In "The Mushroom is the Elf of Plants—" [J1298/F1350], she "feel[s] as if the Grass was pleased" to find mushrooms magically springing to life across its surface. In "What mystery pervades a well!" [J1400/F1433], Dickinson marvels that "The grass does not appear afraid," envying its courage as it "stand[s] so close and look[s] so bold" upon something frightening to her, a void represented in the murky maw of a well. Dickinson's hope that she is as important to nature as it is to her is shown in "Here, where the Daisies fit my Head" [J1037/F985]; she wonders whether the grass, which she considers to be a companion at the very least, "[Will be] sorry, some, for [her]," will mourn and miss her, regret her absence, after she dies.

The poem "Our little Kinsman — after Rain" [J885/F932] also reveals Dickinson's ecological awareness. The fleshy little Angle Worm, or earthworm, serves its purpose by offering "Hospitality" and sustenance to a passing bird. Squirming helplessly, trapped in puddles, these worms are her "Kinsmen," fellow creature subject to the whims of fate, powerless against the hungry bird even as they fulfill their ultimate purpose. Before she witnessed this event, she viewed worms as "A needless life," perhaps influenced by their redundancy and fecundity, by their small, indistinctive appearance, or merely by their position as "bug" in the anthropocentric chain of being. She realizes that there is no real difference between the way she regards and relates to the earthworm and the way God watches and interacts with her, and she leaves more appreciative of the critical position the worm occupies in nature even as she sympathizes with its fate. She begins to understand that she and the worm are both simultaneously insignificant and valuable, and she acknowledges both her own triviality and her own importance to a God that acknowledges and loves each separate particle of creation, realizing that the worm's experience is not much different from hers.

The experience and function of spiders is featured in two of Dickinson's poems, "The Spider holds a Silver Ball" [J605/F513] and "A Spider sewed at Night" [J1138/F1163]. In the essay "Spiders in the Attic: A Suggestion of Synthesis in the Poetry of Emily Dickinson," JoAnne De Lavan Williams interpreted these poems as Dickinson's commentary on the artistic process, especially as a female artist. Williams begins her discussion of "The Spider holds a Silver Ball" [J605/F513] by identifying within the poem the inevitable conflict between the ideal, imaginative world of the artist and the harshness of reality. In this poem, the artist, "[c]laimed by both worlds, ... must 'dangle' between ... spiritual ideality ... and the concrete reality of human existence trapped in a web or irresolvable tensions between mutually destructive worlds,"[21] an interpretation that ignores the ecocritical possibilities the text represents. Rather than interpreting the spider as a symbol for Dickinson's artistic and personal conflicts, this poem can be seen to represent the artistic purpose and existence of that particular spider "Himself." The spider finds personal satisfaction and pleasure by doing what he was intended to do, "dancing softly to Himself" as his "unperceived" and unconsidered "Hands" weave invisible strands, creating substance from nothing, practicing his "unsubstantial Trade," just as "The Soul achieves — Herself—" [J1427/F1145], as she declares in a later poem. His delicate art is superior to ours, and he covers our clumsy attempts at weaving with designs created with a "Yarn of Pearl" gleaming with an ethereal iridescence. He is the master of his trade on "His Continent of Light —," his intricate web, until his world is whisked away by a dutiful and unaware housewife, his art devastated, reduced again to nothing, unacknowledged, "unperceived," and unlamented by anyone but "Himself" and Dickinson.

"A Spider sewed at Night" [J1138/F1163] also projects Dickinson's interest in what possible meaning a spider might find in its existence. Williams is more aware of the ecocritical overtones of this poem, focusing more directly on the spider's creativity, which she characterizes as "reflexive, even solipsistic [..., a] turning inward" that informs and defines itself and its world. According to Williams, Dickinson uses the spider as a symbol for the "autonomous, artistic self-identity" she yearns to develop, a creature "simply pursu[ing] its craft" without apparent concern for the sometimes painful judgments of others.[22] Yet, it is clear that Dickinson also wanted to emphasize the importance of the spider "Himself." As in "The Spider holds a Silver Ball," Dickinson's attitude toward the spider rests on the word "Himself;" in this poem, the spider weaves to "Himself himself inform —," defining himself by doing what he was meant, by God's design, to do. He is defined by his actions, by developing the talents he was given, weaving an "Arc of White —" that gleams even "Without a Light;" being true to "Himself" assures his salvation:

> Of Immortality
> His strategy
> Was physiognomy — [.]

The "Immortality" of the spider rests on his ability to represent, characterize, and "inform himself" by "Himself," by his own nature and being.

Dickinson ponders the purpose and perspective of a caterpillar in "How soft a Caterpillar steps —" [J1449/F1523]. Fascinated by the silken creature determinedly inching across her hand, she is overwhelmed by its presence: "It's soundless travels just arrest/ My slow — terrestrial eye —." As she does in several poems, Dickinson here expresses the flash of wonder, the moment of breathlessness, she experiences when overwhelmed by the intricacies of nature, of life living, an instance of pure anticipation that leaves her frozen and awed. In this moment she comprehends both her insignificance and the caterpillar's "supremacy" over her as it follows its own path, "Intent opon it's own career —[,]" creeping toward a future destiny characterized by inevitable transformation and resurrection. In the final line, which questions "What use it has for me —," Dickinson acknowledges that her existence has no meaning to or influence on the experience of the caterpillar, which focuses only on "it's own career — [,]" its own promise and possibility.

Dickinson even occasionally wonders what it might be like to be an element, such as Water or Wind, or an inanimate object, such as a stone. In "A Dew sufficed itself—" [J1437/F1372], she expresses her understanding that even the dew plays a part in God's plan, fulfilling its "'vast ... Destiny[,]'" defining, fulfilling, and "suffice[ing] itself—[,]" by "satisf[ying] a Leaf" before it evaporates. Either the Dew or the narrator declares, "'How trivial is Life'![,]" a line which refers not to the insignificance of life but to the elegant, simple harmony that supports and sustains it. Dickinson's understanding of environmental processes leads her to imagine the "Tragedy" of that individual dewdrop, which will "not again ... be seen/ By Physiognomy — [,]" which will never be exactly the same once it is struck by the sun. A dewdrop's fate is to evaporate in the sun, mingle with clouds, and unite with the Sea, an existence that is tragic to Dickinson because a dewdrop generally remains unacknowledged and uncelebrated even though its existence, like that of so many things, is "enough."

Dickinson also ponders the experience and viewpoint of the wind in "How lonesome the Wind must feel Nights—" [J1418/F1441]. At night, when people have gone to bed and windows are closed and dim, the wind has no company, no companion, a situation which would have been very familiar to Dickinson, who often wrote and gardened by candlelight. At Noon, she conjectures, the Wind "must feel" "pompous" as it dances to

> incorporeal Tunes
> Correcting errors of the sky
> And clarifying scenery[,]

proudly participating in the design and order of creation. In the morning, "How mighty the Wind must feel," sweeping in the sunrise and greeting each new day. She recognizes that the Wind has a personality and a purpose, and even though she may never be able to understand its experiences, she attempts to relate to them as she imagines what it might be like to have such power and responsibility.

Like the wind, even "a little Stone" [J1510/F1570] is "happy" to fulfill its destiny. Unlike humanity, a stone "does'nt care about Careers" and is not afraid of failure or uncertainty. A stone is eternal and has no fear that its own existence will come to an end; its form might change, crumbling from a large slab into smaller pebbles, rubbed into sandy grit by its neighbors, but a stone will always be comprised of "elemental" particles of creation, building blocks of the "Universe," as important and "independent as the Sun." An individual stone, drab and small and insignificant, was touched and dressed by "a passing Universe," by divinity, designed by Universal constants, equally vital whether it "Associates" with other particles to build a greater form "or glows alone." Even a pebble carries out the function God commanded with grace and dignity, "Fulfilling absolute Decree/ In casual simplicity—" and accepting without question or complaint its place in creation.

Convinced that the seemingly trivial and simple elements of God's creations have a critical effect on and a place in nature, that "God made no act without a cause" [J1163/F1192] and only our ignorance allows us to believe otherwise, she learns to "notice" the multitude of life surrounding her, life that has as much of a right to exist as she, and begins to analyze her relationship with it. In an early poem, "So has a Daisy vanished" [J28/F19], she explains that a Daisy has disappeared "From the fields today," as have "many a slipper," whether they be delicate lady slippers, or dainty slippers of lost ladies, equally inconsequential and unsubstantive, and she wonders whether these exquisite flowers reached "Paradise" and are "with God" as she one day aspires to be. Only Dickinson and God would notice the absence of a single daisy or a cluster of lady slippers in a field, and her use of the word "today" suggests that she frequently inspects the fields, daily tallying the flowers, gleefully anticipating and greeting new arrivals and respectfully mourning those that "tiptoed ... / To Paradise away—." Similarly, in "Except to Heaven, she is nought" [J154/F173], she praises "the smallest Housewife in the grass," perhaps a daisy, spring beauty, or sweet violet, usually noticed only by Angels, Bees, and Butterflies, but essential to creation, something that makes "existence—Home!"

No matter how valued or beloved, every cell and atom of creation must face the same unavoidable ending that she will, a death, a transformation, a return to "Eternity unknown—"; while men in their arrogance of assumed superiority might "swagger," proud of the superiority they assume over nature,

> Death is the Common Right
> Of Toads and Men—
> Of Earl and Midge [J583/F419].

and comes to all equally. Ultimately, even the lowest members, at least in mankind's limited perspective, of nature's society come to the same end; "'Tis Life's award—to die" [F485], after all, and ultimately a "Gnat's supremacy is large as" humanity's. Similarly, in "The Butterfly upon the Sky" [J1521/F1559], the butterfly is nameless, homeless, and moneyless, has no value or identity, no worth, by human standards. However, the butterfly is as worthy of life as we, "Is just as high as you and I,/ And higher, [she] believe[s]," a being that is never dissatisfied with its creation, celebrating its existence as it flutters across the sky, offering invaluable instruction in "the way to grieve" as it accepts what nature has to offer.

Firm in her belief that "The smallest Citizen that flies/ Is heartier than we —" [J1374/F1407], she begins to consider insects to be among the most important members of nature's society. Just as Dickinson comes to regard her plants as "humans," she begins as well to relate to insects as people, her kinsmen, members of a tiny nation. In nature she discovers a "Republic of Delight, ... / Where each is Citizen —" [J1107/F1147], a culture comprised of equal "Forest Folk" [J173/F171]. Nature offers a "mystic Bread" to those able to follow "the Signs to Nature's Inns"; while "Her invitation [is] broad," one must choose to walk through the door of "Nature's House" to participate in the "rites" and receive

> The Hospitality
> That opens with an equal width
> To Beggar and to Bee [J1077/F1106][.]

The "undecaying Cheer" of existence, which is the "Suret[y] of her staunch Estate" and the only universal guarantee, offers reassurance that a divine purpose exists for every life created, reflected in the sunrise that paints the Eastern sky and the North Star dancing across heavens.

In "A Single Clover Plank" [J1343/F1297], Dickinson recounts an event most would deem inconsequential, the salvation of "A Bee [she] personally knew" from an unconcerned wind tossing him through the air. No longer completely an outsider, an observer, she becomes a participant, a friend known to and welcomed by nature:

> The Bee is not afraid of me.
> I know the Butterfly —
> The pretty people in the Woods
> Receive me cordially —
> The Brooks laugh louder when I come —
> The Breezes madder play... [J111/F113][.]

In this poem, all of nature rejoices in her presence, in her willingness to recognize and receive the hospitality nature extends: "Brooks laugh" and "Breezes ... play," bees and butterflies entertain, and she is "cordially" welcomed by all.

Dickinson's interest describing her relationship with "Several of

Nature's People" is reflected in "A narrow fellow in the grass" [J986/F1096], one of her riddle poems. This poem depicts two relationships: the first her tenuous and fearful relationship with a snake and the second her "Cordial[...]" and pleasant relationship with "Several of Nature's People." She believes that she "know[s]" them and that "they know [her]," and she experiences a feeling of friendliness and community towards them. Because these lines are contained within the boundaries of a stanza, it is easy to assume that those feelings of "Cordiality" do not extend to the unnamed, anonymous snake, whose presence, whether encountered "Attended or alone" inspires "a tighter Breathing/ And Zero at the Bone," lines which can be interpreted to represent either a paralyzing and chilling fear or an overpowering sense of awe. It is also likely that the quickening of breath and her allusion to the skin's response to a chill in the air, the raising of goose-bumps, are not only symptoms of fear, especially considering that she once attempted to "secure it," but of wonder and reverence, reactions she has similarly described elsewhere. Despite her interest in naming, which has been discussed by John S. Mann in "Emily Dickinson, Emerson, and the Poet as Namer,"[23] Dickinson does not need to name the snake, as it is defined already by its distinct abilities and characteristics, its "Physiognomy": its appearance, a "narrow," "spotted Shaft"; its motion and speed, "a Whip Lash/ Unbraiding" in an "instant"; its habitat, "a Boggy Acre—" and its overwhelming effect on the human psyche, the instinctive response of fear and awe as it slithers past. Instead, these details indicate her respect for and knowledge about the snake itself, one of "Nature's People," and its "necessaries of life" [W 7], not just the fear it arouses.

At times, Dickinson even appears to envy the existence of the insects, finding more solace and freedom in their experience in nature as she imagines it than she does in her own, and she often compares herself to insects or imagines what it might be like to be one. In "It would have starved a Gnat—" [J512/F444], for example, she describes an existence so frugal and barren that even a Gnat would have been unable to survive. Craving a "necessary" but undefined "Food," a hunger

> like a Claw—[She] could no more remove
> Than [she] could coax a Leech away—
> Or make a Dragon—move—[,]

she feels a certain envy for the Gnat's position in nature. Unlike the Gnat, she does not have "The privilege to fly/ And seek a Dinner for [her]self—[,]" a privilege that makes her wonder "How mightier He—than [she]—" and question whether she is as free as it appears to be.

Dickinson's envy of the freedom of both bees and flowers is evident in "Because the Bee may blameless hum" [J869/F909]; could she fly like a bird or emulate the unabashed gaze of an uplifted blossom, she too would be free, like Robins and bees, to travel to her lover, to gaze and adore without fear of discovery and shame. In "Could I but ride indefinite" [J661/F1056], she again imagines what it would be like to be a bee. As a bee, she would be free to follow her own desires, her own path, to schedule her own social engagements and to avoid unwelcome visitors. Ungoverned by, freed from, social expectation, she could "flirt all Day with Buttercups/ And marry whom [she] may," electing at some times to "dwell a little everywhere" and at others to "run away." Such freedom would have appealed to Dickinson, who, in an earlier poem, describes an overwhelming feeling of oppression, of being trapped in the mundane:

> They shut me up in Prose —
> As when a little Girl
> They put me in the Closet —
> Because they liked me "still" — [F445][.]

To be "shut ... up in Prose —[,]" and not redeemed by Poetry, is to be limited by the proscribed roles and the expectations of others, a punishment that allows no adult decision or action. To Dickinson, who may have sometimes felt like a "Captive[...]" in the "tight ... Dungeons" erected by the expectations of her family, her religion, and her culture, hesitant to speak until spoken to [J661/F473], the prospect of being only a simple, insignificant, and unnoticeable bee rather than a daughter, a sister, a Christian, or a woman offers unimaginable, and unattainable, freedom and autonomy.

In several poems, Dickinson assigns such importance to the idea that nature is self-aware and sentient that she depicts a nature capable of mourning and yearning for lost and absent members. In "Nobody knows this little Rose —" [J35/F11], for example, she explores the notion that a flower she plucked may have been an anonymous "pilgrim" torn from its journey. Even though she offers it to someone, assigning it a rather important meaning in human culture, a gift, a sacrifice to love, she cannot help but remember that it might have remained closer to its nature had she not disturbed it. To be sure,

> Only a Bee will miss it —
> Only a Butterfly,
> [...]
> Only a Bird will wonder —
> Only a Breeze will sigh —[,]

but in Dickinson's experience, those are the citizens of creation that matter most. On some level, Dickinson feels guilty that she is interrupting an essential life, removing it from a cycle that in some trivial way depends upon it, by collecting her scientific and botanical specimens, a conflict she often addresses.

In "The Gentian weaves her fringes—" [J18/F21], even as Dickinson mourns the passing of her garden into autumn as her blossoms droop and fall, she expresses delight in their colorful exhibitions, which "Obviate parade"; in the end, their essential beauty through all stages of their life cycle, their future progeny, and their role in the composition of soil are ample rewards for and reminders of their existence. In "A brief but patient illness—" [J18/F22], a verse until recently paired with "The Gentian weaves her fringes—," it is difficult to determine whether Dickinson is attending a human or floral funeral, as the departed is grieved by only a few select mourners, witnessed by a Bobolink and officiated by a distinguished Bee who offers a eulogy as they, Dickinson included, "knelt in prayer." A more whimsical verse, "Bee! I'm expecting you!" [J1035/F983], is a brief note written from the perspective of a Fly who desperately misses his friend and longs for his return. All of the other harbingers of Spring have returned,

> The Frogs got Home last Week—
> Are settled, and at work—
> Birds, mostly back—
> The Clover warm and thick—[,]

but no Bee. Fly offers no reason to anticipate Bee's return except that he wants bee to "be with [him]," to be his companion once again. Despite the facetious tone of this poem, it also points very clearly to Dickinson's ecological understanding of the process and progression of nature: the frogs, one of the first beings to leave hibernation and emerge in spring, have been "settled" for some time, many but not all birds are back from their winter migrations, the clover has formed flowers, and temperatures have warmed enough that bees should begin to harvest the spring nectar flow and pollinate plants for the next generation of seeds.

Dickinson comes to believe that insects are perhaps "The most important population" [J1746/F1764] in all of nature. As they "Unnoticed dwell," invisible to and oblivious of humanity, the inhabitants of the grass include "bumble bees and other nations," earthworms, ants, beetles, flies, spiders, ladybugs, nematodes, existing not only to replicate and celebrate their creation, offering what she earlier calls a "Sacrament of summer days" [J130/F122], living, to her, in "a heaven each instant" [J1746/F1764], and playing their very vital roles in pollination, soil aeration, decomposition, pest control, and seed dispersal. In "Further in Summer than the Birds—" [J1068/F895], Dickinson's most extensive treatment of the sanctity of insect song, she witnesses the "Pathetic" and "unobtrusive Mass" "celebrate[d]" another "minor Nation" of crickets. According to Wendy Barker, "[m]uch of the power implicit in the crickets' music ... resides in its hiddenness, ... its 'littleness' in the grass"; the crickets' unobtrusive "community," unacknowledged and unappreciated by everyone but Dickinson, has an unfathomable impact on the rest of creation as the voices of the crickets simultaneously arise to revere, and eventually set, the sun. Their chorus evokes in Dickinson "a sense of kinship with a 'minor nation' ... that through its music is beginning to enhance 'Nature' with its own 'Difference.'" Barker somewhat undermines the ecocritical aspects of her argument by emphasizing that, by glorifying the song of crickets and immortalizing their insignificance, only hearing within their chorus the voices of women customarily silenced and deemed negligible, Dickinson is able to "confront ... a dominant cultural metaphoric pattern of assumptions that had enormous implications for women's lives."[24]

Katie Peterson's "Surround Sound: Dickinson's Self and the Hearable" focuses on the humbling experience of submitting one's senses to sound, which can be seen in "Further in Summer than the Birds." Succumbing to the song of crickets results in "a collapse of the self into pure perception without personal history." Essentially losing her self in the music of the crickets, Dickinson is "inspire[d] ... to cast off her interest in expressing individuality while also ... casting-off that which she considers herself." Rather than depending on the senses of the perceiver, as does sight, listening "enables Dickinson to leave pride and self-assertion behind" as she adopts the "even less self-aware and even less self-assertive position of the listener." By attempting to remove herself as perceiver in order to concentrate on the act of auditory perception, by heeding the invisible, inconsequential, and "unnoticed" choir "in the grass," as does Thoreau, Dickinson is able to "achieve the unselfconsciousness of an animal" and "draw nearer to a natural world of which we are only a small part."[25]

Other critics have observed that the crickets' song in American literature traditionally represents a bittersweet harbinger of autumn, a reading that ignores or removes the sacred aspect of their "spectral Canticle."[26] Their song "Enhances Nature," imparts a "Druidic Difference" to the landscape that adds to the ritualistic tone of the poem. Here, crickets take an active part in the progression of the day, of the year, as they do in another poem, where "The Crickets sang/ And set the Sun" [J1104/F1104]. Realizing that "Of bumble-bees and other nations/ The grass is full" [J1746/F1764] and that the Breeze carries "the timid prayer/ Of the minutest Cricket" [J790/F741], Dickinson learns from the songs of the crickets and other "Miniature Creatures" [J606/F523] the most important of creation's lessons, that "Nature is Heaven" [J668/F721] and that all of creation, with the exception of mankind, gloriously and unselfconsciously contributes a voice to the cosmic harmony.

Dickinson most clearly expresses this beatific idea in "'Nature' is what We see—" [J668/F721], a poem that explores the development of faith from the evidence of the senses. At first glance, nature is literally "what we see," a picture composed of landscape and unconnected images, events, and objects: "The Hill—the Afternoon—/ Squirrel—Eclipse—the Bumble bee—." In the fourth line of the poem, "Nay—Nature is Heaven—," Dickinson contradicts the belief that Nature is merely a vision, but does not develop the idea. Instead, she returns to another sensory description of nature, "Nature is what We hear," listing "The Bobolink—the Sea—/ Thunder—the Cricket—" as some of the sounds that might be noticed before she again qualifies her definition: "Nay—Nature is Harmony—." Ultimately, nature becomes "what we know/ Yet have no art to say," inspiring an almost instinctive spirituality that responds to the "Sincerity" of nature. Heavenly landscapes, "what We see—[,]" and universal melodies, "what We hear—[,]" confound "Wisdom," whether it refers to science, theology, or philosophy. Language itself, that which sets humanity above the rest of creation, is "impotent" when confronted with this "Sincerity," an ineffective and insufficient means of translating the meaning, the function, of creation, and "no art," no system created by man, can adequately imitate it, represent it, or speak for it. Nature is what allows Dickinson to "take the Balance" [J576/F546], to negotiate the gulf between the blind faith of her youth and the spiritual estrangement of adulthood. A true understanding of Nature, like the wonder and awe it often inspires, "is not precisely Knowing/ And not precisely Knowing not—," a knowledge poised between the precision of scientific fact—proof—and the certainty of absolute faith—no proof necessary.

In a natural order populated and maintained by insects, blossoms, and birds, Dickinson finds a haven, a heaven, a home. Indeed, she relates that

> The fairest Home [she] ever knew
> Was founded in an Hour
> By Parties also that [she] knew
> A spider and a Flower— [J1423/F1443][.]

The relationship between the spider weaving its web and the flower that forms the foundation for its creation permits the construction of a "home" "founded in an Hour," a haunt more attractive to Dickinson than any elaborate human structure. In nature, Dickinson "learned — at least — what Home could be" [J944/F891], a place "Where Dawn — knows how to be —," "only Birds [will] interrupt/ The Ripple of [her] Theme —" and bees will hum for her. In another poem, Dickinson imagines heaven as

> a small Town —
> Lit — with a Ruby —
> Lathed — with Down — [J374/F577],

evoking earlier images of the "little mortal nest" "cunning[ly] ... wove[n]" by a tender "'Mama.'" An ethereal, peaceful place, "Stiller — than the fields/ At the full Dew —," so illusive and intangible that even as Dickinson attempts to define it, to express it in her language, she realizes that it is unfathomable and inexpressible, as "Beautiful — as Pictures —/ No Man drew." In this "Town" she finds "People — like the Moth —/ Of Mechlin," citizens constructed like delicate, transparent lace and intent on "Duties — of Gossamer —/ And Eider — names —," working with fragile strands of spider threads and plant fibers, fluff and feathers, weaving nests and webs, preparing for both birth and death, beings the "White Moth of Amherst" envies and emulates. Dickinson imagines that

> Almost — contented —
> [She] — could be —
> 'Mong such unique/ Society — [,]

at least more so than she ever felt in human society. Indeed, she even describes those few human companions held close to her soul as members of that "minor Nation": for example, in a brief letter to Sally Jenkins, whom she addresses as Katy Did, she asks, "Will the sweet child who sent me the butterflies, herself a member of the same ethereal nation, accept a rustic kiss, flavored, we trust, with clover?" [L 371], envisioning herself, perhaps, as a bee dusted with clover pollen or honey.

In "A little Road — not made of Man —" [J647/F758], Dickinson reveals that even though her observations of nature have allowed her, "Enabled of the Eye," to perceive a path only

> Accessible to Thill of Bee —
> Or Cart of Butterfly — [,]

she does not, cannot, know with certainty what might lie ahead because nothing can take her there; ultimately, this Heaven is not — yet — intended for her. Even though Dickinson must remain content with the satisfaction and fulfillment she affords as both gardener and poet, the spiritual refreshment and inspiration she finds in her garden, in nature, allow her to catch an occasional glimpse of a ship sailing on "A Sea of Summer Air" whose

> ... Captain was the Butterfly
> For Helmsman was the Bee
> And an entire universe
> For the delighted crew — [J1198/F1199][.]

Dickinson's conviction that nature contains evidence of divine will and order leads her to discover the Heaven that already exists on Earth, if only we could see it. Instead of praying to God in a man-made structure, like the worshippers she refers to in "Some keep the Sabbath going to Church" [J324/F236], she learns to worship

> staying at Home —
> With a Bobolink for a Chorister —
> And an Orchard, for a Dome — [.]

She is closest to God when she listens to the birdsong in her garden, sensing the voice of the divine behind their music as "God preaches." Rather than devoting her life to ensuring the possibility of an afterlife, "instead of getting to Heaven, at last —," when she looks for God in nature, "[She's] going, all along." In another poem, "Heaven is so far of the Mind" [J370/F413], she expresses her belief that paradise is a state of mind, a construction that differs from person to person, so individualized and intimate

> That were the Mind dissolved —
> The Site — of it — by Architect
> Could not again be proved — [.]

No matter how "Vast" and "fair" we imagine it to be, it cannot surpass what we already have: "No further 'tis, than Here." In fact, unless we learn to recognize "The Fact that Earth is Heaven —/ Whether Heaven is Heaven or not" [J1408/F1435], reveling in an earthly Eden to alleviate our doubts in and perhaps even reduce our need for a spiritual Heaven, we will never truly reach paradise: "Who has not found the Heaven — below —/ Will fail of it above —" [J1544/F1609]. In nature, Heaven is always within reach, and a respect and reverence for all members of creation is necessary to salvation.

"From Cocoon forth a Butterfly": Dickinson and Metamorphosis

Louis C. Rutledge's recent essay, "Emily Dickinson's Anthropods" presents an overview of the various insect names included in Dickinson's poetry, including "bee, beetle, borer, bumble bee, butterfly, caterpillar, centipede, cricket, fly, glowworm, gnat, ... midge, monarch, moth and spider." Of these, references to bees, bumble bees, honey, and hives appear in over 100 poems, usually in connection to flowers, pollination, and revelry; and butterflies, caterpillars, and cocoons are featured in 47 verses. Dickinson's diminutive size, ethereal dress, and delicate air reminded many of a fragile, pallid moth, and she encouraged others to think of her as "The White Moth of Amherst," engaging in what Barton Levi St. Armand calls a "private mythologizing of herself."[27] When speaking of Dickinson's reaction to the publication of one of her poems, her sister-in-law, Susan Huntington Dickinson, as related by Martha Dickinson Bianchi, described her as a "little white moth being almost fluttered to death, all a-tremble and ready to die of the experience and be found on the floor next morning a mere hint of winged dust,"[28] an artist blinded, stunned, and potentially destroyed by an unwelcome yet alluring public spotlight, the insubstantial leaves, "wing[s]," of her poems and fascicles, written in a script described by Higginson as "'fossil bird-tracks,'" the only evidence of her earthly existence after she returns to "dust." Higginson, drained, baffled, and somewhat twitterpated after their first meeting, says she is "much too enigmatical a being for me to solve in an hour's interview" and was afraid to pressure or interrogate her too firmly for fear she would "withdraw into her shell."[29] Similarly, novelist Helen Hunt Jackson, in a passage that recounts her first physical encounter with the reclusive poet, says that she "felt like a great ox talking to a white moth" clasping a hand like a "wisp," responding to the vulnerable, fragile persona Dickinson often adopted when meeting unfamiliar people.[30] Dickinson was certainly fond of watching the "drunken" bees [J81/F82] careen and dance across her garden, imagining what it would be like to experience such freedom and seemingly aimless purpose, but in butterflies and their kin she finds subjects for more serious contemplation that she hopes will lead to personal transformation and spiritual comfort and enlightenment.

Dickinson's complex treatment of caterpillars, cocoons, moths, and butterflies explores both the literal facts of their earthly existence and the symbolic possibilities they present. Influenced by her knowledge of and interest in the life cycle of a butterfly and its function and experience in nature, she marvels at the butterfly's ability to transform itself; naturally and seemingly effortlessly spinning its own cocoon and initiating its transformation, the butterfly is a perfect example of nature's continuing endurance. In several poems, concerned about the methods that lead her to these revelations, Dickinson uses the image of a trapped or pinned butterfly to express her conflict and guilt over sacrificing a necessary part of nature to satisfy scientific curiosity. Just as plants spontaneously generate seedpods that both propagate and protect the next generation, so caterpillars instinctively weave cocoons, initiating their transformation and increasing the possibility of another generation. Intrigued by the possibility represented in the process of its metamorphosis, Dickinson also finds in the butterfly's ability to transform or give birth to itself, its true essence and being, by weaving a cocoon and enduring a period of seclusion an ideal symbol for spiritual transformation and regeneration and for her own struggle to find a balance between faith and doubt in an effort to lessen her fear of death and her uncertainty about resurrection.

Dickinson focuses much of her poetic attention to the butterfly's pupa and adult stages of development, but its larval stage, the caterpillar, also interests her. An early poem, "A fuzzy fellow, without feet —" [J173/F171], exemplifies the full range of Dickinson's treatment of butterflies. On an ecocritical level, this poem explores the experience of being a caterpillar: Free to explore nature, to exist where he wills, "Sometime, he dwelleth in the grass!/ Sometime, opon a bough," the caterpillar playfully explores his environment, "descend[ing] in plush/ Opon the Passer-by!" "All this in summer —" occurs until the proper environmental conditions initiate his transformation. In the fall, "when the winds alarm the Forest Folk," he "taketh *Damask* Residence —" to over-winter and recreate himself, taking pride in his transformation, "strut[ting] in sewing silk," displaying a cocoon woven as intricately as "*Damask*" silk. When he "Emerges in the spring!/ A Feather on each Shoulder," he is "scarce[ly] recogniz[able]" from his old self.

Dickinson also reflects upon the daily experience of the butterfly, which often appears at first to lead a completely frivolous, carefree existence. In "Cocoon above! Cocoon below!" [J129/F142], Dickinson earnestly asks the "Stealthy Cocoon, why hide you so/ What all the world suspect?" In this poem, there appears no indication of a harsh season, a time of trial, that the caterpillar must endure to become an adult, as suggested in "A fuzzy fellow, without feet —" [J173/F171]; adopting a rather naive perspective, the speaker wonders why such a beautiful "secret, perched in extasy," must be protected, tucked away into a remote cranny, especially when the secret life itself "Defies imprisonment!" Instead of spending an entire season buffeted by winds, drenched by rain and snow, repeatedly freezing and thawing, after only "An hour in chrysalis to pass —," the butterfly emerges, free to glide "above receding grass" after it takes "A moment" to "interrogate," converse with, explore its new environment, intent upon its new "Career," "The Universe to know!" as it explores with "extasy" the infinite possibilities and adventures of a trivial existence.

In contrast to the bee, whose frolicking and cavalier behavior is somewhat excused because of his role as pollinator, initiator of spring and surveyor of summer, the butterfly in "From Cocoon forth a Butterfly," appears to be "Repairing Everywhere —// Without Design —" [J354/F610], apparently serving no purpose and fulfilling no function, at least none that she could determine or understand Like a flighty, pampered schoolgirl concerned only with her appearance, the butterfly joined "Parties — Phantom as Herself—," an "Audience of Idleness," their "pretty Parasol[s]" flashing in the fields in contrast to the labor of the men in the fields stacking hay and the bee and flower "that worked." The butterfly appears to do nothing, go "Nowhere," flitting about in "purposeless Circumference —" until it is lost in sunset and "Extinguished — in the Sea —." In many ways, there is no obvious ecological importance to the butterfly, which seems to have no true function. Yet, "The Clovers — understood —" the importance of her "Miscellaneous Enterprise," which might simply be "Beauty is nature's fact," the one incontestable truth that governs creation.

In "He parts Himself— like Leaves —" [J517/F655], a poem certainly informed by Dickinson's uncertainly about and experience with sacrificing a part of nature to fulfill her scientific curiosity, the butterfly leads a similar, lighthearted life, until it is interrupted by humanity. This butterfly visits the "Bonnet/ Of Any Buttercup" and races a Rose, "then does Nothing —," then sails "away opon a Jib —[.]" As it explores the Universe, it "dangles" on the horizon like a speck of dust catching the light, "a Mote/ Suspended in the Noon —," and the most difficult decision it must face, its only "uncertain[ty]," is whether "to return Below —/ Or settle in the Moon — [.]" By winter, this butterfly has passed into the unknown, but somewhere, other larva, poised within cocoons to begin the cycle again, are trapped in "Cabinets [to] be shown," metamorphosis suspended, halted. Instead of overwintering in "A Sepulchre of quaintest Floss," a refuge from harsh environmental conditions, a sanctuary in which the larvae will sleep, dormant and numb, until spring, when sun will warm the chrysalis to life, specimens are preserved and stored indefinitely, doomed to "be shown" as artifacts, scientific curiosities, eternally limited to one form, one possibility, unable to return to nature and complete their lifecycles.

Dickinson's reluctant acceptance of and guilt over the sacrifices nature makes to further scientific exploration is also evident in "'Arcturus' is his other name—" [J70/F117], in which she describes herself as "A monster with a glass," ripping a "flower from the woods," ending its life in order to study it in a "'class'" or laboratory. In this poem, science removes the mystery from life, attempting to bridge the gulf between "not precisely Knowing/ And not precisely Knowing not," an effort better served by contemplating the wonder of nature. Dickinson at times believes that "It's very mean of Science/ To go and interfere," to categorize and label, reducing the glory of "'Star'" to a common name and "Comput[ing]" the data gleaned from the microscopic examination of "the stamens" of a flower. The butterfly, "sit[ting] erect in 'Cabinets,'" is no longer a member of nature, and has "forgot[ten]" dancing with the meadow flowers just as "The Clover bells" have forgotten him. Although the butterfly is prized as a specimen, the more exotic the better,

> it obtains
> But little sympathy
> Though favorably mentioned
> In Entomology [J1685/F1701][.]

From a scientific perspective, the butterfly's value lies in the data it generates, and the fact of its beauty is not as important as the physical characteristics that help identify its species. In fact, in an line that reflects an uncharacteristic disregard for the fate of the butterfly, Dickinson, perhaps searching for a way to alleviate her guilt in participating in and benefiting from nature's destruction, proposes that if the butterfly had been less beautiful and more "homely," engaged in "fitter behavior," expressed modestly, it might have been more worthy of "immortality."

In contrast to empirical study, cocoons, seedpods, and bulbs come to represent for Dickinson both the promise of life after death and the possibility of personal transformation. A seedpod or chrysalis, like

> A Coffin — is small Domain,
> Yet able to contain
> A Citizen of Paradise
> In it's diminished Plane —[J943/F890],

and, like death, offers possibilities "ampler than the sun —." The dead, "the meek members of the Resurrection" [J216/F124] are cocooned in coffins, "Untouched" by time and decay, "Safe in their Alabaster Chambers —," biding the passing of the seasons, patiently awaiting salvation, while the planets dance around their suns, timeless and eternal. Like the human dead awaiting salvation, seeds and larvae lie dormant until they are awakened by warmth and rain, "Touched to Conditions," awaiting spring and resurrection.

Dickinson confesses in a brief and powerful poem, "To die — without the Dying" [J1017/F1027], that "liv[ing] — without the Life/ ... is the hardest Miracle/ Propounded to Belief." Maintaining a faith in a literal life after dying was a nearly impossible challenge for Dickinson, no matter how comforting it was. In the life cycles of caterpillars to butterflies and seedpods to seedlings, she finds evidence of a divine plan that relies on transformation for continuance, for growth. A caterpillar hatches and eventually dies, severed from its life, shrouded, and entombed, but then a butterfly is born; a seed is born, encased in a soft pod and a tough shell, released to the elements, swollen by rain and split open by emerging sprouts. In the infinite cycles of nature, the death of one thing always leads to or intersects with the life of another; metamorphosis and growth is impossible without death, and death always leads to transformation, a new life. The possibility for growth and transformation toward a purposeful existence is innate, revealed in the solitary confinement, reflection, and potential growth represented in seedpods and cocoons.

Indeed, the "Revolution is the Pod" [J1082/F1044]; death, decay, and desiccation are unavoidable and essential parts of nature, bringing change and new life. "Every Summer be/ The entomber of itself," leading to autumn, the last brilliant flame of life before death, all manner of life endlessly being born, giving birth, dying, and born again, relying on inert and dormant withered pods that could contain either insects or seeds to continue the cycle, pods that, like dry bones and bare branches, "rattle ... / When the Winds of Will are stirred" until "Revolution" and evolution, life, quivers within and "shakes it for/ Test if it be dead —," triggered, resuscitated, by the proper environmental conditions. Life and death are inseparable and intertwined, unavoidable consequences of each other, an idea inspiring Dickinson to write

> The Opening and the Close
> Of Being, are alike
> Or differ, if they do,

> As Bloom opon a Stalk —
> That from an equal Seed
> Unto an equal Bud
> Go parallel, perfected
> In that they have decayed — [J1047/F1089][.]

In this poem, death and life are as impossible to distinguish from one another as blossoms from the same plant. Life and death are the equalizers of all members of creation; all life follows the "parallel, perfected" course of birth, death, decay, and rebirth, which "beckons spaciously —/ A Miracle for all!" [J1626/F1594], reflecting the flawless order of creation and the intentions of God.

Spring is a seasonal reminder of the possibility of resurrection and change, a promise that life will continue whether on the mortal or heavenly plain. In spring, a "Period/ Express from God" [J844/F948], life cannot begin and

> None stir abroad
> Without a cordial interview
> With God — [.]

When the frosts recede and the soil warms, "ranks of seeds their witness bear" [J130/F122], to the glory of God as they burst forth from the soil, eager to thrive and eventually reproduce, each taking its turn and surrendering to the other plants to follow. Dickinson's faith in the regenerative and transformative powers of spring is also evident in "The Winters are so short —" [J403/F532]. Even though she knows it is necessary, Dickinson doesn't feel "justified" in "sending all the Birds away" or "moving into Pod" because winter feels so brief and spring is always on the horizon. She feels "scarcely settled" into her snug cocoon before the birds return and "it's time to strike [her] Tent —," breaking free of her confinement, and "open House — again —" for the return of life.

Although they at times may be regarded as confining and stifling by their tiny "Captive[s]," pods and cocoons provide a necessary period of seclusion and inner reflection that is impossible to achieve in the normal patterns of everyday life but essential to her personal development. Describing herself as the "slightest in the House" [J486/F473], Dickinson occupies the "smallest Room" in the family home, accompanied by a Book, a solitary Geranium, and the fragrance of Mint, and she cannot "bear to live — aloud" because "The Racket shamed [her] so." In an effort to "dwell in Possibility —" [J657/F466], to explore her own potential, tucked away in her tiny attic, isolated from friends and family, she learns that before there can be a regeneration or a rebirth, a spring, there must be a quiet and solitary winter spent bundled in a snug, cozy space. Just as bulbs and seeds need a cold winter before they respond to the warmth of the sun, Dickinson, concerned about death and restless with uncertainty about an afterlife, uses pod and cocoon imagery to express her desire to hatch into a transcendent life and thus to reinvigorate her faith.

The mysterious process by which plant and insect life grows and transforms itself is still a secret, a hidden process despite Dickinson's curiosity about it. The sacred, "stately air" of "existence" is encapsulated in the tiny Acorn, the "egg of forests," which holds the promise of all life within its fragile shell [F55]. On one level, the acorn exists to give birth to another generation of oak trees to ensure the survival of the species and to contribute to the ecological whole by providing shade, shelter, sustenance, and innumerable other services to all of nature. On another, the resulting trees will serve "To venerate the simple days/ Which lead the seasons by —," worshiping by participating in the eternal cycle of the seasons and of life and death.

In "So from the mould" [J66/F110], Dickinson compares the yearly resurrection of tulips and daffodils, which appear to spring spontaneously from the earth, to "Many a Worm" who burst from their cocoons "Leap[ing] so Highland gay," whirling in ecstasy, free to celebration. Both the bulbs and butterfly larvae have been "Hidden away, cunningly,/ From sagacious eyes," insulated from weather and expectation, confined within accumulated layers of soil or softly spun cocoons, and allowed to develop without scrutiny or criticism until they burst forth in splendor, fulfilling their purpose. "Peasants like" Dickinson, confined to a lowly human existence and limited understanding of nature's order, "Gaze perplexedly," attempting to fathom the conditions that contribute to their growth and somehow emulate their seemingly effortless transformation.

Dickinson's interest in the butterfly as a symbol for spiritual transformation or for the afterlife is also apparent in "A fuzzy fellow, without feet—" [J173/F171]. Dickinson could hardly find a more suitable symbol for the possibility of spiritual transcendence and resurrection—despite lowly, earthly origins—than the caterpillar. After a lifetime of experience, a full summer, the physical caterpillar dies within a self-constructed coffin over the winter, resurrected in spring from the desolate frost of winter, death, and thereby transformed into a creature blessed with "A Feather on each shoulder," angel wings, able to glide between earth and heaven. "[T]he pretty secret/ Of the Butterfly" seems to be twofold: first, transformation from the indistinct and common into the breathtakingly spectacular depends upon a period of isolation and self-reflection, cushioned in softness and seclusion; and second, resurrection brings a natural conclusion to a life spent "inform[ing]" itself, enjoying and contemplating its purpose and its existence.

Dickinson's use of a cocoon to represent both the possibility of an afterlife or an earthly spiritual metamorphosis is also clearly expressed in "Three times — we parted — Breath — and I —" [J598/F514]. In this poem, the narrator describes the sensation of drowning, gasping for a breath that "would not go" as life struggles to survive against violent waves: "Three times — the Billows threw me up —/ Then caught me — like a Ball —[.]" When the waves "grew sleepy — Breath — did not —" and she is eventually "lulled" by the waves she thought would drown her. Washed ashore, she feels the "Sunrise kiss [... her] Chrysalis —/ And [she] stood up — and lived," unfolding and rising to discover a new life and existence. After the trials of life, the unavoidable "Billows" of experience that shake the foundations of faith, leaving her drowning in doubt, the end result is a resurrection in the afterlife or a transformation into a new life blessed by the divine.

In "My Cocoon tightens — Colors teaze —" [J1099/F1107], Dickinson focuses on the moment of birth, of erupting into a new life, and yet the doubt accompanying it. Unable to catch her breath once again, "feeling for the Air —," she believes herself unworthy of the transformation that she has initiated: "A dim capacity for Wings/ Demeans the Dress I wear — [.]" She only has a "dim capacity," a meager talent, for the flight, the journey, ahead of her, and her weakness "Demeans" her "Wings," her new ability to soar, like the bees, "beyond the sun" [J32/F8]. The butterfly's "Aptitude to fly," its readiness and worthiness, for gliding in "easy sweeps of Sky —," is the source of its "power." Unlike the butterfly, who instinctively fulfills its purpose, Dickinson

> must baffle at the Hint
> And cipher at the Sign
> And make much blunder

before she "take[s] the clue divine" [J1099/F1107]. She must endure the painful condition of her mortality, her separation from Eden, "the little mortal nest," until she is able to appreciate and revel in "Joy's insuring quality" [J1434/F1479], reconciling her faith with her "Insecurity."

Dickinson's consideration of caterpillars, butterflies, cocoons, seeds, and seedpods, especially in relation to her conviction that life exists primarily to celebrate and replicate itself in an endless recognition and glorification of God's divine plan, assists her realization that "Each Life converges to some Centre—" [J680/F724]. There is no life without meaning, without a divinely ordained purpose, "A Goal" that whether "Expressed — or still —/ Exists in every Human nature" and every life in nature. If that role remains unrealized or unexpressed, whether by lack of effort or inspiration, heaven offers another opportunity to achieve fulfillment:

> Ungained — it may be — by a Life's low Venture —
> But then —
> Eternity enable the endeavoring
> Again [J680/F724].

Similarly, in "Growth of Man — like Growth of Nature —" [J750/F790], "stir[red]" and "endorse[d]" by sunlight, Dickinson explains that

> Each — it's difficult Ideal
> Must achieve — Itself—
> Through the solitary prowess
> Of a Silent Life —[.]

Dickinson's contemplation of the processes of metamorphosis and genesis in nature leads her to understand that a complete and rewarding life, one that leads to eventual salvation, is gained through self-reflection and sacrifice, a "dwell[ing] in possibilities" fed by faith and seclusion. Only through "Effort," "Patience," and "intact belief" can transformation occur, sometimes unavoidably observed but always essentially solitary and "[un]assisted."

Ultimately, for Dickinson, salvation and transcendence are granted only to those who recognize the delicate balance of creation, the significance of each individual and insignificant life, and the necessity of self-reflection and self-direction. Only the "Consciousness that is aware/ Of neighbors and the Sun" [J822/F817], only those who understand that they are part of a interconnected, united community of friends, a "Nation," governed by natural forces and patterns such as the path of the sun or the certainty of death and rebirth, "Will be ... aware of Death," will understand that death is only another gateway through which we must walk alone:

> itself alone
>
> Is traversing the interval
> Experience between
> And most profound experiment
> Appointed unto Men —[.]

The only purpose of life is to live, as it was meant to be, by its design, its innate abilities and talents; a soul is measured and judged by how well it has lived up to and realized its own goals and prospects, not how it quietly obeyed and abided by the expectations and decisions of others:

> How adequate unto itself
> It's properties shall be
> Itself unto itself and None
> Shall make discovery —
> Adventure most unto itself
> The Soul condemned to be —
> Attended by a single Hound
> It's own identity.

Dickinson realizes that, just as a caterpillar or seed can neither avoid nor independently initiate its own transformation, its birth into a new life, a soul, her soul, cannot escape its essence, its identity, its destiny. To one exceptionally aware of the complex patterns and processes elaborately exhibited in nature, transformation and regeneration, physical and spiritual, are eventually seen as innate and inevitable, inescapable benefits and consequences of living. Those who avoid or deny their instinct, their talent, their nature, are doomed to be "Hound[ed]" by a self never satisfied, haunted by possibilities, and lamenting a life never lived.

IV

John Muir: Translating "Nature's Book"

"Made of the Same Dust as We": Nature's Equality

For John Muir, as for Emerson and Thoreau, nature is the entity through which humanity comes to know God. His travels into the recesses of God's creation lead him to discover that Nature, deliberately crafted and sculpted by God, is a language that communicates to humanity "the proper morals — harmony, joy, and, most importantly, love — that humans aspiring to spiritual perfection should adopt," if only we had ears to listen.[1] In order to interpret this language, Muir hones what he calls his "glacial eye," his own version of Emerson's "transparent eye-ball" or Thoreau's "microscopic eye," attempting to erase his own perspective as he sweeps his gaze across the wilderness, trying to imagine the world as might a glacier, a lake, a Douglas squirrel, a bee, or even a branch. As he dissolves himself into the texts inscribed on Nature, he learns to distinguish the individual and infinite voices carried on the wind. Comprehending that God, like "Nature[,] loves man, beetles, and birds with the same love" [JM 66], Muir realizes that the voices and perspectives of both the large and even the smallest of Nature's citizens, the gnats and mosquitoes, the bees and butterflies, the ants and grasshoppers, demand attention.

This chapter begins with a discussion of the connections between Muir's preservationist beliefs and his religious conviction that nature was divinely ordered and maintained, ideas decidedly informed by his close observation of his environment and the subtle interplay of the residents of creation. The second section of this chapter describes Muir's development of macroscopic and microscopic angles of vision in order explore more completely his ideas that God is an active presence in nature and that his word is written in observable phenomena. From this perspective, it becomes evident to Muir that all creation basks in the loving gaze of its Creator, and he learns that even insects are equal and valuable members of a cosmic brotherhood and family. Muir's extensive interest in bees, creatures that have not lost their connection to nature despite the interference of men, is the focus of the third section of this chapter. As he attempts to see the California landscape as he imagines a bee might see it, envisioning a sort of floral timeline, he realizes that humanity's relationship with bees represents an ideal balance between civilization and wilderness, presenting the possibility that humanity and nature can peaceably and beneficially coexist.

John Muir, unlike Thoreau and Dickinson, is more often viewed as a folk hero than as a literary figure. His travels to Alaska and the Amazon, his thousand mile walk and exploration of the Sierras, and his encounters with alligators and bears contribute to the image of wild "John o' the Mountains," and are overshadowed only by his environmentalist and preservationist activities. Muir climbed trees to get closer to thunderstorms, preferred pine boughs to pillows, conversed with glaciers, squirrels, and grasshoppers, and saved the Sequoias. As John C. Elder notes, "both chronologically and thematically, he stands midway between current writers and the Transcendentalists," and he writes with the hope that his descriptions of sublime landscapes and harmonious existence would ensure their survival. Even though preservationist writing represents only a small segment of his work, most Muir scholarship focuses on Muir the First Environmentalist, the Father of the Sierra Club, and is generally biographical, only briefly addressing Muir the Nature Writer and his literary Transcendental heritage. Like Emerson, he heard the voice of God whispering in the rustling of the leaves; like Thoreau, he looked Nature in the eye and saw joyous Awareness staring back; like Dickinson, he observed and participated in a society of "winged people" [F 189] and "plant people" [NP 211]. His belief that "every purely natural object is a conductor of divinity" [JM 118], that the beauty and joy found in nature lead humanity back to God, forms the foundation for his preservationist stance. Described as "a tree-man, a sky-man, a bug-man, a rock-man," Muir recognizes and responds to all of the voices of creation, revealing a divinely inspired harmony that begins and ends with the songs of the crickets and echoes on the wind as it travels to the stars.[2]

Muir's environmentalism is intricately intertwined with his belief in the transcendent influence of nature and in equality between all members of creation. Elder's essay, "John Muir and the Literature of Wilderness," emphasizes the importance of personal growth and revelation in nature to Muir's position as an environmentalist. Muir understood that his writing "at best [could] only direct the reader's attention towards the *really* important things," because the healing and transforming powers of nature can only be achieved through "immediate experience," direct, unfiltered exposure to and contact with the natural world: "One day's exposure to mountains is better than cartloads of books" [JM 95]. Muir's "own experience of wilderness," his delight in the interconnectedness he discovered in nature, was the "transforming perception ... to which he tried to lead the rest of the nation"; Muir wanted people to experience the inspiration and exhilaration he found in the mountains almost as much as he wanted to preserve the mountains themselves. Even though Muir did not relish reducing his beloved landscapes to commodities and vacation destinations, he was enough of a realist and politician to know that people are more likely to fight to preserve something they have experienced, and enough of an idealist to hope that a people inspirited by nature might create a culture that would naturally protect and cherish it.[3]

While Muir may have understood that it was impossible to restrict human movement into the wild, he did not share the common belief that the world was created for man to use and manipulate. In the nineteenth century, interpretations of nature's position and function in the divine plan varied. In *God's Wilds: John Muir's Vision of Nature*, Dennis C. Williams explains that "many Christian thinkers assumed humans to occupy the penultimate position in Creation; thus, if humans were separated from God by a huge Gulf, then implicitly nature must stand even farther from its Creator." If nature "participated in humanity's sin," it could hardly lead to God. Some believed Saint Paul's assertion that the "design" of nature "provided means for humans to rediscover God," while others saw only a wild and cruel landscape "reordered" by God after the fall to "make life hellish for the fallen creature." In any case, nature was rarely seen as anything but subordinate to humanity, either as a resource at human disposal or as an instrument of divine punishment.[4] Muir, however, more than any other writer or naturalist of his time, was able to cast aside the religiously and culturally inscribed, anthropocentric assumptions of superiority over the natural world. For Muir, all of creation was alive, a breathing, pulsating monument of flesh and stone and ice, a work-in-progress designed, directed, molded, and maintained by God, not for our pleasure or satisfaction or use but for its own sake, thus a radical departure from the usual presumptions about man's place in the universe.

Williams believes Thomas Dick's *Christian Philosophy*, which young Muir read despite his father's disapproval, helped shape his idea that "Nature had functions that limited human minds could not understand." Dick proclaimed that all of nature continuously and gloriously worships its Creator: "The sportive motions, and gesticulations of all the animal tribes — the birds skimming through the air, warbling in the groves, and perching in the trees — the beasts in the Weld, bounding in the forests, and through the lawns — the fishes sporting in the waters — the reptiles wriggling in the dust, and the winged insects, by a thousand wanton mazes — all declare that they are rejoicing in their existence, and in the exercise of these powers with which the Creator has furnished them." This passage would have been very appealing to Muir as he attempted to reconstruct his vision of Nature's place in the universe. He could accept neither the image of a hostile nature, an enemy to man, nor the idea of a benign nature awaiting man's manipulation. Rather, as Williams explains, for Muir, "each organism existed to glorify God. As a product of a Presbyterian culture whose catechism instructed that mankind's chief end was to glorify God and enjoy communication with him forever, such a claim was merely a logical extension. It was an imperative for the whole universe to exist for God's glory and purposes." As a young man, he had already experienced "Nature's pulses ... mysteriously keeping time with [his] own" as he and his boyhood friends explored the "Wisconsin wilderness[,] ... [y]oung hearts, young leaves, flowers, animals, the winds and the streams and the sparkling lake, all wildly, gladly rejoicing together!" [B 34]. He seems always to have known what it had taken Thoreau years to learn, that all creation ecstatically dances with joy and that "goodness" or "love was the core concept around which the universe functioned."[5]

In *My First Summer in the Sierra*, Muir describes the curious appearance of the shepherd who travels with him, "a queer character" [F 226] who despite his oddities interests Muir greatly. The man's "wonderful everlasting" [F 226] trousers, caked with grease from his dripping luncheon bag, are layered with "pine needles, thin flakes and fibers of bark, mica scales and minute grains of quartz, horne-blend, etc., feathers, seed wings, moth and butterfly wings, legs and antennae of innumerable insects, or even whole insects such as the small beetles, moths, and mosquitoes, with flower petals, pollen dust and indeed bits of all plants, animals, and minerals of the region adhere to them and are safely embedded, so that far from being a naturalist he collects fragmentary specimens of everything and becomes richer than he knows" [F 227]. This image leads him to believe that "[m]an is a microcosm" and is especially important to appreciating how Muir wanted to relate to nature. Man can never be separated from nature; every encounter with the "eternal song" [F 226] sung by each separate element of creation, even insects, raindrops, and "rock crystals" [F 226], draws us closer to and makes us a part of nature, adding to the "concentric" [F 226] layers of our relationship with all the participants in this "terrestrial eternity" [F 229].

"To See Better What the Sun Sees": Muir's Divine Vision

Muir's awareness of the critical presence of insects in the landscape does not begin with the development of a microscopic vision, as it does for Thoreau, or stem from a practical, scientifically oriented perspective, as it does for Dickinson. Instead, Muir attempts to see nature from the viewpoint of its Creator, expanding his view to sweep over vast mountain ranges, then contracting it to focus on the smallest particles of creation; he even attempts to imagine a geological perspective that expands the boundaries of time, envisioning the lifecycle of a glacier, the birth, life, and death of a pond and its residents, and the views from Mt. Ritter as they grow and evolve over centuries. Combining macroscopic and microscopic angles of vision allows Muir to recognize the complex harmony that exists between all elements of nature, organic and inorganic, and to find evidence for his theistic conviction that God's message of brotherhood and joy is eternally etched into the landscape. From this position, the superior stance mankind assumes over the rest of nature is undeniably blasphemous and unjust: "How narrow we selfish, conceited creatures are in our sympathies! how blind to the rights of the rest of creation! With what dismal irreverence we speak of our fellow mortals!" [G 98]. Tracing the development of this philosophical and observational technique is therefore important to understanding the role insects played in Muir's intricate world view. Even though he rarely discusses individual insects, Muir frequently notes the swarms that he encounters on his expeditions into the wild; for Muir, these clouds of seemingly insignificant insects joyously cavorting in fields of flowers or skimming a pond's surface, dizzily dancing in the sunlight, are just as important as any other citizens of "Earth-planet" [G xiii] and reinforce his belief that all creatures "are our brothers and sisters" [JM 440], "unfallen, undepraved" [G 98], and equal in the eyes of God.

Muir never had any real doubt that nature was deliberately created by God; he truly never lost the "wild enthusiasm" that "sent [him] flying to the woods and meadows," "charmed" by the knowledge that nature "reveal[s] glorious traces of the thoughts of God," that science's classification systems only reveal what God "'had ... in mind'" [B 139] to begin with. The young Muir described by the adult Muir in *The Story of My Boyhood and Youth* already understands the lessons of nature that he later attempts to translate in his journals. This profound revelation is almost certainly colored by adult experience, and the twelve-year-old Muir had no idea what magnificent natural glories awaited him or what he would decipher from their pages. Still, Muir was a born "lover of nature" in the true Emersonian sense, feeling the throb of nature's call as soon as he met her and "retain[ing] the spirit of infancy even into the era of manhood" [E 10]. More than Emerson and Thoreau were ever able to do, Muir accepts that he is Nature's "creature" and succumbs to the "wild delight run[ning] through" him in her "presence" [E 10]. While Emerson might have experienced moments of "perfect exhilaration" as he "cross[es] a bare common" [E 10], it is difficult to imagine him climbing a tree during a storm to surrender himself to the whims of the wind. Thoreau may have imagined submerging himself in the swamplands, but he never does; he successfully climbs Ktaadn, but the moment of unity and transcendence of himself that he experiences at the summit is as temporary as it is overwhelming, and he never catches more than occasional glimpses of what Muir devotes his life to experiencing. Emerson and Thoreau may have eventually felt nature's harmony coursing through them and heard the infinite voices of the wind calling them forward to participate, but they never fully relinquished themselves to it; they always returned home to contemplate and interpret what they had seen. For Muir, however, "intercourse with heaven and earth, bec[ame] part of his daily food" [E 10], his "daily spirit bread" [JM 118], a Eucharist, and he is only ever truly at home when in nature.

Many critics have noticed Muir's ability to erase personal awareness from his vision, to become Emerson's "transparent eye-ball"; in nature, Muir at times becomes "nothing" and "sees all," allows "the currents of the Universal Being [to] circulate through [him]," and becomes "part or particle of God" [E 10]. Gretel Ehrlich describes Muir as "an Emersonian eye — whole, transparent, curious." Sherman Paul describes *My First Summer in the Sierra* as "one of his versions of Emerson's transparent eyeball" and believes that "Muir effortlessly achieves the egoless stance within the field that some poets and naturalists now value.... He eliminates the personal pronoun in order to enact the central fact of his experience: that the 'I' has merged with the 'eye.'" Frank E. Buske says that "The 'transparent self' might well describe Muir's ideal literary persona, and his narrative style might be characterized as one of self-*effacement*— an attempt to *erase* the obstructive presence of self in the interest of opening the view of nature."[6] Muir easily achieves this selflessness, and never consciously has to seek it, as Thoreau does; indeed, it seems at times to possess him, seizing control of his senses and improving them so overwhelmingly that he melts into the pulse of the landscape: "you seem dissolved in it, yet everything about you is beating with warm, terrestrial, human love and life delightfully substantial and familiar.... Bees hum as in a harvest noon, butterflies waver above the flowers, and like them you lave in the vital sunshine, too richly and homogeneously joy-filled to be capable of partial thought. You are all eye, sifted through and through with light and beauty" [MC 395]. Basking in the sunshine, he becomes "all eye," so conscious of the abundant life swarming around him that he cannot help but notice their ecstatic joy as they celebrate their creation and their Creator. The mountains infect him, entering his body and forever changing it, returning him for a time to a prelapsarian condition: "We are now in the mountains and they are in us, kindling enthusiasm, making every nerve quiver, filling every pore and cell of us. Our flesh-and-bone tabernacle seems transparent as glass to the beauty about us, as if truly an inseparable part of it, thrilling with the air and trees, streams and rocks, in the waves of the sun,—a part of all nature, neither old nor young, sick nor well, but immortal.... How glorious a conversion, so complete and wholesome it is, scarce memory enough of old bondage days left as a standpoint to view it from! In this newness of life we seem to have been so always" [F 161].

One reason Muir more successfully immerses himself in nature more than other naturalists is his unswerving, constant faith that every creature, every thing, every moment, is in the hands of the Creator; as Williams explains, "Muir accepted the *a priori* assumption proposed by natural theologians, such as [John] Ray and Dick, that the natural world operated on the basis of divine harmony and order."[7] Like Emerson's ideal "lover of nature," he believes that "nothing can befall [him] in life,—no disgrace, no calamity ... which nature cannot repair" [E 10]. For example, after experiencing an earthquake in Yosemite National Park and witnessing Eagle Rock "pouring to the valley floor in a free curve luminous from friction, making a terribly sublime and beautiful spectacle — an arc of fire fifteen hundred feet span" [NP 197], he begins to understand that "every boulder is prepared and measured and put in its place more thoughtfully than are the stones of temples" [NP 200]. He is able to see beyond the rubble and chaos created by the earthquake and understands that "by what at first sight seemed pure confusion and ruin, the landscapes were enriched; for gradually every talus, however big the boulders composing it, was covered with groves and gardens, and made a finely proportioned and ornamental base for the sheer cliffs" [NP 200]. There are no accidents in God's creation; everything is planned, orchestrated by God's hand. Those who don't believe in this natural order are advised to "climb to the top of one of them, tie your mountain shoes firmly over the instep, and with braced nerves run down without any haggling, puttering hesitation, boldly jumping from boulder to boulder with even speed" [NP 200]. One can easily imagine Muir joyously bounding from boulder to boulder, his "feet playing a tune," dancing to "the music and poetry of rock piles" [NP 200], his faith that God will guide his feet secure.

Muir's faith in the perfection of God's design is evident in another rather famous event narrated in "A Wind-storm in the Forests." Not content to weather out a wind-storm in the home of his friend, Muir "los[es] no time in pushing out into the woods to enjoy it" [MC 467] and, like Goldilocks, sets out to find a tree that is just right to climb. He finally settles on a Douglas Spruce and shimmies up to the top, where he and the trees "flapped and swished in the passionate torrent, bending and swirling backward and forward, round and round, tracing indescribable combinations of vertical and horizontal curves" [MC 469]. Perched in the treetop like a squirrel, whipping about in "an arc of from twenty to thirty degrees" [MC 469–70], he still "felt sure of its elastic temper, having seen others of the same species ... bent almost to the ground indeed, in heavy snows, without breaking a fiber. [He] was therefore safe, and free to take the wind into [his] pulses and enjoy the excited forest from [his] superb outlook" [MC 470]. He never thinks of the risk to his own life, certain that the tree has been deliberately designed to endure much more than his weight and the force of the winds. After several hours, he "dismount[s]" [MC 47] the tree as easily as if it were a horse, turns once more to contemplate the landscape from the ground, and witnesses "the setting sun fill[ing the forests] with amber light, [which] seemed to say, while they listened, 'My peace I give unto you'" [MC 473]. Storms, like every other natural force, originate from God and speak a language that takes a lifetime to learn.

Rather than agents of destruction and ruin, "[s]torms of every sort, torrents, earthquakes, cataclysms, 'convulsions of nature,' etc., however mysterious and lawless at first sight they may seem, are only harmonious notes in the song of creation, varied expressions of God's love" [NP 200], and Muir fears them no more than he does a gentle rain or snowfall.

On another occasion, while attempting to climb a "narrow avalanche gully" [MC 354] on Mount Ritter, he becomes frozen with fear when he is unable to find a hand- or foot-hold, "unable to move hand or foot either up or down," and he believes that he "*must* fall" [MC 355]. After he surrenders himself to the possibility that he might wind up a "lifeless rumble ... [on] ... the glacier below" [MC 355], he "seemed suddenly to become possessed of a new sense. The other self, bygone experiences, Instinct, or Guardian Angel,—call it what you will,—came forward and assumed control. Then my trembling muscles became firm again, every rift and flaw in the rock was seen as through a microscope, and my limbs moved with a positiveness and precision with which I seemed to have nothing at all to do. Had I been borne aloft upon wings, my deliverance could not have been more complete" [MC 355]. The adrenaline rush his body undergoes as he clings to the side of the icy cavern might support his state of hyper-awareness of his environment, allowing him to discern the small crack in the ice that he uses to climb to safety, but for Muir, something other than himself guides him out of that crevasse. In *The Pathless Way*, Michael P. Cohen describes this event as something that "happened to" Muir, something that "he could only observe.... He was not certain what force had assumed control." Cohen declares that Muir's dissolution of self into Nature begins earlier in the Mount Ritter account, when Muir describes the sensation of "limbs moving of themselves, every sense unfolding like the thawing flowers" [MC 352], pointing out that it is much easier to achieve this selflessness while strolling through the woods than it is to do so "in the midst of intense effort and tension." Muir's "fusion of self and other" is for Cohen "a key step to ecological thinking," and a critical part of Muir's "awakening" to Nature, but he fails to acknowledge that Muir is opened to more than a selfless unity with nature.[8] More specifically, he is exposed to and seized by the hand of God, for one moment a puppet dangling on very thin strings over a precipice. Unlike Jonathan Edwards, who imagines an irate, vengeful God dropping a cringing sinner into hell-fire, Muir conceives that his body is guided by hands "sufficiently gentle and tender for the folding and unfolding of petaled bundles of flowers" [JM 25]. Muir's ability to disconnect himself from himself, to find a center, a calmness, even when facing death and danger, also stems from his belief that neither his success nor his failure to scale Ritter will, in the long run, matter; as Williams explains, for Muir, "death as well as life" was an essential part of the "divine order" and "[t]o live in communion with God was to live a joyful life and die a joyful death."[9] While his success might expose him to new visions of God's handiwork to celebrate and decipher, his flesh would provide a meal to whatever lucky critters happen to find it, and his bones might someday be covered by a boulder, a grove, or a lake; either way, it would be part of God's design and he is more than willing to sacrifice himself to play his part.

Muir's confidence that "landscapes were God's predestined works of art," part of an "ongoing process performed by an immanent creative being,"[10] leads him to believe that God's plan was written, layer upon layer, like the concentric circles that mark a tree's life span or the travels of Thoreau's water-skaters, upon nature itself. He compares this terrestrial evidence of God's plan to a page "written over and over with characters of every size and style, ... [which] soon becomes unreadable, although not a single confused meaningless mark or thought may occur among all the written characters to mar its perfection" [G 164]. When attempting to interpret the infinitely more complex pages of nature's book, "[o]ur limited powers are similarly perplexed and overtaxed..., for they are written over and over uncountable times, written in characters of every size and color, sentences composed of sentences, every part of a character a sentence. There is not a fragment in all nature, for every relative fragment of one thing is a full harmonious unit in itself. All together form the one grand palimpsest of the world" [G 164]. Every grain, cell, and molecule of creation, no matter how minute or insignificant humanity might believe it to be, was a "particle of God," a letter inscribed by his hand. As he learns to listen to the "wind ... telling the wonders of the upper mountains" [F 163-64], as he sharpens his vision to decipher the multiple strata of God's living text, he realizes that the actions and voices of even the most inconsequential creatures are recorded in stone and carried on the wind.

This belief that even the tiniest creatures have a divine purpose, a direct role, in the "grand play ... being acted with scenery and music and incense" [F 187] under God's direction is another reason Muir is able to dissolve himself so readily into the landscape. As Lawrence Buell states, "Muir never seriously considered that the 'pathetic fallacy' might be fallacious"; because he "imagine[s] God as having created the universe as a vast interwoven fraternity of absolutely equal members," he does not hesitate to assume that they experienced fear, pain, love, and rapture as we do. According to John Gatta, Muir "challeng[es] the view that other creatures are simply our underlings, [and] describes them instead as 'earthborn companions & fellow mortals.'" Williams recognizes that some have been tempted to label this understanding of nature as "some kind of druidism or Paleolithic paganism," but he explains that this stance denies Muir's Judeo-Christian roots. Only man, in his fallen state, is removed from God; the rest of creation "exist[s] for God's glory and purposes." Cohen believes that when Muir tries to "see [creation] as the builder saw it, [and] take as nearly as possible a God's-eye view," he discovers, like Thoreau, that all of nature pulses with the rhythm of the universe. If, as Williams asserts, the function of nature is to teach man to "be content to live in joyful, harmonious fellowship with God like the rest of Creation," Muir can find no better instructors than the insects endlessly dancing through the landscape.[11]

While Thoreau's exploration of the importance of insects in the natural order of things begins with his deliberate development of a microscopic vision, Muir's appreciation of the individual particles of creation develops through his attempts, as Cohen states, to "take ... a God's eye view" of creation in order to translate the sublime messages of Nature "written in mountain ranges along the sky, rising to heaven in triumphant songs in long ridge and dome and clustering peak" [JM 98], transcribed in "characters ... so large it is difficult to see them from top to bottom in one view" [JM 88]. As John Dolis explains, Thoreau's concentrated perspective, his emphasis on the minute details of Nature's design, perhaps confined by the shores of Walden itself, "moves toward compression and intimacy, shuns the grand, the ornate, as unimaginable, unmanageable, unwieldy" and "wants nothing to do with the sublime." Unlike Thoreau, Muir does not need to close his "transparent" eye in order to envision the world from a "microscopic" standpoint, and his effort to reconstruct and transcend his personal perspective to catch a glimpse of God's, the growth of his "glacial eye," is rooted in his acknowledgment and appreciation of both the infinite and the imperceptible. Cohen observes that as Muir tries "to see the landscape as a glacier might" or adopt the "outlook," the experience, of "a young tree, rocking and swirling in wild ecstasy" in a wind-storm, he also discovers the individual elements and characters in the landscape, seeking to experience not only what it might be like to be a glacier or a tree but an individual branch or bee.[12]

Muir's glacial eye teaches him to see the divine lesson behind all creation, that there can be no resplendent vista, no sublime landscape, no transcendent experience, without the individual "particles" of life and matter that compose it, that nothing God has written will ever truly disappear. Muir's glacial eye, his conflation of Emerson's transparent eye-ball and Thoreau's microscopic lens, is always tempered by his unwavering faith in God's ever-constant observance of and participation in his universe. For example, as I discussed earlier, Muir clearly believes his deliverance from certain death on Mt. Ritter was directed by divine purpose, and that salvation was achieved by his sudden ability to perceive "every rift and flaw in the rock ... as through a microscope" [MC 355]. When he finally reaches the summit, a climb guided, he believes, by the hand and vision of God, which Cohen describes as an "ascent ... greater than the parts," he beholds a landscape that is more than a vision, one that transcends the "mechanical combination of foregrounds, middlegrounds, and backgrounds." Muir's glacial eye allows him to see "not four static views, but a harmonious sequence[,] ... a manifestation of flow" not limited or bound by space or time: "he had entered cosmic time, at the origin of creation, and only the wheeling of the sun reminded him that he was also a part of the historical present as well as the cosmic eternal. He was standing at the intersection where space and time began."[13] The writing of God on the landscape is eternal, every event leaves its mark: "Nothing goes unrecorded. Every word of leaf and snowflake and particle of dew, shimmering, fluttering, falling, as well as earthquake and avalanche, is written down in Nature's book, though human eye cannot detect the handwriting of any but the heaviest. Every event is both written and spoken" [JM 88]. At the peak of Mt. Ritter, his vision enhanced by the direct touch of God, Muir sees not only creation as it is but creation as it has been and will be, as God sees it, an angle of perspective that perceives "[b]eauty beyond thought everywhere, beneath, above, made and being made forever" [F 160].

In his attempt to see creation from the perspective of its Creator, Muir imaginatively attempts to transcend not only his limited human perspective but also his place in the human timeline. To comprehend more than "the heaviest" messages etched into the landscape, to read the elegant and "divine hieroglyphics written with sunbeams" [F 164], he must learn to exist within the "eternal time" of the bears rather than the chronological frame of human experience.[14] On one occasion, upon encountering a glacier meadow, he is so stricken by the significance and influence of the glaciers in the design of creation that he becomes disoriented in time: "So fully are the works of these vanished glaciers recorded upon the clean, unblurred pages of the mountains that it is difficult to assure ourselves that centuries have elapsed since they vanished" [JM 71]. Creation plays itself out before Muir's eyes, and for a brief moment, time collapses, condenses upon itself, and Muir stands not only in his time, but in eternal time, sacred time, cosmic time: "As I gazed, notwithstanding the kindly sunshine, the waving of grass, and the humming of flies, the stupendous canyon ... seemed to fill again with creeping ice" [JM 71]. The totality and harmony of the universe, the equally magnificent and subtle connection between a long-forgotten glacier and a buzzing fly or single trembling blade of grass, the process of Nature as Muir imagines God must see it, briefly flashes before his eyes as the imaginary ice recedes.

On another occasion, Muir imagines the birth and life experience of a lake, allowing his glacial eye to roam "from century to century" [MC 379] to trace its origin and track its influence. The lake is a living entity, beginning life as "an irregular, expressionless crescent," an embryo spawned by "bare, glaciated rock" and "the rugged snout of a glacier," "inclosed in banks of rock and ice," in the womb of Nature. Even before it "is born," it is aware, a "young eye ... open [...] to the light" [MC 379] of the sun, the touch of God. It gestates "for many a year, until at length, toward the end of some auspicious cluster of seasons, the glacier recedes beyond the upper margin of the basin, leaving it open from shore to shore for the first time, thousands of years after its conception beneath the glacier that excavated its basin" [MC 379]. Like a father, the glacier carves out a basin, a cradle, a home, for the infant lake, while patiently waiting, like any mother, for the "auspicious cluster of seasons" and signs that mark a pregnancy and announce an imminent birth. As the lake ages and the "glacier continues to recede, ... numerous rills, still younger than the lake itself, bring down glacier-mud, sand-grains, and pebbles, giving rise to margin-rings and plats of soil" [MC 379] and the rest of Nature takes its turn in nurturing and providing for, parenting, the infant lake. Plants begin to emerge, clothing its shores and enhancing its soil for the next generations of plant life, and "[i]nsects [begin to] enrich the air, frogs pipe cheerily in the shallows, soon followed by the ouzel, which is the first bird to visit a glacier lake, as the sedge is the first of plants" [MC 379]. Every fragment of creation, from ice crystals and grains of sand to mosses and blue gentians, from water ouzels and spring peepers to melodious insects and mountain streams, participates in the life of the lake, becoming, in essence, its relatives, extending Muir's images of conception, pregnancy, birth, and family.

Just as Muir's glacial eye allows him to compress centuries of geological evolution into the blink of an infant lake's eye, so he understands the language of nature enough to interpret the future death of this lake as well. As "the young lake grows in beauty, becoming more and more humanly lovable from century to century" [MC 379], the elements of creation that gave it life ultimately begin to take it away. Like the rest of creation, the lake is mortal, subject to the decay of time and the ravages of reproduction and creation. In time, the beds of soil that once encouraged plant and animal life to flourish along the lake's shores will be covered with "[g]roves of aspen ... and hardy pines, and the Hemlock Spruce, until it is richly overshadowed and embowered. But while its shores are being enriched, the soil-beds creep out with incessant growth, contracting its area, while the lighter mud-particles deposited on the bottom cause it to grow constantly shallower, until at length the last remnant of the lake vanishes" [MC 379]. After a long and fertile life, surrounded by generations of plants and insects and birds and other citizens of creation, for which it was parent or grandparent or distant ancestor, the eye of the lake is "closed forever in ripe and natural old age. And now its feeding-stream goes winding on without halting through the new gardens and groves that have taken its place" [MC 380]. Even though the lake will eventually no longer exist as itself, it nevertheless has been born and given birth, raised a family, and played with grandchildren, and so it necessarily continues on, endlessly influencing and sustaining future generations of life that will eventually "take [...] its place" [MC 380], recorded in the stones of the earth, its entire existence planned and acknowledged by the God that watches over it, the first and last light that strikes its eye.

The image of the sun as a representation of God's gaze sweeping over his creation is crucial in understanding Muir's attempt to translate the words of God in the text of Nature. Under sunlight, "everything seems equally divine," its radiance revealing and "opening a thousand windows to show us God" [F 187]. For example, the "alpenglow" [MC 350], the passage of the sun across the mountains, is to Muir "one of the most impressive of all the terrestrial manifestations of God" [MC 350]. Sunlight is the physical presence of the divine, the touch of God, and inspires all of Nature to worship: "At the touch of this divine light, the mountains seemed to kindle to a rapt, religious consciousness, and stood hushed and waiting like devout worshipers" [MC 350]. The mountains and trees do not merely inspire a religious experience in a perceiver, they participate in it, awaiting and expecting a rapturous encounter with the divine in every sunbeam. The sun fertilizes creation, blesses it, and the flowers it brings to life, like the rest of nature, are its offspring: "Well may the sun feed them with his richest light, for these shining sunlets are his very children — rays of his ray, beams of his beam!" [G 208] Just as Walden endlessly mirrors heaven and earth for Thoreau, the rays of the sun, both absorbed by and reflected from the golden petals of the Yellow *Compositae,* cause "The earth [to] indeed become a sky; and the two cloudless skies, raying toward each other flower-beams and sun-beams, are fused and congealed into one glowing heaven" [G 208]. In Nature, sunlight fills the void between heaven and earth with "God's shoreless atmosphere of beauty and love" [G 211]. Even the rocks "seemed responsive to the vital heat" [MC 352] of the sun, as "thrill[ed]" and "exhilarated" [MC 352] as Muir is himself. Under the sun's gaze, God's sight and touch, Muir surrenders himself to divine purpose as he did in the icy crevasse on Mt. Ritter: he "strode on exhilarated, as if never more to feel fatigue, limbs moving of themselves, every sense unfolding like the thawing flowers, to take part in the new day harmony" [MC 352]. Like the bees, fed by the rays of the sun, which "shines not on [him] but in [him]" [JM 92], Muir once again relinquishes control of his body and his vision to God's will, allowing himself at least momentarily to experience the "new day harmony," unencumbered by yesterday's fears and tomorrow's concerns. Like the flowers, Muir tries to live in the moment, a moment both fleeting and eternal, bound only by the course of the rising and setting sun reflecting and reflected by its creation.

Immersion in sunlight becomes for Muir as much of a baptism as immersion in water. In his recollection of his exploration of Twenty Hills Hollow, he describes an experience he refers to as a "baptism" by sunlight: "Never shall I forget my baptism in this font.... [T]he Hollow overflowed with light, as a fountain.... Light, of unspeakable richness, was brooding the flowers" [G 211]. Awash "in metallic gold, in sun gold, and in plant gold" [G 211], he imagines that "[t]he sunshine for a whole summer seemed condensed into the chambers of that one glowing day" [G 211]. This concentrated sunlight once again links terrestrial earth and celestial heaven, revealing the resplendence of God's divine plan, and the overwhelming distance between earth and sky, mountain and Hollow, becomes insignificant: "To lovers of the wild, these mountains are not a hundred miles away. Their spiritual power and the goodness of the sky make them near, as a circle of friends" [G 212]. In the sunlight, everything is united, nothing is distant, and "plain, sky, and mountains ray beauty which you feel" [G 212]. Luxuriating in the comfort of this divine glow, Muir "bathe[s] in these spirit-beams, turning round and round, as if warming at a campfire. Presently [he] lose[s] consciousness of [his] own separate existence: [he] blend[s] with the landscape, and become[s] part and parcel of nature" [G 212]. Under God's eye, caressed and pierced by the same sunbeams that unite the rest of creation, Muir escapes the confines of his human perspectives and disappears into the landscape, no more or less important than any other speck of matter in creation. Reduced to a "part" of nature, a particle, an elemental speck instead of a human being supposedly entitled to a privileged position in the chain of being, Muir loses his awareness of the dividing line between himself and Nature, himself and Other, himself and God: "as soon as we are absorbed in the harmony, plain, mountain, calm, storm, lilies and sequoias, forests and meads are only different strands of many-colored Light -are one in the sunbeam!" [JM 92].

"[L]av[ing] in the vital sunshine," pierced by divine rays reflecting off of creation, Muir's vision is again touched by God, transcending the transparency of Emerson's eye-ball, which "become[s] nothing" and "see[s] all" but is unable to participate in the cosmic dance or swim in the Universal currents. Muir's selfless stance in nature is not rooted in a void, an absence of self, but in a self infused with Nature, "filled with the Holy Ghost" [JM 118], his whole body attuned to and electrified by the divine rays and currents passing through it: "The radiance in some places is so great as to be fairly dazzling, keen lance rays of every color flashing, sparkling in glorious abundance, joining the plants in their fine, brave beauty-work,—every crystal, every flower a window opening into heaven, a mirror reflecting the Creator.... In the midst of such beauty, pierced with its rays, one's body is all one tingling palate" [F 243]. He does not only "dissolve" into Nature, into beauty, he is "absorbed" by it, losing his sense of self, time, and mortality; suddenly "[l]ife seems neither long nor short, and we take no more heed to save time or make haste than do the trees and stars" [F 175], he is "neither old nor young, sick nor well, but immortal," "truly an inseparable part of" the beauty that surrounds him [F 161]. His body becomes a prism, "sound as a crystal" and "transparent as glass" [F 161], beauty and sunlight "entering not by [his] eyes alone, but equally through all [his] flesh like radiant heat, making a passionate ecstatic pleasure glow not explainable" [F 228]. Muir's baptism in sunlight, another "submergence in fountain God" [JM 79] his "conversion" to a perspective that imitates not a God distant and removed from creation but one painstakingly and lovingly immersed in it, "working ... in a glow of enthusiasm" [F 187], does not remove his own perspective from his vision. Rather than dissipating into the landscape, his "individualism" is "washed and clean, ... more clearly defined than ever, unified yet separate" [JM 80], humanity purified, and he learns to "see better what the sun sees" [MC 517] as it, like the wind, "visit[s] the humblest flower, ... tr[ies] the temper of every leaf, tuning them, fondling and caressing them, stirring them in lusty exercise, ... playing on every needle, on every mountain spire, on all the landscape as on a harp" [JM 98–99].

Muir's critical question, "What is 'higher,' what is 'lower' in Nature?" [JM 137] is linked to his interpretation of light as the direct touch or gaze of God. In God's plan, "all of the individual 'things' or 'beings' into which the world is wrought are sparks of the Divine Soul variously clothed upon with flesh, leaves, or that harder tissue called rock, water, etc" [JM 137–38]. The origin of all life, all creation, in the beginning, is light directly emanating from the Creator: "All of these varied forms, high and low, are simply portions of God, radiated from Him as a sun" [JM 138]. Born from and bathed in divine light, all of Nature, the "eagle soaring above a sheer cliff, ... deer in the forest caring for their young; the strong, well-clad, well-fed bears; the lively throng of squirrels; the blessed birds, great and small, stirring and sweetening the groves; and the clouds of happy insects filling the sky with joyous hum" is "part and parcel of the down-pouring sunshine" [F 244], comprised of the particles of God. Unlike "the astronomer [who] looks high, [and] the geologist low" [JM 67], when Muir attempts to peer "between ... the surface of the earth" [JM 67] and heaven, he can no longer recognize a "higher" or "lower" order of creation. Under the sun, "Benevolent, solemn, fateful, pervaded with divine light, every landscape glows like a countenance hallowed in eternal repose; and every one of its living creatures, clad in flesh and leaves, and every crystal of its rocks, whether on the surface shining in the sun or buried miles deep in what we call darkness, is throbbing and pulsing with the heartbeats of God" [NP 57]. Blessed by the rays of God, infused by the Holy Ghost, Muir realizes that there is no hierarchy, no division, in Nature: a "[w]arm, sunny day, thrill[s] plant and animals and rocks alike, making sap and blood flow fast, and making every particle of the crystal mountains throb and swirl and dance in glad accord like star-dust" [F 196]. All creation participates in a joyous daily ritual of baptism by sunlight: "Innumerable insects begin to dance, the deer withdraw from the open glades and ridgetops to their leafy hiding-places in the chaparral, the flowers open and straighten their petals as the dew vanishes, every pulse beats high, every life-cell rejoices, the very rocks seem to tingle with life, and God is felt brooding over everything great and small" [MC 423].

Muir's God's-eye view, his prismatic, glacial eye, allows him, to borrow a term from Dolis, to "appreciate" the unique particles of the landscape and the individual characters living within it. While Emerson and Thoreau attempt to allow nature to speak for itself, to permit the distinct voices of the smallest parts of creation to speak, they never really truly believe, as Muir and Dickinson do, that the Creator intended a creation comprised of equal individuals. His "[a]ppreciation" of the landscape, informed by his divinely-oriented point of view, "lets things in, allows them to be, to (co)exist...[,] permit[ing] the greatest number of things to enter the picture; it sees how things belong, their different fit, in maximum complexity."[15] He is able not only to see the pattern of creation as it is displayed before him, the complex web of intersecting pulses and heartbeats, but also to follow that web beyond the confines of time, apprehending all of creation in a single moment in which past, present, and future simultaneously coexist. The "wonders ... [that] lie in every mountain day" are not limited to "the awful enthusiasm of booming falls, the roar of cataracts, the crash and roll of thunder, [or] earthquake shocks," but also include "[c]rystals of snow, plash of small raindrops, hum of small insects, booming beetles, the jolly rattle of grasshoppers, chirping crickets, the screaming of hawks, jays, and Clark crows, the 'coo-r-r-r' of cranes, the honking of geese, partridges drumming, trumpeting swans, frogs croaking, the whirring rattle of snakes, ... the whisper of rills soothing to slumber, the piping of marmots, the bark of squirrels, the laugh of a wolf, the snorting of deer, the explosive roaring of bears, the squeak of mice, [and] the cry of the loon" [JM 92]. As God contemplates and sanctifies his creation, "Not a single cell or crystal [is] unvisited or forgotten" [F 196]; from this perspective, every particle is recognized and acknowledged, not as an attempt to classify or divide, but to comprehend its relationship with everything else in Nature. Unlike an entomologist attempting to understand, for example, the life-habits of ants or locusts, or an ornithologist tracing the migratory patterns of certain birds, Muir is not as interested in discovering information about a species as he is in encountering and forming a relationship with every individual tree, plant, insect, bird, and boulder of God's creation that he can find.

Muir's appreciation of Nature allows him to recognize the smallest and unacknowledged citizens of creation as special recipients of God's attention. Regarded as insignificant or ignored, or, more often, disdained or abhorred by humanity, insect life, Muir begins to believe, is especially important to God. Witnessing "Butterflies colored like the flowers ... and many other beautiful winged people, numbered and known and loved only by the Lord, ... waltzing together high over head, seemingly in pure play and hilarious enjoyment of their little sparks of life" [F 246], Muir is captivated by the marvelous display of God's creativity and ingenuity: "Regarded only as mechanical inventions, how wonderful they are! Compared with these, Godlike man's greatest machines are as nothing" [F 246–47]. The lowliest of insects, a common gnat or housefly, is more remarkable than any of the achievements of science and medicine, art and architecture, that mankind uses to reinforce the belief that humanity is superior to nature. Contemplating "How do they get a living, and endure the weather? How are their little bodies, with muscles, nerves, organs, kept warm and jolly in such admirable exuberant health?" [F 246] leads him to discover that "[e]very rock, mountain, stream, plant, lake, lawn, forest, garden, bird, beast, insect seems to call and invite [him] to come and learn something of its history and relationship" [F 295] and to wonder whether he, a "poor ignorant scholar," will "be allowed to try the lessons they offer?" [F 295]. Dissolved into the landscape, permeated with creation, "Drifting about among flowers and sunshine, [Muir is] like a butterfly or bee, though not half so busy or with so sure an aim" [JM 108], and learns that the language of the insects is one of playful, exuberant celebration. Just as Thoreau's water-skater glides on the margin between earth and heaven, so Muir's "innumerable hosts of the insect kingdom" [MC 518], "singing every summer the songs sung a thousand years ago" [JM 93] soar along the sunbeams radiating from both God and creation, "shak[ing] all the air into music" [JM 54], "joy in every wingbeat" [NP 212]. Sailing across the divine landscape like all other "insect people" [JM 106], Muir explores another way of translating the "line[s] of writing" formed by "a thousand peaks, pinnacles, spires ... thrust into the sky" [JM 94]: "But in the midst of these methodless rovings I seek to spell out by close inspection things not well understood" [JM 108]. Observing that "[t]he air on the divide is full of insects, [which] when seen in the sunlight ... appear like transparent flecks of silver" [JM 162], Muir learns that "surely all God's people, however serious and savage, great or small, like to play. Whales and elephants, dancing, humming gnats, and invisibly small mischievous microbes,—all are warm with divine radium and must have lots of fun in them" [B 91]. Insects teach Muir, as they do Thoreau, that "joy is the condition of life" and that Nature continually offers this lesson to humanity, if only we could comprehend it. While "in the work of grave science [Muir] make[s] but little progress" [JM 108], his imitation of and appreciation for the position of insects assists him in his attempt to translate the language of God, which all of nature speaks.

Muir's initial contemplations of the sublime landscape lead to his discovery of the "many small soothing voices in sweet accord whispering peace" [F 170] that are carried on the wind, in the mountain streams, and on the sunbeams themselves. Awakening each morning to these "thousand other facts so small and spoken ... in so low a voice the human ear cannot hear them" [JM 95], Muir hears the voice of Nature "wooingly whisper[ing], 'Come higher,' [F 240], beckoning him, entreating him to explore the "glorious landscapes ... about [him], new plants, new animals, new crystals, and multitudes of new mountains..., towering in glorious array along the axis of the range, serene, majestic, snow-laden, sun-drenched, vast domes and ridges shining below them, forests, lakes, and meadows in the hollows, the pure blue bell-flower sky brooding them all" [F 240]. Unlike Thoreau's experience on Ktaadn, which inspires him momentarily to attain and thereafter yearn for "'Contact!'" with the sublime, the divine, in nature and leaves him trembling, Muir's translation of Nature's message is based in his desire to forge an intimately personal relationship with all of "God's people" [B 91]. The voice of Nature, "the happy plants and all our fellow animal creatures great and small, and even the rocks, seemed to be shouting, 'Awake, awake, rejoice, rejoice, come love us and join in our song. Come! Come!'" [F 190]. Like the crickets calling for Thoreau to join in the universal choir, Williams believes that Nature entreats Muir to awaken from the slumber of his human existence and to learn that "joyful existence should [be] ... the norm among humans ... as ... it was in Nature."[16] Mankind should emulate the grasshopper that visits Muir as he is "perched like a fly" [F 228] on a summit, "the mountain's merriest child, [who] seems to be made up of pure, condensed gayety" [F 232]. Like the Douglas squirrel, one of Muir's favorite "mountaineers" [F 234] and companions, the grasshopper exhibits nothing but "exuberant, rollicking, irrepressible jollity" and "Nature in him seems to be snapping her fingers in the face of all earthy dejection and melancholy with a boyish hip-hip-hurrah" [F 232]. Rather than dwelling on petty, manmade concerns, people should learn to accept and live with the spirit of celebration, the "spiritual reality available to humans," continually reflected and displayed by and in Nature. As Cohen says, "To Muir's 'glacial eye' the mystery of Nature became a living truth and could be known by those who were willing to repeat the mystical experience of living *in* the wilderness, as a Christian would live *in* Christ," and learn the language of joy and fraternity written on Nature's infinite pages.[17]

Muir's recognition of the brotherhood that exists between mankind and all of creation, informed by his glacial eye, his crystalline vision, permits him to see all creation as a family, a society, of individuals. He "ask[s] the boulders [he meets] whence they came and whither they were going" [JM 69] and "[w]hen [he] discover[s] a new plant, [he sits] down beside it, for a minute or a day, to make its acquaintance and hear what it had to tell" [JM 69]. For Muir, every living and nonliving thing on earth speaks the language of God, and he does not doubt their sentience, self-awareness: "Plants are credited with but dim and uncertain sensation, and minerals with positively none at all. But why may not even a mineral arrangement of matter be endowed with sensation of a kind that we in our blind exclusive perfection can have no manner of communication with?" [G 140]. Muir "fancies a heart like [his] own must be beating in every crystal and cell," which makes him "feel like stopping to speak to the plants and animals as friendly fellow mountaineers" [F 245]. Whether through imagination or direct exploration, "it is a good thing, therefore, to make short excursions now and then to the bottom of the sea among dulse and coral, or up among the clouds on mountain-tops, or in balloons, or even to creep like worms into dark holes and caverns underground, not only to learn something of what is going on in those out-of-the-way places" [MC 517], but to experience creation as God intended it to be experienced. Instead of determining the worth and purpose of the individual members of creation according to human standards, measuring their importance to the advancement of science or society or finance, Muir comes to believe that "nature's object in making animals and plants might possibly be first of all the happiness of each one of them, not the creation of all for the happiness of one. Why should man value himself as more than a small part of the one great unit of creation?" [G 138–39], a statement that perfectly encapsulates his "proto-awareness" of ecological concerns and convictions.

Contemplation of the complex insect societies frolicking throughout creation permits Muir "to think of many that are smaller still [that] lead [him] on and on into infinite mystery" [F 253]. Beneath the barely perceptible elements of creation, gleaming silver and gold in divine light, "the smallest transmicroscopic creature[s] that dwell [...] beyond our conceitful eyes and knowledge" [G 139] also exist, without which the "universe ... would ... be incomplete" [G 139]. Every "creature of all that the Lord has taken the pains to make," from the magnificent to the microscopic, is "essential to the completeness of that unit — the cosmos" [G 139]. All of creation is formed from particles of God, specks of divine light, "the dust of the earth" [G 139] and all citizens of Nature, "however noxious and insignificant to us ... are earth-born companions and our fellow mortals" [G 139], participating and existing in the divine order of creation and its Creator.

Creation is made up of "[m]yriads of rejoicing living creatures, daily, hourly, perhaps every moment sink[ing] into death's arms, dust to dust, spirit to spirit — waited on, watched over, noticed only by their Maker, each arriving at its own heaven-dealt destiny" [JM 440]. The insects and microbes, birds and innumerable plant-life, animal life and the very stones that make up the earth "all are our brothers and sisters and they enjoy life as we do, share heaven's blessings with us, die and are buried in hallowed ground, come with us out of eternity and return into eternity" [JM 440]. Only mankind is separate from this glorious existence, viewing death as "horrifying ... punishment" rather than as a "part of God's plan," allowing that fear of death to remove humanity even farther from a condition of joyful existence.[18] In sacred time, eternal time, time as it is measured by God and Nature, "[t]his star, our own good earth, made many a successful journey around the heavens ere man was made, and whole kingdoms of creatures enjoyed existence and returned to dust ere man appeared to claim them" [G 140]. Like the timeless lake, born from rock and ice and slowly consumed by the cells of matter and being that assisted in its creation, "[a]fter human beings have also played their part in Creation's plan, they too may disappear without any general burning or extraordinary commotion whatever" [G 140]. Even after humans, the supposed pinnacle of creation, disappear, as they eventually will, the "one general harmony of all nature's voices ... — winds, waters, insects, and animals" [JM 17] will continue to be written on the divine landscape, carried on the rays of the "stars ... streaming through space[,] puls[ing] on and on forever like blood globules in Nature's warm heart" [F 292].

"In the Eyes of a Bee": The "Bee-Garden" of California

Of all insects, Muir appears to be most interested in bees. While he devotes significant attention to the many races of "merry insect people" [B 208] basking in the gaze of God as he attempts to translate the language of nature, he does not often attempt to imagine the world through their eyes. The joyous grasshopper that visits him on the summit of Yosemite is a new acquaintance, as is the house fly that also buzzes about him, but his relationship with them is temporary, and he rarely mentions them again unless they are included in the "clouds of happy insects" [F 244] swirling around him, "filling the sky with joyous hum" [F 244]. The ants he describes in *My First Summer* receive, which he imagines as "the master existence of this vast mountain world" [F 176] because of their ferocious savagery, remind him of the unnecessary and unavoidable blind violence in a society far removed from Nature and its Creator: "When I contemplate this fierce creature so widely distributed and strongly intrenched, I see that much remains to be done ere the world is brought under the rule of universal peace and love" [F 178]. Unlike Thoreau, Muir does not focus on the warlike nature of ants or the fate of the solitary soldier sacrificed for the benefit of his colony; he admires their industry and determination, even in relation to their ferocity, and their seemingly infinite numbers lead him to consider "How many mouths Nature has to feed, how little we know about them, and how seldom we get in each other's way! Then to think of the infinite numbers of smaller fellow mortals, invisibly small, compared with which the smallest ants are as mastadons" [F 179]. Like the swarms of insects that fascinate him, Muir views ants as example of how nature endlessly recreates and celebrates itself. In the bee, however, a creature that lives on the product of sunbeams and manages to preserve its wild nature even when domesticated, Muir discovers a potential teacher and partner in mankind's attempt to live more harmoniously in Nature, and he attempts to imagine the past experiences and future fate of the California floral landscape as they might be seen "in the eyes of a bee" [MC 547].

It is possible that Muir was attracted to bees because they represented an alternative to domesticated sheep, which Muir often describes as "hoofed locusts" [MC 530] and certainly blames for a majority of the devastation of California's sacred "sweet bee-garden" [MC 523], "sweeping over the ground like a fire, and trampling down every rod that escapes the plow as completely as if the whole plain were a cottage garden-plot without a fence" [MC 530]. If tamed flocks of sheep represent for Muir all that is destructive and unnatural about domestication, apiculture exemplifies a more proper, balanced relationship between humanity and Nature. Speaking of Muir's "The Bee-Pastures" essay, Williams "find[s] some irony in Muir's bee economics," observing that "honeybees are domesticated animals, and Muir knew it. Honeybees had been bred to be greedy nectar harvesters meant to fill their combs plumb full of honey, just as apple breeders plumped and sweetened crab apples and sheepmen bred avaricious mounds of mutton and wool. They were part of human culture." Williams believes that Muir ignores their domestication because they are not as "terribly destructive" as sheep, and says that "he could see them as going feral, a process that may have inclined him to imagine them as mostly wild anyway." The fact that honeybees had been manipulated by human interests and yet still managed to flourish in the wild without human intervention would have been very pleasing to Muir, who could also be described as "going feral" as he wanders for months at a time without or with scarcely any human contact. Muir, like the bee, balances on the line between wild and tame, wilderness and culture, and it is the bee's perspective he seeks to imitate while he saunters through the Sierras. He attempts to experience the mountains "like a butterfly or bee" [JM 108], witnessing "[t]he great yellow days circl[ing] by uncounted, while [he] drifted toward the north, observing the countless forms of life thronging about [him], lying down almost anywhere on the approach of night" [MC 525]. In "The Bee-Pastures," he tries to imagine the geography of California as a bee would perceive it, constructing a calendar of bee-time and a reconstruction of bee history. As he expressed to Jeanne Carr, his "last efforts were on the preservation of the Sierra forests, and the wild and trampled condition of our flora from a bee's point of view."[19]

Muir's intimate relationship with bees begins before his efforts to preserve the bee-gardens of California. In *My Boyhood and Youth*, Muir recounts his first attempt to find a bee tree. After constructing a small wooden box with a glass lid and filling it with honeycomb, Muir captures a bee and carefully observes as it "first ... groped around trying to get out, [and then], smelling the honey, ... seemed to forget everything else [B 114]. Muir assumes that the bee will head straight for its hive in the proverbial bee-line after it is released, and was pleasantly surprised when "it was in no hurry to fly.... [I]nstead of making what is called a bee-line for home, it buzzed around the box and minutely examined it as if trying to fix a clear picture of it in its mind so as to be able to recognize it when it returned for another load, then circled around at a little distance as if looking for something to locate it by. I was the nearest object, and the thoughtful worker buzzed in front of my face and took a good stare at me, and then flew up on to the top of an oak on the side of the open spot in the centre of which the honey-box was. Keeping a keen watch, after a minute or two of rest or wing-cleaning, I saw it fly in wide circles round the tops of the trees nearest the honey-box, and, after apparently satisfying itself, make a bee-line for the hive" [B 114]. Muir moves the box "a few rods" [B 115] away from its original position "to test the worth of the impression [he] had that the little insect found the way back to the box by fixing telling points in its mind" [B 115] and waits for the bee's arrival. When it returns, it "c[a]me bouncing down right to the spaces in the air which had been occupied by [his] head and the honey-box, and when the cunning little honey-gleaner found nothing there but empty air it whirled round and round as if confused and lost" [B 115].

Muir repeats the entire process with another bee and is eventually led to the hive. Like the first bee, it seemed to recognize Muir as a potential landmark, "buzzing in front of [him] and staring [him] in the face to be able to recognize [him]" [B 115]. By observing that the bee acted "as if the adjacent trees and bushes were sufficiently well known" [115], Muir concludes that the hive is near, but he is disappointed and saddened when he finally finds it: "some lucky fellow had discovered it before me and robbed it. The robbers had chopped a large hole in the log, taken out most of the honey, and left the poor bees late in the fall when winter was approaching, to make haste to gather all the honey they could from the latest flowers to avoid starvation in the winter" [B 116]. The fate of the hive certainly would be less tragic in Muir's eyes were "the entire establishment, ... before time is given for a general buzz, bees old and young, larvæ, honey, stings, nest, taken in one ravishing mouthful" [MC 539] by an appreciative bear. Instead, they were left to suffer miserably through the upcoming winter without adequate food supplies despite their frantic efforts to "avoid starvation" [B 116].

Muir never loses his empathy for the bees. His poignant description of the fate of the Sierran wildlife during times of drought culminates with the death of millions of bees that could have easily been prevented had mankind intervened. Cattle, birds, and squirrels

> were in distress, ... falling one by one in slow, sure starvation along the banks of the hot, sluggish streams, while thousands of buzzards correspondingly fat were sailing above them, or standing gorged on the ground beneath the trees, waiting with easy faith for fresh carcasses. The quails, prudently considering the hard times, abandoned all thought of pairing. They were too poor to marry, and so continued in flocks all through the year without attempting to rear young.... The squirrels, leaving their accustomed feeding-grounds, betook themselves to the leafy oaks to gnaw out the acorn stores of the provident woodpeckers, but the latter kept up a vigilant watch upon their movements. I noticed four woodpeckers in league against one squirrel, driving the poor fellow out of an oak that they

claimed. He dodged round the knotty trunk from side to side, as nimbly as he could in his famished condition, only to find a sharp bill everywhere. But the fate of the bees that year seemed the saddest of all. In different portions of Los Angeles and San Diego counties, from one half to three fourths of them died of sheer starvation. Not less than 18,000 colonies perished in these two counties alone, while in the adjacent counties the death-rate was hardly less [MC 542].

Muir attempts to write his essay "The Bee-Pastures" by adopting a perspective that is sympathetic to the needs of a bee, that surveys the landscape "from a bee point of view" [MC 532], that sees the world as it is seen "in the eyes of a bee" [MC 547].

"The Bee-Pastures" begins with an image from bee history: before the intrusion of Spanish shepherds and their flocks, "[when] California was wild, it was one sweet bee-garden throughout its entire length, north and south, and all the way across from the snowy Sierra to the ocean.... Wherever a bee might fly within the bounds of this virgin wilderness — through the redwood forests, along the banks of the rivers, along the bluffs and headlands fronting the sea, over valley and plain, park and grove, and deep, leafy glen, or far up the piny slopes of the mountains — throughout every belt and section of climate up to the timber line, bee-flowers bloomed in lavish abundance" [MC 523]. Muir immediately contrasts this image of Bee Eden with a description of its current condition, ravaged and tainted by hordes of homesteaders, intent on manipulating land to produce crops that only they deem valuable: "But of late years plows and sheep have made sad havoc in these glorious pastures, destroying tens of thousands of the flowery acres like a fire, and banishing many species of the best honey-plants to rocky cliffs and fence-corners, while, on the other hand, cultivation thus far has given no adequate compensation, at least in kind; only acres of alfalfa for miles of the richest wild pasture, ornamental roses and honeysuckles around cottage doors for cascades of wild roses in the dells, and small, square orchards and orange-groves for broad mountain belts of chaparral" [MC 523]. As Cohen states, "[f]rom a bee's point of view it appeared that agri-culture had destroyed a boundless garden and replaced it with circumscribed plots."[20] In this essay, Muir interprets the landscape from the history of the bee, using his previously discussed glacial eye and his imagined bee perspective to recreate a history that emphasizes what he thinks would have been most important to the bees: a floral timeline, past, present, and its possible futures.

Williams describes "The Bee-Pastures" as "a paean to the lost floral paradise that existed there before the sheep and plow decimated the landscape."[21] Muir's essay emphasizes the past glory of the Great Central Plain of California in an attempt to preserve and maintain what remained. The Plains were once "one smooth, continuous bed of honey-bloom, so marvelously rich that, in walking from one end of it to the other, a distance of more than 400 miles, your foot would press about a hundred flowers at every step. Mints, gilias, nemophilas, castilleias, and innumerable compositæ were so crowded together that, had ninety-nine per cent. of them been taken away, the plain would still have seemed to any but Californians extravagantly flowery" [MC 523]. Much of the essay is dominated by Muir's extensive catalogues of the plant life that had flourished in the bee zones of the Sierras, which represent, after all, the landmarks most noticeable and important to bees. As he recounts his first entrance into "this central garden, ... it seemed all one sheet of plant gold, hazy and vanishing in the distance, distinct as a new map along the foot-hills at [his] feet" [MC 524]. Muir imagines what the landscape would have been like, and his later accounts of the cycles of annual plant growth are colored by what would have been there in the past as well as what manages to survive in the present. As he remembers his first footsteps into this wild garden and "wade[s] into the midst of it" [MC 524], it is difficult to determine whether he is drifting into a California he remembers from actual experience or a California he reconstructs from what he imagines was there before the intrusion and destruction of the "hoofed locusts." Once again, Muir seems to be lost in time, existing in "eternal" or "cosmic" time, transcending history and witnessing Nature's endless flow, the days "uncounted" and blurring together, time marked by the appearance and disappearance of the annual blooms.

According to Muir, the California plains are ideal for bee culture because, "although the main bloom and honey season is only about three months long, the floral circle, however thin around some of the hot, rainless months, is never completely broken" [MC 528]. This floral circle, in the eyes of a bee, must in some way represent a sort of floral calendar, the passing of the year. Brought to life by the rains of November and December, [b]y the end of January four species of plants were in flower" [MC 527] violets were born in February, and by

> March, the vegetation was more than doubled in depth and color.... In April, plant-life, as a whole, reached its greatest height, and the plain, over all its varied surface, was mantled with a close, furred plush of purple and golden corollas.... In May, the bees found in flower only a few deep-set lil-

iaceous plants and eriogonums.... June, July, August, and September is the season of rest and sleep,—a winter of dry heat,—followed in October by a second outburst of bloom at the very driest time of the year. Then, after the shrunken mass of leaves and stalks of the dead vegetation crinkle and turn to dust beneath the foot, as if it had been baked in an oven, *Hemizonia virgata*, a slender, unobtrusive little plant, from six inches to three feet high, suddenly makes its appearance in patches miles in extent, like a resurrection of the bloom of April.... It remains in flower until November, uniting with two or three species of wiry eriogonums, which continue the floral chain around December to the spring flowers of January [MC 527–28].

From a bee's perspective, time is measured by the development of buds, the blooming of flowers, the formation of seedpods, and their yearly resurrection.

After establishing the floral calendar of the region, Muir also relays the apicultural history of the region. The plains were an Eden for "wild bees" [MC 528], who have "probably" flourished "in this honey-garden ... ever since the main body of the present flora gained possession of the land, toward the end of the glacial period" [MC 528]. The domesticated honeybee was brought to San Francisco in 1853 [MC 528] and, like Muir, never really witnessed the spectacular "sheet of bloom bounded only by the mountains" [MC 524]. For them, as for Muir, "the present condition of the Grand Central Garden is very different from that we have sketched" [MC 529], subjected to "the attention of fortune-seekers—not home seekers—[who] ... began experiments in a kind of restless, wild agriculture" [MC 530]. Even as recently as "twenty years" [MC 529] before Muir wrote this essay, "the greater portion" of the plains were "still covered every season with a repressed growth of bee-flowers, for most of the species are annuals, and many of them are not relished by sheep or cattle, while the rapidity of their growth enables them to develop and mature their seeds before any foot has time to crush them. The ground is, therefore, kept sweet, and the race is perpetuated, though only as a suggestive shadow of the magnificence of its wildness" [MC 530].

After giving an account of the "floral circle" and explaining that many of the best bee-pastures are "already lost to the bees by cultivation" [MC 531], Muir begins to consider how the remaining resources of California might be preserved, keeping the needs of both the bees and "home-seekers" in balance. While his suggestions for an organized effort to develop the industry of beekeeping as both an economic and preservationist pursuit might be "half-whimsical, half-serious," as Williams says, it is obvious that bees represent for Muir what an ideal relationship with Nature, one that brings mankind closer to the intentions of God, might be like. Muir's idea that man's efforts to create a more economically valuable product from a wild sheep by "breed[ing] the hair out of its wool and the bones out of its body" [WW 602] have resulted in animals that have "cease[d] to be ... sheep" [WW 602] anticipates Annie Dillard's lament that she can find no spark of life in a cow's eye because it was no longer truly alive, just another human product, "like rayon," and exemplifies the largest problem Muir has with domesticated animals.[22] The "hoofed locusts" have lost their sheep-ness, and can no longer survive without the care of humans; as the "wild" has been bred out of them so they can better fulfill human needs, their connection to Nature is lost. They are as lost as humanity, victims of human manipulation, but as far removed from God as those who created them, and thus they become active agents of the mindless destruction of nature. Eventually, under the footsteps of sheep and their keepers, "The time will undoubtedly come when the entire area of this noble valley will be tilled like a garden.... Then, I suppose, there will be few left, even among botanists, to deplore the vanished primeval flora. In the mean time, the pure waste going on — the wanton destruction of the innocents — is a sad sight to see, and the sun may well be pitied in being compelled to look on" [MC 530].

Unlike sheep, however, bees can be domesticated without reducing them to products. It is possible to form an economic relationship with them that neither ravages the landscape nor destroys their bee-ness. Bees are able to survive without human intervention, and they are never limited by any boundaries, garden plots, or fence lines. Even in the face of the sheep's rampant destruction, the land can more than adequately support bees; even though many of the "tender plants" and shrubs are "badly bitten, ... neither sheep nor cattle care to feed on the manzanita, spiræa, our adenostoma; and these fine honeybushes are too stiff and tall, or grow in places too rough and inaccessible, to be trodden under foot" [MC 534]. Bees go where sheep fear to tread, and many "cañon walls and gorges, ... while inaccessible to domestic sheep, are well fringed with honey-shrubs, and contain thousands of lovely bee-gardens, lying hid in narrow side-cañons and recesses fenced with avalanche taluses, and on the top of flat, projecting headlands, where only bees would think to look for them" [MC 534]. Despite the disappearance of countless annual plants, the plains could still support a "thousand swarms of bees ... for every one now gathering honey" [MC 530] and a single *Magnolia grandiflora* tree, "[w]hen in full bloom" can feed "a whole hive of bees at once, and the deep hum of such a multitude makes the listener guess that more than the ordinary work of honey-winning must be going on" [MC 532].

Indeed, the land seems to be meant for bees, historically and geographically, despite mankind's efforts to "make improvements in order to make a home." Cohen believes that "[i]n trying to make peace with the society in which he would have to live, [Muir] had chosen to accept Man's right to find a home in Nature," and that he knew "[i]t was too late to save the Central Valley."[23] Apiculture represented a possible compromise, a way of forming a relationship with a member of Nature's society without changing its nature or its purpose. Williams says that the prospect of bee-culture proposes a "radical" yet "rational solution to the degradation caused by overgrazing" and addresses one of Muir's critical concerns: "Could people use [the land] in a manner that still preserved the attributes Muir believed it necessary to preserve in order for the landscape to fulfill it[s] highest purpose? Compromise on the domestication issue was acceptable if it led to respecting those elements of the natural world that he valued."[24] As he describes "the three main divisions of the bee-lands of the State" [MC 533] and their subdivisions, the foot-hill regions, the forest region, and the alpine region, he claims to have found bees flourishing "at a height of 13,000 feet above the sea" [MC 534]. If Californians were to employ the apicultural techniques of other countries, including Scotland, where "bees are carried in carts to the Highlands," France and Poland, where "they are carried from pasture to pasture," and Egypt, where "they are taken far up the Nile, and floated slowly home, ... the productive season would last all year" [MC 535]. Bees represent a continual cycle of production, one that does not interrupt the natural order, and human assistance can enhance their productivity, benefiting both the hive and its keeper without destroying their integrity, and drawing humanity, at least, closer to God. The bees are already there.

Despite their intimate connections to human culture, bees have not lost their connection to Nature. Swarms beyond human control still fill the air, and even those that will return to Langstroth hives at sundown retain the ability to "rove and revel, rejoicing in the bounty of the sun, clambering eagerly through bramble and hucklebloom, ringing the myriad bells of the manzanita, now humming aloft among polleny willows and firs, now down on the ashy ground among gilias and buttercups, and anon plunging deep into snowy banks of cherry and buckthorn" [MC 537]. Despite humanity's efforts to tame them, remove them from their wildness, the bees, "impelled by sun-power" [MC 537] have not forgotten their connection to Nature. As humanity is entreated to do in Matthew 6:28–29, "[t]hey consider the lilies and roll into them, and, like lilies, they toil not" [MC 537], but instead, "thrilling and quivering in wild ecstasy" [MC 536], they participate in a "perpetual feast[,] ... hug[ging] their favorite flowers with profound cordiality, and push[ing] their blunt, polleny faces against them, like babies on their mother's bosom" [MC 538]. Unforgotten and always noticed by God, uncorrupted by the stain of mankind's division from Nature, bees, even when domesticated, are still the children of sunlight, "[a]nd fondly, too, with eternal love, does Mother Nature clasp her small bee-babies, and suckle them, multitudes at once, on her warm Shasta breast" [MC 538]. Bees, half-wild, half-tame, have not ceased to inscribe their messages on the text of the natural world, and thus for Muir they represent the possibility that mankind might one day begin once again to coexist harmoniously with all the citizens of nature.

Chapter Notes

Introduction

1. Lawrence Buell, *The Environmental Imagination: Thoreau, Nature Writing, and the Formation of American Culture* (Cambridge: Belknap Press of Harvard University Press, 1995), 104.

2. C. L. Hogue, "Cultural Entomology," *Cultural Entomology Digest*, First Issue (June 1993): http://www.insects.org/ced1/cult_ent.html. See for example, Christopher Hollingsworth, *The Poetics of the Hive: The Insect Metaphor in Literature* (Iowa City: University of Iowa Press, 2001) and Eric C. Brown, ed., *Insect Poetics* (Minneapolis: University of Minnesota Press, 2006).

3. The history of ecocriticism is influenced and addressed by several authors. Leo Marx's *Machine in the Garden: Technology and the Pastoral Ideal in America* (New York: Oxford University Press, 1964) established a critical foundation for discussing the relationship between nature and technology, and Joseph W. Meeker first defined the term literary ecology in *The Comedy of Survival: Studies in Literary Ecology* (New York: Scribner's, 1972). *The Idea of Wilderness: From Prehistory to the Age of Ecology* (New Haven: Yale University Press, 1991) by Max Oelschlaeger provides an extensive historical study of humanity's interaction with nature. Daniel G. Payne examines the links between environmentalism and nature writing in *Voices in the Wilderness: American Nature Writing and Environmental Politics* (Hanover, NH: University Press of New England, 1996). In *Nature Writing: The Pastoral Impulse in America* (New York: Twayne Publishers, 1996), Don Scheese traces the emergence of the genre itself. Cheryll Glotfelty and Harold Fromm's *The Ecocriticism Reader: Landmarks in Literary Ecology* (Athens: University of Georgia Press, 1996) is generally regarded to be the cornerstone text of ecocritical studies. Other essential texts to consult include *Reading the Earth: New Directions in the Study of Literature and the Environment*, eds. Michael P. Branch, Rochelle Johnson, Daniel Patterson, and Scott Slovic (Moscow: University of Idaho Press, 1998); *Writing the Environment: Ecocriticism and Literature*, eds. Richard Kerridge and Neil Sammells (London: Zed Books, 1998); *Reading Under the Sign of Nature*, eds. Hank Harrington and John Tallmadge (Salt Lake City: University of Utah Press, 2000); *Beyond Nature Writing: Expanding the Boundaries of Ecocriticism*, eds. Karla Armbruster and Kathleen Wallace (Charlottesville: University Press of Virginia, 2001); *The Greening of Literary Scholarship: Literature, Theory, and the Environment* by Steven Rosendale (Iowa City: University of Iowa Press, 2002); and *The ISLE Reader: Ecocriticism 1993–2003*, ed. Michael P. Branch and Scott Slovic (Athens: University of Georgia Press, 2003).

4. Glotfelty, "Introduction: Literary Studies in an Age of Environmental Crisis," *The Ecocriticism Reader*, xviii; xix; xviii; xxii–xxiv; Branch and Slovic, "Introduction: Surveying the Emergence of Ecocriticism," *The ISLE Reader*, xxiii.

5. Lynn White, "The Historic Roots of Our Ecologic Crisis," *The Ecocriticism Reader*, 12; Payne 2.

6. Payne 3.

7. L. White 14.

8. Meeker 4, 6–7.

9. Glen A. Love, "Revaluing Nature: Toward an Ecological Criticism," *The Ecocriticism Reader*, 225–40: 227, 229, 237.

10. Buell 2.

11. Glotfelty xix.

12. Buell 7.

13. Branch et al., "Introduction," *Reading the Earth*, xiii.

14. Branch and Slovic xix.

15. Buell 2.

16. Martin Heidegger, *The Basic Problems of Phenomenology*, trans. Albert Hofstadter, rev. ed. (Bloomington: Indiana University Press, 1988), 18; Christopher Manes, "Nature and Silence," *The Ecocriticism Reader*, 15, 16.

17. David Mazel, *American Literary Environmentalism* (Athens: University of Georgia Press, 2000), xxiii; Glotfelty xx.

18. Manes 24.

19. Manes 17. For a summary of scientific attitudes toward animal emotion and language, see Jeffrey Moussaieff Masson and Susan McCarthy, *When Elephants Weep: The Emotional Lives of Animals* (New York: Delta Books, 1995). For a brief yet interesting discussion of intelligence and language use in animals, see Virginia Morell, "Animal Minds," *National Geographic* 213 (March 2008): 36–61.

20. Masson 2, 3, 21, 32, 33, 41–42.

21. Roger Fouts and Stephen Tukel Mills, *Next of Kin: My Conversations with Chimpanzees* (New York: William Morrow Paperbacks of HarperCollins, 1998), ix, 107, 157; accuracy 101; autism, 188.

22. The Chimpanzee Human Communication Institute, "Mission Statement," http://www.cwu.edu/~cwuchci/mission.html, 2004–2009; Roger Fouts, "Interview," The Chimpanzee Human Communication Institute, http://www.cwu.edu/~cwuchci/next_of_kin_book.html, 2004–2009.

23. Waggle dance: Subhash C. Kak, "The Honey Bee Dance Language Controversy," *The Mankind Quarterly* 31 (1991): 357–365, http://www.beesource.com/point-of-view/adrian-wenner/dance-language-controversy/; low frequency sounds and robotic bee: Wolfgang H. Kirchner and William F. Towne, "The Sensory Basis of the Honeybee's Dance Language," *Scientific American* (1994): http://www.beekeeping.com/articles/us/bee_dance_2.htm; CCD and Einstein: Richard Thomas Gerber, *Mysterious, Massive Disappearance/Death of U.S. Honey Bees—Colony Collapse Disorder (CCD)*, Target Health Global, 2007–2012, http://blog.targethealth.com/?p=58.

24. Louis M. Herman, "Language Learning," The Dolphin Institute, 2002, http://www.dolphin-institute.org/resource_guide/animal_language.htm.

25. Dolphin Research Center, "Communication," 2007, http://www.dolphins.org/marineed_communication.pp; Herman, "Language Learning."

26. Michael J. McDowell, "The Bakhtinian Road to Ecological Insight," *The Ecocriticism Reader*, 372–73.

27. Huxley quoted in Masson 34; Thomas Nagel, "What Is It Like to Be a Bat?" *The Philosophical Review* 83 (October 1974): 435–50: 449; McDowell, *The Ecocriticism Reader*, 386, 372–73. Sharon Cameron, *Writing Nature: Henry Thoreau's Journal* (Chicago: University of Chicago Press, 1989), 44.

28. McDowell 372–75, 381.

29. Buell 103, 104–8, 117.

30. Gunn quoted in Scott Slovic, *Seeking Awareness in American Nature Writing: Henry Thoreau, Annie Dillard, Edward Abbey, Wendell Berry, Barry Lopez* (Salt Lake City: University of Utah Press, 1992), 4.

31. Buell 21.

32. Slovic, *Seeking Awareness in American Nature Writing*, 4; Buell 103; Slovic 4.

33. For information about the history behind the idea of nature as a reflection of God's intention and will, see Peter Harrison, *The Bible, Protestantism, and the Rise of Natural Science* (Cambridge: Cambridge University Press, 2001); Buell 143.

34. *OED. Insect*: (1) A small invertebrate animal, usually having a body divided into segments, and several pairs of legs, and often winged; in popular use comprising, besides the animals scientifically so called (see 2), many other arthropods, as spiders, mites, centipedes, wood-lice, etc., and other invertebrates, as the "coral-insect"; formerly (and still by the uneducated) applied still more widely, e.g. to earthworms, snails, and even some small vertebrates, as frogs and tortoises. (2) Zool. An animal belonging to the class Insecta of Arthropoda. *Insecta*: Zool. (With capital initial.) A class of invertebrate animals; formerly (as by Linnæus) made to comprise the whole of the division now called Arthropoda or (as by Latreille) all these except the Crustacea and Arachnida; now restricted to that division of these otherwise called Hexapoda, having the body divided or distinguishable into three regions (head, thorax, and abdomen), with six legs (all borne upon the thorax), and usually two or four wings (but in some cases none); constituting the largest class of Arthropoda, and outnumbering all the rest of the animal kingdom, nearly a million species being now known (1988). Willis Conner Sorenson, *Brethren of the Net: American Entomology 1840–1880* (History of American Science and Technology Series, Tuscaloosa: University of Alabama Press, 1995), 2, 3, 22.

35. Michelle Tolini, "'Beetle Abominations' and Birds on Bonnets: Zoological Fantasy in Late-Nineteenth Century Dress," *Nineteenth-Century Art Worldwide: A Journal of Nineteenth Century Visual Culture*, 1.1 (2002): http://19thc-artworldwide.org/spring_02/articles/toli.html.

36. Sorenson 93.
37. Tolini.
38. Stephen Nissenbaum, *The Battle for Christmas* (New York: Vintage, 1997), 138.
39. Select articles include Frank Davidson, "Melville, Thoreau, and 'The Apple-Tree Table,'" *American Literature* 25.4 (1954): 479–88; Francis D. Ross, "Rhetorical Procedure in Thoreau's 'Battle of the Ants,'" *College Composition and Communication* 16.1 (1965): 14–18; Thomas W. Ford, "Thoreau's Cosmic Mosquito and Dickinson's Terrestrial Fly," *The New England Quarterly* 48 (1973): 487–504; Michael Tritt, "Thoreau's Skillful Use of an Entomological Text," *The American Transcendental Quarterly* 52 (1981): 259–62; Patrick F. O'Connell, "'The Battle of the Ants': Two Notes," *Thoreau Journal Quarterly* 7.4 (1984): 9–13; and Diana J. Swanson, "'Born Too Far Into Life': The Metaphor of the Bee in *Walden*," *American Transcendental Quarterly* 4.2 (1990): 123–34.
40. Critics who address insects in Dickinson include John Q. Anderson, "Emily Dickinson's Butterflies and Tigers," *ESQ: A Journal of the American Renaissance* 47 (1967): 43–48; Cynthia Chaliff, "The Bees, the Flowers, and Emily Dickinson," *Research Studies* 42 (1974): 93–103; Steven K. Hoffman, "Emily Dickinson's Bees: Development of an Agglutinative Symbol," *Dickinson Studies* 29 (1976): 30–35; JoAnne De Lavan Williams, "Spiders in the Attic: A Suggestion of Synthesis in the Poetry of Emily Dickinson," *Dickinson Studies* 29 (1976): 21–29; David Landrey, "The Spider Self of Emily Dickinson and Susan Howe," *Talisman: A Journal of Contemporary Poetry and Poetics* 4 (1990): 107–9; and Jane Donahue Eberwein, "Emily Dickinson and the Bumble Bee's Religion," *Dickinson Studies* 77 (1991): 23–33.
41. For a detailed discussion of Muir's textual chronology, see Cronon's "Note on the Texts" in *John Muir: Nature Writings* (New York: Library of America, 1997). To summarize, *The Story of My Boyhood and Youth*, published in 1913, covers 1838–1863; published in 1916, *A Thousand Mile Walk to the Gulf* was based on journals written in 1867; *My First Summer in the Sierra*, published in 1911, deals with Muir's trip to California in 1869; *Mountains of California* was published in 1894 and is comprised of 18 essays previously published between 1875–1882; *Our National Parks* appeared in 1901 and included essays originally written between 1897–1901; and *John of the Mountains: The Unpublished Journals of John Muir* spans 1868–1914 and was published in 1979.

42. Buell 193.
43. Michael P. Cohen, *The Pathless Way: John Muir and American Wilderness* (Madison: The University of Wisconsin Press, 1984), 117.

Chapter I

1. C. L. Hogue, "Cultural Entomology," *Cultural Entomology Digest*, First Issue (June 1993): http://www.insects.org/ced1/cult_ent.html.
2. Erich Hoyt and Ted Schultz, eds., *Insect Lives: Stories of Mystery and Romance from a Hidden World* (New York: John Wiley & Sons, 1999), 3.
3. See Diana J. Swanson, "'Born Too Far Into Life': The Metaphor of the Bee in *Walden*," *American Transcendental Quarterly* 4.2 (1990): 123–34. Tammy Horn, *Bees in America: How the Honey Bee Shaped A Nation* (Lexington: University Press of Kentucky, 2005), 130.
4. Unless noted otherwise, the information in this section is summarized from Willis Conner Sorenson, *Brethren of the Net: American Entomology 1840–1880*, chapters one through eight, (History of American Science and Technology Series, Tuscaloosa: University of Alabama Press, 1995); see page 93.
5. Corn planting: Personal interview, Mabel Wilson, Waynesburg, Pennsylvania, March 15, 2002. Woolly Bear Caterpillar: Lucy W. Clausen, *Insect Fact and Folklore* (New York: Macmillan Company, 1958), 19. Spider: David Pickering, *Cashell's Dictionary of Superstitions* (New York: Sterling Publishing Group, Inc., 2003), 440.
6. Vincent M. Holt, *Why Not Eat Insects?* (London: Field & Tuer, The Leadenhall Press, 1885), 5.
7. Sorenson 2.
8. Sorenson 5. Attitudes about entomology as a hobby: May Berenbaum, *Bugs in the System: Insects and Their Impact on Human Affairs* (New York: Basic Books, 1995), 274.
9. Sorenson 8; see chapter one, "Entomology in the American Context to 1840," 1–14. Harris's relationship with Thoreau: see J. S. Wade, "The Friendship of Two Old-Time Naturalists," *The Scientific Monthly* 23 (August 1926): 152–60. JSTOR.org. Harris' relationship with Colonel Thomas Wentworth Higginson: Higginson, "Butterflies in Poetry," *Part of a Man's Life*, (Boston: Houghton and Mifflin and Company, 2005), 179–203: 179–80. Books.Google.com.
10. Sorenson 15–17; see chapter two, "'A Few Literary Gentlemen': The Entomological Society of Pennsylvania, 1842–1853," 15–32.

11. Sorenson 34, 58. Number of entomologists: 253. See chapter three, "Of Cabinets and Collections," 33–59 and chapter four, "Agricultural Entomologists and Institutions," 60–91.
12. Sorenson 60, 61; see chapter four.
13. Sorenson 64; see chapter four.
14. Sorenson 125; see chapter four.
15. Tammy Horn, *Bees in America*, 20, 42, 43; wagons 93.
16. Horn 42–43.
17. Horn 65.
18. Horn 121–22.
19. Horn 104–9, 114–15.
20. Tammy Horn, "Piping Up: Women Beekeepers in Nineteenth-Century North America," *Bee Craft* (October 2007): 4–7. *Ladies' Home Journal* and Dickinson information: Horn, *Bees in America*, 130, 134, 136.
21. Steve Kellert, "Values and Perceptions," *Cultural Entomology Digest* First Issue (June 1993): http://www.insects.org/ced1/val_perc.html; see also Sorenson 107.
22. Sorenson 108–10.
23. Sorenson 110–14.
24. Sorenson 116–20.
25. Sorenson 121–25.
26. Jeffrey A. Lockwood. *Locust: The Devastating Rise and Mysterious Disappearance of the Insect that Shaped the American Frontier* (New York: Basic Books, 2004), xxvii; 8; xviii; 12. In the spirit of not "spoiling" the ending, I have chosen not to reveal the solution to this mystery. Those interested in the ending will find it an interesting and intricate explanation.
27. Lockwood 15, 16, 36, 37.
28. See L. O. Howard, "Striking Entomological Events of the Last Decade of the Nineteenth Century," *The Scientific Monthly* 31 (July 1930): 5–18, 115–116, 118, 119–124, 127, 129.
29. Howard 132.
30. Gilbert Waldbauer, *Fireflies, Honey, and Silk* (Berkeley: University of California Press, 2009), 154–156.
31. Terry Devitt, "Modern medicine goes medieval?" *University of Wisconsin-Madison News*, 2001, http://www.news.wisc.edu/6900; "Leeches and a History of Medicine," Niagra Leeches, 2005–2011, http://www.leeches.biz/medicine-leech.htm.
32. Waldbauer 161–164; Paré: Josie Glausiusz and Volker Steger, *Buzz: The Intimate Bond Between Humans and Insects* (San Francisco: Chronicle Books, 2004), 53.
33. Waldbauer 164–174; homeopathic remedies: Katherine Mariaca, "Homeopathic Remedies with Honey," Livestrong.com, April 28, 2010, http://www.livestrong.com/article/113493-homeopathic-remedies-honey/ and Carole Franske, "Facts on Honey and Cinnamon," February 4, 2009, http://forums.hpathy.com/forum_posts.asp?TID=9086.
34. Leeches and Cockroaches, Lice, Entomed: Glausiusz and Steger 16, 20, 70; Fruit flies: Waldbauer 172.
35. Medical Entomology Center, "Insect Research and Development," http://www.insectresearch.com/commercial.htm.
36. Christine Dell'Amore, "Cockroach Brains May Hold New Antibiotics?" *National Geographic Daily News*, September 9, 2010. http://news.nationalgeographic.com/news/2010/09/100909-cockroach-brains-mrsa-ecoli-antibiotics-science-health/.
37. Jack Claridge, "Insects and Flies in Forensic Medicine," *Explore Forensics*, June 16 2011, http://www.exploreforensics.co.uk/insects-and-flies-in-forensic-medicine.html.
38. Yao Ge Huang et. al., "Cytotoxic Activities of Various Fractions Extracted from Some Pharmaceutical Insect Relatives, *Archives of Pharmacal Research* 20:2 (1997): 110–114; Robert Lamb, "Parasitic Wasps' Genome May Yield New Drugs," *Discovery News*, January 14 2010, http://news.discovery.com/animals/wasps-genome-drugs-pest-control.html; "Russian Scientists Develop Anticancer Medicines on the Base of Insect Immune System," April 21, 2005, http://english.pravda.ru/science/tech/21-04-2005/8108-insect-0/.
39. The information in this section was primarily drawn from Lucy W. Clausen, *Insect Fact and Folklore*; see page viii. For additional information about superstitions, consult David Pickering, *Cashell's Dictionary of Superstitions*. Useful articles from the period about insect superstitions include: "Legends of Insects: What Popular Superstition Says About the Bee," *Atchinson Daily Champion*, Tuesday, August 28, 1888, Issue 134 Column B. 19th Century U.S. Newspapers Database; and "Superstitions About Insects," *The Atchinson Daily Globe*, Thursday, August 30, 1888, Issue 3,348 Column E. 19th Century U.S. Newspapers Database.
40. Clausen 29–30.
41. Beetles and ladybugs: Clausen 47–49; also see "Superstitions About Love," *St. Louis Globe-Democrat*, Tuesday, October 10, 1882, 4 Issue 142, Column D. 19th Century U.S. Newspapers Database. Cockroaches: Clausen 55; Grasshoppers: Clausen 59; Crickets: Clausen 60; also see "Chirping Crickets: Habits of These Hearthstone Genii — Their Peculiarities Discussed," *St. Louis Globe-Democrat*, Thursday, September 23, 1886, 15, Issue 123 Column D. 19th Century U.S.

Newspapers Database. Mantids: Jean-Henri Fabre, *The Life of the Grasshopper*, trans. Alexander Teixeira de Mattos (New York: Dodd, Mead and Company, 1917), 168. Books.Google.com. Digitized October 9, 2007. Also refer to Margaret M. Fagan, "The Uses of Insect Galls," *The American Naturalist* LII (February–March 1918): 155–76.

42. Flies: Clausen 81. Dragonflies: Clausen 143–44. Bees: Clausen 93–94; Pickering discusses offering food to bees on 59–60; also consult "Superstitions of Bees," *Daily Evening Bulletin*, San Francisco, CA, Saturday, November 22, 1873, Issue 40 Column D. 19th Century U.S. Newspapers Database. Hornets and Wasps: Clausen 118–19; Vance Randolph discusses the practice of using wasp nests to attract husbands on page 8 of "Ozark Superstitions," *Journal of American Folklore* 46 (January–March 1933): 1–21.

43. The information in this section is drawn from Waldbauer, *Fireflies, Silk, and Honey*, 30, 47.

44. Waldbauer 52.
45. Waldbauer 89.
46. Waldbauer 108.
47. Jan Thomas, "Early Victorian or Romantic Era: 1837–1860," http://www.jantiques.com/jewelryhistory/lesson3.html; Tolini.
48. Gene Kritsky and Ron Cherry, *Insect Mythology* (Lincoln, NE: Writers Club Press, 2000), 49, 57, 59, 60–61.
49. Tolini, "Beetle Abominations"; fireflies: Waldbauer 66.
50. Paul Beckman, "The Art of Beetles," http://www.living-jewels.com/art.htm; William H. Rideing, "At the Exhibition," *Appleton's Journal of Literature, Science and Art 1869–1876*, xv: 376 (June 3, 1876): 376. APS Online; E. B. D., "The Great Centennial Exhibition: Our First Visit," *Arthur's Illustrated Home Magazine*, 1873–1879 44 (July 1876): 7. APS Online; J. Thomas; Tolini.
51. Sheila Lemon, "Royal Belgian Ceiling Glows with Flemish Sculptor's Beetles Arrangement," *Providence Journal*, September 3, 2009, http://shenews.projo.com/2009/09/royal-belgian-c.html#.Tx0Nwm-JerZ; caddisfly jewelry: Waldbauer 77.
52. U.S. Food and Drug Administration, *Defects Level Handbook*, 1995–2012, http://www.fda.gov/food/guidancecomplianceregulatoryinformation/guidancedocuments/sanitation/ucm056174.htm#CHPT3; Waldbauer 119–120.
53. Holt 5, 11–13, 15, 18, 31.
54. Holt 31–44.
55. Holt 56, 58, 64, 79, 87.
56. Waldbauer 150.
57. Kritsky 65.
58. Unless otherwise noted, the information in this section is from William Carpenter and Dummer Gorham Abbot, *Scripture Natural History: Containing a Descriptive Account of the Quadrupeds, Birds, Fishes, Insects, Reptiles, Serpents, Plants, Trees, Minerals, Gems, and Precious Stones, Mentioned in the Bible*, chapter VI: Insects (Boston: Lincoln, Edmands, & Co, 1833): 197–227: 197–198. Books.Google.com. Digitized January 12, 2007.
59. F. S. Bodenheimer, "The Manna of Sinai," *The Biblical Archaeologist* 10 (Feb., 1947): 1–6. JSTOR.org. DOI:10.2307/3209227.
60. Carpenter 200–1.
61. Carpenter 213–15.
62. Carpenter 201–3.
63. Carpenter 202–4.
64. Carpenter 124, 205–7.
65. Carpenter 208.
66. Carpenter 209–10.
67. Carpenter 211–213. Honey and eloquence: Joann E. Lauck, *The Voice of the Infinite in the Small: Re-Visioning the Insect-Human Connection*, 1998, rev. ed. (Boston: Shambhala Publications: 2002), 138.
68. Carpenter 216–19.
69. Berel Dov Lerner, "Timid Grasshoppers and Fierce Locusts: An Ironic Pair of Biblical Metaphors," *Vetus Testamentum* 49, Fasc. 4 (Oct, 1999): 545–48. JSTOR.org; 546.
70. Robert Patterson, *Natural History of the Insects Mentioned in Shakespeare's Plays* (London: A. K. Newman, 1841).
71. Jonathan Edwards, "Sinners in the Hands of an Angry God," *Works of Jonathan Edwards Online*, The Jonathan Edwards Center of Yale University, http://edwards.yale.edu/archive/documents/page?document_id=7810&search_id=13505156&source_type=edited&pagenumber=1.
72. Spurgeon, Moody, Robertson, and Bushnell references taken from *Master Sermons of the Nineteenth Century*, ed. Gaius Glenn Atkins (Norwood, MA: The Plimpton Press, 1940), 227–256. Books.Google.com. "Regret[...]: Bushnell 152; the Rev. Davies's sermon is included in *Sermons of Rev. Samuel Davies, A. M.* (Ann Arbor: University of Michigan, 1864), 302. Books.Google.com. Digitized February 17, 2006.
73. R. Hunter, *Dialogues on Entomology, in Which the Forms and Habits of Insects are Familiarly Explained*, London: privately printed, 1819, v–vi, Books.Google.com.
74. Maria E. Catlow, *Popular British Entomology; Containing A Familiar and Technical Description of the Insects Most Common to the*

Various Localities of the British Isles, London: Reeve, Benham, and Reeve, 1848, v, vi, Books.Google.com.

75. John George Wood, *Insects at Home: A Popular Account of British Insects* (Oxford: Oxford University, 1872), 1, Books.Google.com.

76. Higginson, "Butterflies in Poetry," 182, 184, 191.

77. "Insects in English Poetry," *The Scientific Monthly* 33 (July 1931): 53–73. JSTOR.org; see pages 53–55; see also Pearl Faulkner Eddy, "Insects in English Poetry," *The Scientific Monthly* 33 (August 1931): 148–63. JSTOR.org.

78. May Berenbaum, "On the Lives of Insects in Literature," *Insect Poetics*, 3–12; see pages 4 and 11.

79. Hollingsworth 32, 41, 48, 49, 50, 85, 97, 123.

80. Hollingsworth 101.

Chapter II

1. Sattelmeyer, Robert. "Introduction." *"A Natural History of Massachusetts," "Wild Apples" and Other Natural History Essays*; see xiv.

2. J. S. Wade, "The Friendship of Two Old-Time Naturalists," *The Scientific Monthly* 23 (August 1926): 152–60. JSTOR.org, 152; David Spooner, *Thoreau's Vision of Insects & the Origins of American Entomology* (Philadelphia: Xlibris Corporation, 2002), 30.

3. Wade 153.

4. Wade 156.

5. Daniel H. Peck, *Thoreau's Morning Work: Memory and Perception in A Week on the Concord and Merrimack Rivers, The Journal, and Walden* (New Haven: Yale University Press, 1990), 118.

6. Wade 155; Peck 118, 119.

7. Joan Burbick, *Thoreau's Alternative History: Changing Perspectives on Nature, Culture, and Language* (Philadelphia: University of Pennsylvania Press, 1987), 1, 5, 9.

8. Frederick Garber, *Thoreau's Redemptive Imagination* (New York: New York University Press, 1977), 19, 187.

9. Sharon Cameron, *Writing Nature: Henry Thoreau's Journal* (Chicago: University of Chicago Press, 1989), 47, 75, 88, 149, 151.

10. Annie Marble Russell, *Thoreau: His Home, Friends, and Books*, 1902, (New York: AMS Press, 1969), 126, 271.

11. Nina Baym, "Thoreau's View of Science," *Journal of the History of Ideas* 26:2 (Apr.–Jun., 1965): 221–34. JSTOR.com. DOI:10.2307/2708229: 231; Cameron 6.

12. Bradford Torrey, "Introduction," *Journal of Henry David Thoreau in Fourteen Volumes Bound as Two Volumes: 8–14 (November 1855–1961)*. Reprint Ed. Mineola, NY: Dover Publications, 1982; see page 11 (xxix); also see Charles R. Anderson, *Thoreau's Vision: The Major Essays* (Englewood Cliffs, N.J.: Prentice-Hall, 1973), 18.

13. John Dolis, *Tracking Thoreau: Double-Crossing Nature and Technology*. (Madison, NJ: Fairleigh Dickinson University Press, 2005), 18, 23, 28, 34, 40, 69–70, 55.

14. Cameron 137; Baym 232, 236.

15. James Hedges, "The Cricket in Thoreau's Journal," *Thoreau Quarterly Journal* X (April 1979): 11–16: 15.

16. Michael Tritt, "Thoreau's Skillful Use of an Entomological Text," *The American Transcendental Quarterly* 52 (1981): 259–62.

17. Buell 297; Dolis 34, 190.

18. C. Anderson 18.

19. Tony McGowan, "Imperfect States: Thoreau, Melville, and the 'Insectivorous Fate.'" *Insect Poetics*, 58–86: 62.

20. Spooner 75, 77, 81.

21. See Hollingsworth, *The Poetics of the Hive*; Swanson 126, 127.

22. Swanson 124.

23. Stanley Cavell, *The Senses of Walden: An Expanded Edition* (Chicago: University of Chicago Press, 1992), 168.

24. Swanson 123, 126–27, 128, 129.

25. Patrick F. O'Connell, "'The Battle of the Ants': Two Notes," *Thoreau Journal Quarterly* 7.4 (1984): 9–13: 9.

26. O'Connell 10. Francis D. Ross, "Rhetorical Procedure in Thoreau's 'Battle of the Ants,'" *College Composition and Communication* 16.1 (1965): 14–18: 16, 28.

27. O'Connell 10.

28. Ross 18.

29. Swanson 129–31.

30. Spooner 84.

31. Walter Harding, "The Apple-Tree Table Tale," *Boston Public Library Quarterly*, VIII (1956): 213–5.

32. Frank Davidson, "Melville, Thoreau, and 'The Apple-Tree Table,'" *American Literature* 25.4 (1954): 479–88.

33. Donald Worster, *Nature's Economy: A History of Ecological Ideas*, Second Edition, (Cambridge: Cambridge University Press, 1994), 60; Spooner 38.

34. Spooner 40.

Chapter III

1. Romanticism: Joanne Feit Diehl, *Dickinson and the Romantic Imagination* (Prince-

ton: Princeton University Press, 1981), 7. "Proto-ecological": Christine Gerhardt, "'Often Seen — But Seldom Felt': Emily Dickinson's Reluctant Ecology of Place," *The Emily Dickinson Journal* 15 (Spring 2006): 56–78. 59. Science: James R. Guthrie, *Emily Dickinson's Vision: Illness and Identity in her Poetry* (Gainesville: University Press of Florida, 1998): 54. "Neighbors": Sister Mary James Power, *In the Name of the Bee: The Significance of Emily Dickinson* (New York: Biblo and Tannen, 1970), 66.

2. Judith Farr, *The Gardens of Emily Dickinson* (Cambridge: Harvard University Press, 2005), 3, 11; Gerhardt 63, 64, 68, 69, 73; Martin quoted in A. James Wohlpart, "A New Redemption: Emily Dickinson's Poetic in Fascicle 22 and 'I Dwell in Possibility,'" *South Atlantic Review* 66 (Winter 2001): 50–83: 53.

3. Inder Nath Kher, *The Landscape of Absence: Emily Dickinson's Poetry* (New Haven: Yale University Press, 1974), 101. Gerhardt 57, 60; Farr 127, 181, 270; Gerhardt 57.

4. Douglas Anderson, "Presence and Place in Emily Dickinson's Poetry," *The New England Quarterly* 57 (June 1984): 205–24: 205; Steven Winhusen, "Emily Dickinson and Schizotypy," *The Emily Dickinson Journal* 13.1 (2004): 77–96: 88, 91; D. Anderson 205; James McIntosh, *Nimble Believing: Dickinson and the Unknown* (Ann Arbor: University of Michigan Press, 2004), 124.

5. Joan Burbick, "'One Unbroken Company': Religion and Emily Dickinson," *The New England Quarterly* 53.1 (March 1980): 62–75: 62, 63, 66, 67, 73. Other texts that address Dickinson's religious concerns include Emily Dickinson and Martha Dickinson Bianchi, *The Life and Letters of Emily Dickinson* (New York: Biblo & Tannen Publishers, 1972); Roger Lundin, *Emily Dickinson and the Art of Belief* (Grand Rapids, MI: Wm. B. Eerdmans Publishing, 2004); Wendy Martin, *The Cambridge Introduction to Emily Dickinson* (Cambridge: Cambridge University Press, 2007); James McIntosh, *Nimble Believing: Dickinson and the Unknown*; Richard Benson Sewell, *The Life of Emily Dickinson* (Cambridge: Harvard University Press, 1980); and Barton Levi St. Armand, *Emily Dickinson and Her Culture* (Cambridge: Cambridge University Press Archive, 1986.

6. Nadean Bishop, "Queen of Calvary: Spirituality in Emily Dickinson," *University of Dayton Review* 19 (Winter 1987–1988): 49–60: 50, 53, 55.

7. Bishop 49; "she alternately believed": Patrick J. Keane, *Emily Dickinson's Approving God: Divine Design and the Problem of Suffering* (Columbia, MO: University of Missouri Press, 2008), 36; McIntosh 129.

8. Bishop 55.

9. Keane 2.

10. Gerhardt 56, 57, 58.

11. Emily Dickinson and Martha Dickinson Bianchi, *The Life and Letters of Emily Dickinson* (New York: Biblo & Tannen Publishers, 1972), 238. Books.Google.com; Fred D. White, "'Sweet Skepticism of the Heart': Science in the Poetry of Emily Dickinson," *College Literature* 19 (February 1992): 121–128: 121, 122, 123.

12. Guthrie, *Vision*: 2, 5, 33, 54, 55, 56; F. White 123.

13. Midori Asahina, "'Fascination' Is Absolute of Clime': Reading Dickinson's Correspondence with Higginson as Naturalist," *The Emily Dickinson Journal* 14 (Fall 2005): 103–119: 103; Frank D. Rashid, "Higginson the Entomologist," *The New England Quarterly* 56 (December 1983): 577–582: 578, 581–82.

14. Bulb forcing is a cultivation technique that "forces" bulbs to bloom indoors, usually out of season. Keane 33; Domhnall Mitchell, *Emily Dickinson: Monarch of Perception* (Amherst: University of Massachusetts Press, 2000), 113, 115–18, 146, 149.

15. Farr 4, 71, 72, 180, 181.

16. See Sister Mary James Power, *In the Name of the Bee: The Significance of Emily Dickinson*; Steven K. Hoffman, "Emily Dickinson's Bees: Development of an Agglutinative Symbol," *Dickinson Studies* 29 (1976): 30–35; Jane Donahue Eberwein, "Ed and the Bumble Bee's Religion," *Dickinson Studies* 77 (1991): 23–33; James R. Guthrie, "Darwinian Dickinson: The Scandalous Rise and Noble Fall of the Common Clover," *The Emily Dickinson Journal* 16.1 (2007): 73–91; John Q. Anderson, "Emily Dickinson's Butterflies and Tigers," *ESQ: A Journal of the American Renaissance* 47 (1967): 43–48; Thomas W. Ford, "Thoreau's Cosmic Mosquito and Dickinson's Terrestrial Fly," *The New England Quarterly* 48 (December 1975): 487–504; Sandra M. Gilbert and Susan Gubar, *The Madwoman in the Attic: The Woman Writer and the Nineteenth-Century Literary Imagination* (New Haven: Yale University Press, 1979); and Wendy Barker, *Lunacy of Light: Emily Dickinson and the Experience of Metaphor* (Carbondale: Southern Illinois University Press, 1987).

17. Gerhardt 63, 64, 68, 69, 73.

18. Gerhardt 62, 63, 66.

19. Gerhardt 57, 60; Farr 127, 181, 270.

20. Keane 74.

21. JoAnne De Lavan Williams, "Spiders in the Attic: A Suggestion of Synthesis in the

Poetry of Emily Dickinson," *Dickinson Studies* 29 (1976): 21–29; 24.
22. J. Williams 25, 26, 26.
23. John S. Mann, "Emily Dickinson, Emerson, and the Poet as Namer," *The New England Quarterly* 51 (December 1978): 467–88.
24. Wendy Barker, *Lunacy of Light: Emily Dickinson and the Experience of Metaphor* (Carbondale: Southern Illinois University Press, 1987), 107, 130, 132.
25. Katie Peterson, "Surround Sound: Dickinson's Self and the Hearable," *The Emily Dickinson Journal* 14 (Fall 2005): 76–88: 76, 79, 82.
26. James Hedges, "The Cricket in Thoreau's Journal," *Thoreau Quarterly Journal* X (April 1979): 11–16.
27. Louis C. Rutledge, "Emily Dickinson's Anthropods," *American Entomologist* 49 (Summer 2003): 70–74: 72; St. Armand 19, 80.
28. Dickinson and Bianchi 86.
29. Meyers, Howard N., *The Magnificent Activist: The Writings of Thomas Wentworth Higginson (1823–1911)* (New York: Da Capo Press, 2000), 544, 558.
30. St. Armand 19, 80.

Chapter IV

1. Dennis C. Williams, *God's Wilds: John Muir's Vision of Nature* (Number Eighteen, Environmental History Series, College Station: Texas A & M University Press, 2002), 203.
2. Elder, John C., "John Muir and the Literature of Wilderness," *Massachusetts Review: A Quarterly of Literature, the Arts and Public Affairs* 22 (Summer 1981): 376; Ehrlich, Gretel, *John Muir: Nature's Visionary* (Washington, DC: National Geographic, 2000), 144.
3. Elder 377, 386.
4. D. Williams 17, 18.
5. D. Williams 19; Thomas Dick quoted in D. Williams 20; D. Williams 8, 14.
6. Ehrlich 8; Sherman Paul, *For Love of the World: Essays on Nature Writers* (Iowa City: University of Iowa Press 1992), 254; Michael P. Branch, "Telling Nature's Story: John Muir and the Decentering of the Romantic Self," in *John Muir in Historical Perspective*, ed. Sally Miller and Frank E. Buske (New York: Peter Lang, 1999), 99–122: 108.
7. D. Williams 28.
8. Michael P. Cohen, *The Pathless Way: John Muir and American Wilderness* (Madison: University of Wisconsin Press, 1984), 68, 69, 70.
9. D. Williams 28.
10. D. Williams 72.
11. Buell, *The Environmental Imagination*, 192, 193; John Gatta, *Making Nature Sacred: Literature, Religion and Environment in American from the Puritans to the Present* (New York: Oxford University Press, 2004), 155; D. Williams 8, 60; Cohen 117; D. Williams 20.
12. Dolis 34; Cohen 43, 143.
13. Cohen 74–75, 79, 80.
14. Cohen 24.
15. Dolis 69–70.
16. D. Williams 25, 34.
17. Cohen 127.
18. D. Williams 28.
19. D. Williams 156; Muir quoted in Cohen 230–31.
20. Cohen 231.
21. D. Williams 155.
22. D. Williams 154; Annie Dillard, *Pilgrim at Tinker Creek* (New York: Harper's Magazine Press, 1974), 4.
23. Cohen 232, 235.
24. D. Williams 157.

Works Cited

Anderson, Charles R. *Thoreau's Vision: The Major Essays*. Englewood Cliffs, NJ: Prentice-Hall, 1973.

Anderson, Douglas. "Presence and Place in Emily Dickinson's Poetry," *The New England Quarterly* 57 (June 1984): 205–224.

Anderson, John Q. "Emily Dickinson's Butterflies and Tigers," *ESQ: A Journal of the American Renaissance* 47 (1967): 43–48.

Armbruster, Karla, and Kathleen R. Wallace, eds. *Beyond Nature Writing: Expanding the Boundaries of Ecocriticism*. Charlottesville: University Press of Virginia, 2001.

Asahina, Midori. "'Fascination' Is Absolute of Clime': Reading Dickinson's Correspondence with Higginson as Naturalist," *The Emily Dickinson Journal* 14 (Fall 2005): 103–119.

Atkins, Gaius Glenn, ed. *Master Sermons of the Nineteenth Century*. Norwood, MA: The Plimpton Press, 1940. Books.Google.com.

Barker, Wendy. *Lunacy of Light: Emily Dickinson and the Experience of Metaphor*. Carbondale: Southern Illinois University Press, 1987.

Baym, Nina. "Thoreau's View of Science," *Journal of the History of Ideas* 26 (Apr.–Jun., 1965): 221–34. JSTOR.com. DOI: 10.2307/2708229.

Beckman, Paul. "The Art of Beetles," http://www.living-jewels.com/art.htm.

Berenbaum, May. *Bugs in the System: Insects and Their Impact on Human Affairs*. New York: Basic Books, 1995.

———. "On the Lives of Insects in Literature," in *Insect Poetics*, Eric C. Brown, ed. Minneapolis: University of Minnesota Press, 2006, 3–12.

Bishop, Nadean. "Queen of Calvary: Spirituality in Emily Dickinson," *University of Dayton Review* 19 (Winter 1987–1988): 49–60.

Blake, William. "The Fly," *The Poetry of William Blake: The Works in Illuminated Printing: Songs of Innocence and of Experience*. New York: Doubleday, 1965. Literature Online. http://gateway.proquest.com.ezaccess.libraries.psu.edu/openurl?ctx_ver=Z39.88-2003&xri:pqil:res_ver=0.2&res_id=xri:lionus&rft_id=xri:lion:ft:po:Z400282022:4

———. "The Human Abstract," *The Poetry of William Blake*. http://gateway.proquest.com.ezaccess.libraries.psu.edu/openurl?ctx_ver=Z39.88-2003&xri:pqil:res_ver=0.2&res_id=xri:lionus&rft_id=xri: lion:ft:po:Z400282013:4

———. "Milton a Poem in 2 Books," *The Poetry of William Blake*. http://gateway.proquest.com.ezaccess.libraries.psu.edu/openurl?ctx_ver=Z39.88-2003&xri:pqil:res_ver=0.2&res_id=xri:lionus&rft_id=xri: lion:ft:po:Z200282254:2

Bodenheimer, F. S. "The Manna of Sinai," *The Biblical Archaeologist* 10 (Feb. 1947): 1–6. JSTOR.org. DOI:10.2307/32092 27.

Branch, Michael P., and Scott Slovic, eds. *The ISLE Reader: Ecocriticism 1993–2003*. Athens: University of Georgia Press, 2003.

Branch, Michael P. "Telling Nature's Story:

John Muir and the Decentering of the Romantic Self," in *John Muir in Historical Perspective*, Sally Miller and Frank E. Buske, eds. New York: Peter Lang, 1999, 99–122.

_____, Rochelle Johnson, Daniel Patterson, and Scott Slovic, eds. *Reading the Earth: New Directions in the Study of Literature and the Environment*. Moscow: University of Idaho Press, 1998.

Brown, Eric C., ed. *Insect Poetics*. Minneapolis: University of Minnesota Press, 2006.

Buell, Lawrence. *The Environmental Imagination: Thoreau, Nature Writing, and the Formation of American Culture*. Cambridge: Belknap Press of Harvard University Press, 1995.

Burbick, Joan. "'One Unbroken Company': Religion and Emily Dickinson," *The New England Quarterly* 53 (March 1980): 62–75.

_____. *Thoreau's Alternative History: Changing Perspectives on Nature, Culture, and Language*. Philadelphia: University of Pennsylvania Press, 1987.

Bushnell, Horace. "The Power of an Endless Life," *Master Sermons of the Nineteenth Century*, Gaius Glenn Atkins, ed. Norwood, MA: The Plimpton Press, 1940, 134–54. Books.Google.com.

Cameron, Sharon. *Writing Nature: Henry Thoreau's Journal*. Chicago: University of Chicago Press, 1989.

Carpenter, William, and Dummer Gorham Abbot. *Scripture Natural History: Containing a Descriptive Account of the Quadrupeds, Birds, Fishes, Insects, Reptiles, Serpents, Plants, Trees, Minerals, Gems, and Precious Stones, Mentioned in the Bible*. Boston: Lincoln, Edmands, & Co, 1833. Books. Google.com. Digitized January 12, 2007.

Catlow, Maria E. *Popular British Entomology; Containing A Familiar and Technical Description of the Insects Most Common to the Various Localities of the British Isles*. London: Reeve, Benham, and Reeve, 1848. Books.Google.com.

Cavell, Stanley. *The Senses of Walden: An Expanded Edition*. Chicago: University of Chicago Press, 1992.

Chaliff, Cynthia. "The Bees, the Flowers, and Emily Dickinson," *Research Studies* 42 (1974): 93–103.

The Chimpanzee Human Communication Institute. "Mission Statement," http://www.cwu.edu/~cwuchci/mission.html, 2004–2009.

"Chirping Crickets: Habits of These Hearthstone Genii — Their Peculiarities Discussed," *St. Louis Globe-Democrat* Thursday, September 23, 1886, 15, Issue 123 Column D. 19th Century U.S. Newspapers Database. Duq.edu.

Claridge, Jack. "Insects and Flies in Forensic Medicine," *Explore Forensics*, June 16 2011, http://www.exploreforensics.co.uk/insects-and-flies-in-forensic-medicine.html

Clausen, Lucy W. *Insect Fact and Folklore*. New York: MacMillan Company, 1958.

Cohen, Michael P. *The Pathless Way: John Muir and American Wilderness*. Madison: University of Wisconsin Press, 1984.

Cronon, William. "Note on the Texts," in *John Muir: Nature Writings: The Story of My Boyhood and Youth; My First Summer in the Sierra; The Mountains of California; Stickeen; Essays*. William Cronon, ed. New York: Library of America, 1997.

Davidson, Frank. "Melville, Thoreau, and 'The Apple-Tree Table,'" *American Literature* 25.4 (1954): 479–88.

Davies, Samuel. "Sermon IX: The Connection Between Present Holiness and Future Felicity," *Sermons of Rev. Samuel Davies, A. M.* Ann Arbor: University of Michigan, 1864. Books.Google.com. Digitized February 17, 2006.

Dell'Amore, Christine. "Cockroach Brains May Hold New Antibiotics?" *National Geographic Daily News*, September 9, 2010, http://news.nationalgeographic.com/news/2010/09/100909-cockroach-brains-mrsa-ecoli-antibiotics-science-health/

Devitt, Terry. "Modern Medicine Goes Medieval?" *University of Wisconsin-Madison News*, 2001, http://www.news.wisc.edu/6900

Dickinson, Emily. *The Complete Poems of Emily Dickinson*. Thomas H. Johnson, ed. Boston: Little, Brown, and Company, 1960.

_____. *The Letters of Emily Dickinson*. 3 Vols. Thomas H. Johnson, ed., with Theodora Ward. Cambridge: The Belknap Press of Harvard University Press, 1955.

_____. *The Poems of Emily Dickinson*. 3 Vols. R. W. Franklin, ed. Cambridge: The Belknap Press of Harvard University Press, 1998.

Dickinson, Emily, and Martha Dickinson Bianchi. *The Life and Letters of Emily Dickinson*. New York: Biblo & Tannen Publishers, 1972. Books.Google.com.

Diehl, Joanne Feit. *Dickinson and the Romantic Imagination*. Princeton: Princeton University Press, 1981.

Dillard, Annie. *Pilgrim at Tinker Creek*. New York: Harper's Magazine Press, 1974.

Dolis, John. *Tracking Thoreau: Double-Crossing Nature and Technology*. Madison, NJ: Fairleigh Dickinson University Press, 2005.

Dolphin Research Center. "Communication," 2007, http://www.dolphins.org/marineed_communication.php

Donne, John. "The Canonization," *Poems*. 1633. Printed for private circulation: 1872. Literature Online, http://gateway.proquest.com.ezaccess.libraries.psu.edu/openurl?ctx_ver=Z39.88-2003&xri:pqil:res_ver=0.2&res_id=xri:lion-us&rft_id=xri:lion:ft:po:Z200340897:2

_____. "The Flea," *Poems*. 1633. Literature Online, http://gateway.proquest.com.ezaccess.libraries.psu.edu/openurl?ctx_ver=Z39.88-2003&xri:pqil:res_ver=0.2&res_id=xri:lion-us&rft_id=xri:lion:ft:po:Z300317613:3

_____. "On a Flea on His Mistress' Bosom," *The Complete Poems (1872): Lyrical, Songs and Sonnets, and Miscellaneous*. Printed for private circulation 1872. Literature Online, http://gateway.proquest.com.ezaccess.libraries.psu.edu/openurl?ctx_ver=Z39.88-2003&xri:pqil:res_ver=0.2&res_id=xri:lion-us&rft_id=xri:lion:ft:po:Z300340680:3

E. B. D. "The Great Centennial Exhibition: Our First Visit," *Arthur's Illustrated Home Magazine, 1873–1879* 44 (July 1876): 7. APS Online. Duq.edu.

Eberwein, Jane Donahue. "Ed and the Bumble Bee's Religion," *Dickinson Studies* 77 (1991): 23–33.

Eddy, Pearl Faulkner. "Insects in English Poetry," *The Scientific Monthly* 33 (July 1931): 53–73. JSTOR.org.

_____. "Insects in English Poetry," *The Scientific Monthly* 33 (August 1931): 148–63. JSTOR.org.

Edwards, Jonathan. "Of Insects," in *The Complete Works of Jonathan Edwards, Vol. VI: Scientific and Philosophical Writings*, Wallace E. Anderson, ed. New Haven: Yale University Press, 1989, 154–62.

_____. "Sinners in the Hands of an Angry God," *Works of Jonathan Edwards Online*. The Jonathan Edwards Center of Yale University, http://edwards.yale.edu/archive/documents/page?document_id=7810&search_id=13505156&source_type=edited&pagenumber=1

_____. "The 'Spider' Letter," *The Complete Works of Jonathan Edwards, Vol. VI: Scientific and Philosophical Writings*, 162–69.

Ehrlich, Gretel. *John Muir: Nature's Visionary*. First Ed. Washington, DC: National Geographic, 2000.

Elder, John C. "John Muir and the Literature of Wilderness," *Massachusetts Review: A Quarterly of Literature, the Arts and Public Affairs* 22 (Summer 1981): 375–86.

Emerson, Ralph Waldo. "Nature," *Essays and Lectures: Nature: Addresses and Lectures/ Essays: First and Second Series/ Representative Men/ English Traits/ The Conduct of Life*. New York: Library of America, 1983.

Fabre, Jean-Henri. *The Life of the Grasshopper*. Trans. Alexander Teixeira de Mattos. New York: Dodd, Mead and Company, 1917. Books.Google.com. Digitized October 9, 2007.

Fagan, Margaret M. "The Uses of Insect Galls," *The American Naturalist* LII (February–March 1918): 155–176.

Farr, Judith. *The Gardens of Emily Dickinson*. Cambridge: Harvard University Press, 2004.

Ford, Thomas W. "Thoreau's Cosmic Mosquito and Dickinson's Terrestrial Fly," *The New England Quarterly* 48 (1973): 487–504.

Fouts, Roger. "Interview," The Chimpanzee Human Communication Institute. 2004-2009. http://www.cwu.edu/~cwuchci/next_of_kin_book.html.

_____, and Stephen Tukel Mills. *Next of Kin: My Conversations with Chimpanzees*. New York: William Morrow Paperbacks of HarperCollins, 1998.

Franske, Carole. "Facts on Honey and Cinnamon," February 4, 2009, http://forums.hpathy.com/forum_posts.asp?TID=9086

Garber, Frederick. *Thoreau's Redemptive Imagination*. New York: New York University Press, 1977.

Gatta, John. *Making Nature Sacred: Literature, Religion and Environment in American from the Puritans to the Present*. New York: Oxford University Press, 2004.

Gerber, Richard Thomas. *Mysterious, Massive Disappearance/Death of US Honey Bees — Colony Collapse Disorder (CCD)*. Target Health Global: 2007-2012. http://blog.targethealth.com/?p=58.

Gerhardt, Christine. "'Often Seen — But Seldom Felt': Emily Dickinson's Reluctant Ecology of Place," *The Emily Dickinson Journal* 15 (Spring 2006): 56-78.

Gilbert, Sandra M., and Susan Gubar. *The Madwoman in the Attic: The Woman Writer and the Nineteenth-Century Literary Imagination*. New Haven: Yale University Press, 1979.

Glausiusz, Josie, and Volker Steger. *Buzz: The Intimate Bond Between Humans and Insects*. San Francisco: Chronicle Books, 2004.

Glotfelty, Cheryll, and Harold Fromm, eds. *The Ecocriticism Reader: Landmarks in Literary Ecology*. Athens: University of Georgia Press, 1996.

Guthrie, James R. "Darwinian Dickinson: The Scandalous Rise and Noble Fall of the Common Clover," *The Emily Dickinson Journal* 16.1 (2007): 73-91.

_____. *Emily Dickinson's Vision: Illness and Identity in her Poetry*. Gainesville: University Press of Florida, 1998.

Harding, Walter. "The Apple-Tree Table Tale," *Boston Public Library Quarterly* VIII (1956): 213-5.

Harrington, Hank, and John Tallmadge, eds. *Reading Under the Sign of Nature*. Salt Lake City: University of Utah Press, 2000.

Harrison, Peter. *The Bible, Protestantism, and the Rise of Natural Science*. Cambridge: Cambridge University Press, 2001.

Hedges, James. "The Cricket in Thoreau's Journal," *Thoreau Quarterly Journal* X (April 1979): 11-16.

Heidegger, Martin. *The Basic Problems of Phenomenology*. Rev. Ed. Trans. Albert Hofstadter. Bloomington: Indiana University Press, 1988.

Herman, Louis M. "Language Learning," The Dolphin Institute. 2002, http://www.dolphin-institute.org/resource_guide/animal_language.htm.

Higginson, Colonel Thomas Wentworth. "Butterflies in Poetry," in *Part of a Man's Life*. Boston: Houghton and Mifflin and Company, 2005, 179-203. Books.Google.com.

Hoffman, Steven K. "Emily Dickinson's Bees: Development of an Agglutinative Symbol," *Dickinson Studies* 29 (1976): 30-35.

Hogue, C. L. "Cultural Entomology," *Cultural Entomology Digest*. First Issue (June 1993): http://www.insects.org/ced1/cult_ent.html.

Hollingsworth, Christopher. *The Poetics of the Hive: The Insect Metaphor in Literature*. Iowa City: University of Iowa Press, 2001.

Holt, Vincent M. *Why Not Eat Insects?* London: Field & Tuer, The Leadenhall Press, 1885.

Horn, Tammy. *Bees in America: How the Honey Bee Shaped A Nation*. Lexington: University Press of Kentucky, 2005.

_____. "Piping Up: Women Beekeepers in Nineteenth-Century North America," *Bee Craft* (October 2007): 4-7.

Howard, L. O. "Striking Entomological Events of the Last Decade of the Nineteenth Century," *The Scientific Monthly* 31 (July 1930): 5-18.

Hoyt, Erich, and Ted Schultz, eds. *Insect Lives: Stories of Mystery and Romance from a Hidden World*. New York: John Wiley & Sons, 1999.

Huang, Yao Ge, et. al. "Cytotoxic Activities of Various Fractions Extracted from Some Pharmaceutical Insect Relatives," *Archives of Pharmacal Research* 20:2 (1997): 110–114.

Hunter, R. *Dialogues on Entomology, in Which the Forms and Habits of Insects Are Familiarly Explained.* London: privately printed, 1819. Books.Google.com.

Kak, Subhash C. "The Honey Bee Dance Language Controversy," *The Mankind Quarterly* 31 (1991): 357–365. http://www.beesource.com/point-of-view/adrian-wenner/dance-language-controversy/

Keane, Patrick J. *Emily Dickinson's Approving God: Divine Design and the Problem of Suffering.* Columbia: University of Missouri Press, 2008.

Kellert, Steve. "Values and Perceptions," *Cultural Entomology Digest.* First Issue (June 1993): http://www.insects.org/ced1/val_perc.html.

Kerridge, Richard, and Neil Sammells, eds. *Writing the Environment: Ecocriticism and Literature.* New York: St. Martin's Press, 1998.

Kher, Inder Nath. *The Landscape of Absence: Emily Dickinson's Poetry.* New Haven: Yale University Press, 1974.

Kirchner, Wolfgang H., and William F. Towne. "The Sensory Basis of the Honeybee's Dance Language," *Scientific American* (1994): http://www.beekeeping.com/articles/us/bee_dance_2.htm.

Kritsky, Gene, and Ron Cherry. *Insect Mythology.* Lincoln, NE: Writers Club Press, 2000.

Lamb, Robert. "Parasitic Wasps' Genome May Yield New Drugs," *Discovery News,* January 14 2010, http://news.discovery.com/animals/wasps-genome-drugs-pest-control.html.

Landrey, David. "The Spider Self of Emily Dickinson and Susan Howe," *Talisman: A Journal of Contemporary Poetry and Poetics* 4 (1990): 107–109.

Lauck, Joann E. *The Voice of the Infinite in the Small: Re-Visioning the Insect-Human Connection.* 1998. Rev. Ed. Boston: Shambhala Publications, 2002.

"Legends of Insects: What Popular Superstition Says About the Bee," *Atchinson Daily Champion,* Tuesday, August 28, 1888, Issue 134 Column B. 19th Century U.S. Newspapers Database. Duq.edu.

Lemon, Sheila. "Royal Belgian Ceiling Glows with Flemish Sculptor's Beetles Arrangement," *Providence Journal,* September 3, 2009, http://shenews.projo.com/2009/09/royal-belgian-c.html#.Tx0Nwm-JerZ.

Lerner, Berel Dov. "Timid Grasshoppers and Fierce Locusts: An Ironic Pair of Biblical Metaphors," *Vetus Testamentum* 49, Fasc. 4 (Oct, 1999): 545–48. JSTOR.org

Lockwood, Jeffrey A. *Locust: The Devastating Rise and Mysterious Disappearance of the Insect that Shaped the American Frontier.* New York: Basic Books, 2004.

Love, Glen A. "Revaluing Nature: Toward an Ecological Criticism," in *The Ecocriticism Reader,* 225–40.

Lundin, Roger. *Emily Dickinson and the Art of Belief.* Grand Rapids, MI: Wm. B. Eerdmans Publishing, 2004.

Manes, Christopher. "Nature and Silence," in *The Ecocriticism Reader,* 15–29.

Mann, John S. "Emily Dickinson, Emerson, and the Poet as Namer," *The New England Quarterly* 51 (December 1978): 467–88.

Mariaca, Katherine. "Homeopathic Remedies with Honey," Livestrong.com, April 28, 2010, http://www.livestrong.com/article/113493-homeopathic-remedies-honey/

Martin, Wendy. *The Cambridge Introduction to Emily Dickinson.* Cambridge: Cambridge University Press, 2007.

Marx, Leo. *Machine in the Garden: Technology and the Pastoral Ideal in America.* New York: Oxford University Press, 1964.

Masson, Jeffrey Moussaieff, and Susan McCarthy. *When Elephants Weep: The Emotional Lives of Animals.* New York: Delta Books, 1995.

Mazel, David. *American Literary Environmentalism.* Athens: University of Georgia Press, 2000.

McDowell, Michael J. "The Bakhtinian Road to Ecological Insight," in *The Ecocriticism Reader,* 371–92.

McGowan, Tony. "Imperfect States: Thoreau, Melville, and the 'Insectivorous Fate,'" in *Insect Poetics*, 58–86.

McGregor, Robert Kuhn. *A Wider View of the Universe: Henry Thoreau's Study of Nature*. Urbana: University of Illinois Press, 1997.

McIntosh, James. *Nimble Believing: Dickinson and the Unknown*. Ann Arbor: University of Michigan Press, 2004.

Medical Entomology Center. "Insect Research and Development," http://www.insectresearch.com/commercial.htm.

Meeker, Joseph W. *The Comedy of Survival: Studies in Literary Ecology*. New York: Scribner's, 1972.

Meyers, Howard N. *The Magnificent Activist: The Writings of Thomas Wentworth Higginson (1823–1911)*. New York: Da Capo Press, 2000.

Miller, Sally M., and Frank E. Buske, eds. *John Muir in Historical Perspective*. New York: Peter Lang, 1999.

Mitchell, Domhnall. *Emily Dickinson: Monarch of Perception*. Amherst: University of Massachusetts Press, 2000.

Moody, Dwight Lyman. "Good News," *Master Sermons of the Nineteenth Century*. Gaius Glenn Atkins, ed. Norwood, MA: The Plimpton Press, 1940, 230–56. Books.Google.com.

Morell, Virginia. "Animal Minds," *National Geographic* 213 (March 2008): 36–61.

Muir, John. *John Muir: Nature Writings: The Story of My Boyhood and Youth; My First Summer in the Sierra; The Mountains of California; Stickeen; Essays*. William Cronon, ed. New York: Library of America, 1997.

_____. *John of the Mountains: The Unpublished Journals of John Muir*. Linnie Marsh Wolfe, ed. Madison: University of Wisconsin Press, 1979.

_____. *Our National Parks*. 1901. San Francisco: Sierra Club Books, 1991.

_____. *A Thousand Mile Walk to the Gulf*. 1916. William Frederic Bade, ed. New York: Mariner Books, 1998.

Nagel, Thomas. "What Is It Like to Be a Bat?" *The Philosophical Review* 83 (October 1974): 435–50.

Niagra Leeches. "Leeches and a History of Medicine," 2005–2011, http://www.leeches.biz/medicine-leech.htm.

Nissenbaum, Stephen. *The Battle for Christmas*. New York: Vintage, 1997.

O'Connell, Patrick F. "'The Battle of the Ants': Two Notes," *Thoreau Journal Quarterly* 7.4 (1984): 9–13.

Oelschlaeger, Max. *The Idea of Wilderness: From Prehistory to the Age of Ecology*. New Haven: Yale University Press, 1991.

Oxford English Dictionary. "Insect," Online Edition, http://www.oed.com

Patterson, Robert. *Natural History of the Insects Mentioned in Shakespeare's Plays*. London: A. K. Newman, 1841.

Paul, Sherman. *For Love of the World: Essays on Nature Writers*. Iowa City: University of Iowa Press, 1992.

Payne, Daniel G. *Voices in the Wilderness: American Nature Writing and Environmental Politics*. Hanover: University Press of New England, 1996.

Peck, Daniel H. *Thoreau's Morning Work: Memory and Perception in A Week on the Concord and Merrimack Rivers, The Journal, and Walden*. New Haven: Yale University Press, 1990.

Peterson, Katie. "Surround Sound: Dickinson's Self and the Hearable," *The Emily Dickinson Journal* 14 (Fall 2005): 76–88.

Pickering, David. *Cashell's Dictionary of Superstitions*. New York: Sterling Publishing Group, Inc., 2003.

Power, Sister Mary James. *In the Name of the Bee: The Significance of Emily Dickinson*. New York: Biblo and Tannen, 1970.

Randolph, Vance. "Ozark Superstitions," *Journal of American Folklore* 46 (January–March 1933): 1–21.

Rashid, Frank D. "Higginson the Entomologist," *The New England Quarterly* 56 (December 1983): 577–82.

Rideing, William H. "At the Exhibition," *Appleton's Journal of Literature, Science and Art 1869–1876* xv: 376 (June 3, 1876): 376. APS Online. Duq.edu.

Robertson, Frederick William. "The Three Crosses on Calvary," *Master Sermons of the Nineteenth Century*. Gaius Glenn Atkins, ed. Norwood, MA: The Plimpton Press, 1940, 106–16. Books.Google.com.

Rosendale, Steven. *The Greening of Literary Scholarship: Literature, Theory, and the Environment.* Iowa City: University of Iowa Press, 2002.

Ross, Francis D. "Rhetorical Procedure in Thoreau's 'Battle of the Ants.'" *College Composition and Communication* 16.1 (1965): 14–18.

Russell, Annie Marble. *Thoreau: His Home, Friends, and Books.* 1902. New York: AMS Press, 1969.

"Russian Scientists Develop Anticancer Medicines on the Base of Insect Immune System," April 21, 2005,. http://english.pravda.ru/science/tech/21-04-2005/8108-insect-0/

Rutledge, Louis C. "Emily Dickinson's Anthropods," *American Entomologist* 49 (Summer 2003): 70–74.

St. Armand, Barton Levi. *Emily Dickinson and Her Culture.* Cambridge: Cambridge University Press Archive, 1986.

Sattelmeyer, Robert. "Introduction," in *"A Natural History of Massachusetts," "Wild Apples" and Other Natural History Essays.* Henry David Thoreau, William John Rossi, ed. Athens: University of Georgia Press, 2002.

Scheese, Don. *Nature Writing: The Pastoral Impulse in America.* New York: Twayne Publishers, 1996.

Sewell, Richard Benson. *The Life of Emily Dickinson.* Cambridge: Harvard University Press, 1980.

Shakespeare, William. *The Riverside Shakespeare: The Complete Works.* G. Blakemore Evans and J. J. M. Tobin, eds. 2d ed. Boston: Houghton Mifflin, 1997.

Slovic, Scott. *Seeking Awareness in American Nature Writing: Henry Thoreau, Annie Dillard, Edward Abbey, Wendell Berry, Barry Lopez.* Salt Lake City: University of Utah Press, 1992.

Sorensen, Willis Conner. *Brethren of the Net: American Entomology 1840–1880.* History of American Science and Technology Series. Tuscaloosa: University of Alabama Press, 1995.

Spooner, David. *Thoreau's Vision of Insects & the Origins of American Entomology.* Philadelphia: Xlibris Corporation, 2002.

Spurgeon, Charles Haddon. "Everybody's Sermon," *Master Sermons of the Nineteenth Century.* Gaius Glenn Atkins, ed. Norwood, MA: The Plimpton Press, 1940, 207–26. Books.Google.com.

"Superstitions About Insects," *The Atchinson Daily Globe*, Thursday, August 30, 1888, Issue 3,348 Column E. 19th Century U.S. Newspapers Database. Duq.edu.

"Superstitions About Love," *St. Louis Globe-Democrat*, Tuesday, October 10, 1882, 4 Issue 142, Column D. 19th Century U.S. Newspapers Database. Duq.edu.

"Superstitions of Bees," *Daily Evening Bulletin*, San Francisco, CA, Saturday, November 22, 1873, Issue 40 Column D. 19th Century U.S. Newspapers Database. Duq.edu.

Swanson, Diana J. "'Born Too Far Into Life': The Metaphor of the Bee in *Walden*," *American Transcendental Quarterly* 4.2 (1990): 123–134.

Thomas, Jan. "Early Victorian or Romantic Era: 1837–1860," http://www.jantiques.com/jewelryhistory/lesson3.html.

Thoreau, Henry David. *"A Natural History of Massachusetts," "Wild Apples" and Other Natural History Essays.* William John Rossi, ed. Athens: University of Georgia Press, 2002.

_____. *Journal of Henry David Thoreau in Fourteen Volumes Bound as Two Volumes: I-VII (1837–October 1855).* Bradford Torrey and Francis H. Allen, eds. Reprint Edition. Mineola, NY: Dover Publications, 1982.

_____. *Journal of Henry David Thoreau in Fourteen Volumes Bound as Two Volumes: VIII-XIV (November 1855–1961).* Bradford Torrey and Francis H. Allen, eds. Reprint Edition. Mineola, New York: Dover Publications, 1982.

_____. *Walden, Civil Disobedience, and Other Writings.* 3d ed. William Rossi, ed. Norton Critical Edition. New York: W. W. Norton, 2008.

Tolini, Michelle. "'Beetle Abominations' and Birds on Bonnets: Zoological Fantasy in Late-Nineteenth Century Dress," *Nineteenth-Century Art Worldwide: A Journal of Nineteenth Century Visual Culture* 1.1 (2002). http://19thc-artworldwide.org/spring_02/articles/toli.html.

Torrey, Bradford. "Introduction," in *Journal of Henry David Thoreau*. Vol. I.
Tritt, Michael. "Thoreau's Skillful Use of an Entomological Text," *The American Transcendental Quarterly* 52 (1981): 259–62.
Twain, Mark. *The Adventures of Huckleberry Finn*. 1884. 3d ed. Thomas Cooley, ed. Norton Critical Edition. New York: W.W. Norton, 1998.
U.S. Food and Drug Administration. *Defects Level Handbook*. 1995–2012. http://www.fda.gov/food/guidancecompliance regulatoryinformation/guidance documents/sanitation/ucm056174.htm#CHPT3
Wade, J. S. "The Friendship of Two Old-Time Naturalists," *The Scientific Monthly* 23 (August 1926): 152–160. JSTOR.org.
Waldbauer, Gilbert. *Fireflies, Honey, and Silk*. Berkeley: University of California Press, 2009.
White, Fred D. "'Sweet Skepticism of the Heart': Science in the Poetry of Emily Dickinson," *College Literature* 19 (February 1992): 121–28.
White, Lynn. "The Historic Roots of Our Ecologic Crisis," in *The Ecocriticism Reader*, 3–14.
Wilder, Laura Ingalls. *On The Banks of Plum Creek*. 1937. New York: HarperTrophy, 2007.
Williams, Dennis C. *God's Wilds: John Muir's Vision of Nature*. College Station: Texas A & M University Press, 2002.
Williams, JoAnne De Lavan. "Spiders in the Attic: A Suggestion of Synthesis in the Poetry of Emily Dickinson," *Dickinson Studies* 29 (1976): 21–29.
Wilson, Mabel. Personal Interview. Waynesburg, Pennsylvania, March 15, 2002.
Winhusen, Steven. "Emily Dickinson and Schizotypy," *The Emily Dickinson Journal* 13.1 (2004): 77–96.
Wohlpart, A. James. "A New Redemption: Emily Dickinson's Poetic in Fascicle 22 and 'I Dwell in Possibility,'" *South Atlantic Review* 66 (Winter 2001): 50–83.
Wood, John George. *Insects at Home: A Popular Account of British Insects*. Oxford: Oxford University, 1872. Books.Google.com.
Worster, Donald. *Nature's Economy: A History of Ecological Ideas*. 2d ed. Cambridge: Cambridge University Press, 1994.

Index

Abbot, John 34
The ABC and XYZ of Bee Culture 39
Achilles 99
Adamson, Joy 16
Aeacus 99
Akeakamai 14–15
Alcott, Bronsen 73
alpenglow 158
American Association of Agricultural Entomologists 36
American Bee Journal 39
American Entomology; or, Descriptions of the Insects of North America 34
American Ornithology 34
Anderson, Charles R. 77, 88
angels 126, 141, 153
animals 120, 148, 161–167, 173; adornment 22, 53–54; bats 10, 16; bears 156, 161–162, 169; cattle 169, 172–173; chimpanzees 10–17; deer 161–162; dogs 10; dolphins 11, 14–16, 93; elephants 163; foxes 72, 87; frogs 21, 76, 90, 130, 157, 162; hounds 144; hyla 72; language 11–19; lizards 114; marmots 162; mice 75, 162; muskrats 72; pit bulls 44; platypus 16; sheep (hooved locusts) 167, 171, 173; snakes 50, 95, 100, 128, 162; spring peepers 157; squirrels 2, 25, 30, 75, 110, 132, 145–146, 152, 161–164, 169; treatment 13; turtles, snapping 72; weasels 44; whales 11, 163; wolves 162; woodchucks 25, 87
anthropocentrism 8, 11, 17, 123, 147
anthropods 135
anthropology 12, 46–47
anthropomorphism 11
antibiotics 46–47
anticoagulant 46
ants 2, 23, 29, 32, 44, 47, 57–59, 62, 66–70, 75, 82–85, 91, 145, 162, 167; "The Battle of the Ants" 97–101; honeypot 57; mythology 99; sutures 44–45
aphids 55, 120

apiculture 28–29, 37–39, 50, 167, 174
"The Apple-Tree Table" 101
arachnids 27
Aristotle 27
armyworms 40, 43
arsenic insecticides 22, 43; *see also* pesticides
art 28, 31, 50–54, 68, 100, 132; of beekeeping 26, 37–38; medical 45; of spider 123–124
arthropods 21, 27
artists 31, 51–54, 117, 58, 123, 135
Asahina, Midori 114
"Augeries of Innocence" 64
Austin, Mary 18
autumn 79, 130–131, 139; *see also* fall
avalanche 153, 156, 173

bacteria 46
bagworm 52
Bakhtin, Mikhail 17
"The Bakhtinian Road to Ecological Insight" 16
balance 8, 23–25, 33, 78, 93–94, 103, 109–111, 117–118, 132, 136, 143, 146, 167–168, 172; *see also* divine; faith; soul
balm 81, 111
Barber, J.W. 101
Barker, Wendy 131
batiking 51
"'The Battle of the Ants': Two Notes" 98
Baym, Nina 70, 78
Bee Culture 39
beekeeping 29, 31, 37–39, 50, 172; bellows smoker 38; extraction 29, 38; Langstroth hive 38–39, 174; wax comb foundation 38–39; *see also* bees; hive; honey
bees 2–3, 6, 11, 16–17, 24–32, 37–40, 50, 53, 57–69, 76, 97–100, 105, 115–137, 142, 145–146, 151, 155, 159, 163, 166–175; American foulbrood 38; bee-line 31, 168–169; bee-ness 173; bumble bees 130, 132, 135; Colony Collapse Disorder 14; dance

and language 11–14; humble-bee 76; propolis 97; robotic 13; royal jelly 97; venom 97; *see also* entomology; hive; honey
Bees in America: How the Honey Bee Shaped a Nation 37
beeswax 38, 51, 97
beetles 22, 40–44, 49–50, 53–58, 66, 68, 80, 130, 135, 145, 148, 162; borer 135; Brazilian 31, 54; buprestid 53; Colorado potato 40–42; death-watch 49–50, 80, 89; elaterid 53; fabric 53; as food 56; jewel 53–54; scarabs 31, 53; staghorn 56; tenebrionid 53
Berenbaum, May 68
bess bug (*Passalus cornutus*) 49
Bianchi, Martha Dickinson 135
Bible 6, 28, 32, 42, 56–62, 108
biodebridement 45–46
birds 31, 37, 76, 89, 92–94, 110–11, 118, 123, 129–135, 140, 145, 148, 157–158, 161–163, 166, 169; as adornment 22, 31, 53–54; bitterns 72; bobolink 130–134; cranes 98, 162; crows 72, 162; ducks 72; eagles 87, 161; geese 162; hawks 89, 162; hummingbird 22, 53; jays 162; loons 75, 87–88, 100, 162; partridges 162; phoebes 72, 75; robin 75, 118, 129; sparrows 91, 110; squall 89; swans 162; water bird 12; water ouzel 157; woodpeckers 169; *see also* eggs; feathers; hatching; nests; ornithology; ova
birth 80, 88, 93, 95, 120, 133, 136, 139–144, 149, 157–158; *see also* lake; mother; resurrection
Bishop, Nadean 107–108
Blake, William 62, 64
bloodletting 45
blossoms 105, 116–121, 129–132, 140; brain 120; exuviae 95–96; *see also* bees; flowers; gardens; plants
bones 63, 128, 139, 151, 154, 173; fossil bird-tracks 135; skeletons 95
Bones 47
botany 20, 29, 33, 104–105, 112–118; crystalline 70–71
botfly 96; *see also* human insect; ova
boulders 152, 154, 162, 165
Bowles, Samuel 111
Branch, Michael P. 9
Brethren of the Net: American Entomology, 1840–1880 33
bridges 89, 111
Brown, Eric C. 28
Bryson, Norman 18
buckthorn 174
Buell, Lawrence 8–9, 18, 20, 25, 86, 154
bug 22, 23, 31, 55, 62, 85, 91, 101, 102, 123; bug-hunter 35, 44; bug-man 146; *see also* entomology; insects; nature

bulbs 115–116, 138, 141, 183; *see also* cultivation; flowers; plants
Burbick, Joan 74–75, 107
Bushnell, Horace 65
Buske, Frank E. 151
butterflies 2, 6, 22–26, 29–31, 34, 48, 53, 64–72, 95, 100, 114–117, 122, 126–129, 133–148, 151, 162–163, 168; monarch 135; *see also* caterpillar; cocoons; metamorphosis; moths
"Butterflies and Poetry" 67

caddisfly 54
Calliphoridae fly 47
Calvinism 107
Cameron, Sharon 75, 77–78
"The Canonization" 64
Carpenter, William 32, 57–60, 73
Carr, Jeanne 168
Carson, Rachel 18
casting, lost wax 51
Catalogue of the Insects of Pennsylvania 34
caterpillar 30, 43, 52, 56–57, 68, 96, 100, 120–125, 135–144; as food 52, 56–57; woolly bear 30; *see also* butterflies; cocoons; metamorphosis; moths
Catlow, Maria E. 66–67
"Catterpiller and Fly" 64
Cavell, Stanley 97
cells 38, 52, 57, 98, 126, 151, 154, 161–166
centipedes 21
Chaucer, Geoffrey 68
chinch bugs 40–41
choir 23, 79, 80–82, 85, 88, 90–92, 131, 164; *see also* chorus; crickets; music; quire; universe
chorus 1, 2, 23–24, 70, 79, 90, 131; *see also* choir; crickets; music; quire; universe
Christ 107, 164
Christian Philosophy 148
Christianity 8–11, 113, 129, 147, 155, 164
Christmas stockings 22
chrysalides 23, 66, 94–95, 137–138, 142; *see also* butterflies; caterpillar; cocoons; metamorphosis; moths
church 108, 134; *see also* nature; prayer; worship
cicada 47, 100
cinnamon 47
circles: floral circle 171–172; tree growth 102; Walden's surface 24, 70, 92, 102, 154
Civil War 30, 39, 45
Clausen, Lucy W. 48–50
clouds 42, 93, 125, 149, 159, 165; of insects 161, 167
cochineal 52
cockroach 6, 47–49
cocoons 23, 51, 94, 102, 106, 135–44; but-

Index

terflies; caterpillar; chrysalides; metamorphosis; moths; transformation
coffin 138–141
Cohen Michael P. 26, 153, 155–156, 164, 170, 174
Cole, Jane 39
Colony Collapse Disorder 14; *see also* bees
Comstock, Anna Botsford 39
Comstock, John Henry 35, 39, 43
Connery, Sean 47
contraception 46
cosmic 95; botfly 96; choir 82, 90, 132; dance 82, 160; mosquito 23, 83–84; order 10, 46; time 156–157, 171; truth 122; *see also* choir; chorus; insects; music; nature; quire; universe
cosmos 84, 119, 95, 165; *see also* mosquito; nature; universe
Cowan, Frank 54
Cowper, William 28
creation 1–6, 10–11, 20–26, 58, 66, 69–73, 77–97, 101–111; citizens 84, 130, 158, 162; pulse 71, 84; rhythm 84; voice 84, 94; *see also* divine; god; nature; particles; universe
Crèvecoeur, Hector St. John de 37
crickets 1–2, 23–26, 49, 63, 66, 70–72, 79–95, 105, 110, 115, 135, 146, 162, 164; Mass 106, 131; nation 24, 106, 131–133; set sun 24, 111, 131–132; *see also* choir; chorus; quire; sun
crops: barley 41; barley sugar candy 22; beans 76–77, 97; cotton 40, 43, 46, 51; grain 63, 80, 88, 148, 154, 157; oats 41; pea 20; rye 41; sorrel 76; tobacco 40–41; *see also* pesticides; plants
Crucifixion 108
crystals 78, 91, 93, 149, 157, 160–165; crystalline botany 71–72; crystalline vision 165; *see also* creation; particles
cultivation 37, 41, 115, 170, 172; of self 77; *see also* botany; crops; horticulture; plants
"Cultural Entomology" 27
cutworms 120

Dadant, Charles 39
dance 1–4, 79, 135, 155; cosmic 82, 88–90, 95, 122–123, 127, 138–139, 148–149, 152, 160–163; insects on Walden 88–95; Muir 152; waggle 11–14, 135; wind 125; *see also* choir; chorus; cosmos; divine; god; insects; music; nature; universe
Dante 62, 69
Darwin, Charles 17, 28, 56, 103
Davidson, Frank 101
Davies, Samuel 65
death 58, 65, 92, 100, 104–110, 115, 122, 126, 133, 135, 139–143, 149, 154–158, 166; fear 25, 65, 80, 136, 141, 166; Harris' 73;

honeybees 14, 30, 169–170; notify hive 31, 47, 50; prediction 48, 49, 80; *see also* butterflies; coffin; funeral; resurrection; salvation
de Hruschka, Fransesco 38
Devitt, Terry 45
dew 120–122, 125, 133, 156, 161
Dialogues on Entomology, in Which the Forms and Habits of Insects Are Familiarly Explained 66
Dick, Thomas 148
Dickinson, Edward 116
Dickinson, Emily: Amherst Academy 113; beekeeping 39; conservatory 116; exotropia 113; fascicles 105, 135; as flower 120; Mount Holyoke 108; poetic eye 106; proto-ecological stance 104–105, 112, 121; Scientist of Faith 104, 113; White Moth of Amherst 133
Dickinson, Lavinia Norcross 110, 120–121
Dickinson, Susan Huntington 135
Dickinson and the Romantic Imagination 104
Diehl, Joanne Feit 104
Dillard, Annie 18, 174
divine: authority 108; breath 80; Dickinson's doubt 108, 117; justice 42; love 3; message 6; music 83, 88, 90, 100, 121, 134, 146; notice 111; order 3, 78, 151, 154; plan 20–26, 66, 70, 78, 82, 85, 89, 105–107, 112, 118, 121, 127, 134–135, 143–147, 154–166; power 60; presence 5, 78, 102, 158; separation from 65; text 26; voice 106, 134; will 64; *see also* creation; god; insects; nature
Dolis, John 77, 86, 155, 162
Donne, John 62–64
dragonflies 6, 49–50, 53, 92, 95
drought 30, 169
dust 59–65, 135–137, 148, 166, 172; stardust 161; with pollen 133, 148, 175
Dwight, Timothy 101–102
dye 31, 51–52

Eagle Rock 151
earthquake 47, 151–153, 156, 162
earthworm 21, 64, 123, 130
earwig 66
ecocriticism 1, 5–11, 18, 67; canon 9, 25
The Ecocriticism Reader 7
ecology 6, 17, 20, 26, 104, 118–122; awareness of 8, 21–25, 54, 70–71, 104, 112, 118–123, 130, 165; crisis 8; Dickinson 118–124; literary 8, 17; *see also* ecocriticism; nature; science
ecosystems 6–10, 19, 70, 103
Eddy, Pearl Faulkner 68
Eden 2, 84, 108, 118, 134, 142, 170–172
Edwards, Jonathan 59, 64–65, 153
eggs 59, 95, 96, 102, 141; cockatrice 59;

Index

Drosophilia 55; of forest 141; mantis egg sac 49–50; silkworm 51; *see also* birds; hatching; insects; metamorphosis; ova; shell; transformation
Ehrlich, Gretel 150
Elder, John C. 146–147
elytra 54; *see also* insects; wings
Emerson, Ralph Waldo 18, 73–74; transparent eye-ball 86, 150–151
"Emily Dickinson, Emerson, and the Poet as Namer" 128
Emily Dickinson: Monarch of Perception 115
"Emily Dickinson's Anthropods" 135
Emily Dickinson's Vision: Illness and Identity in Her Poetry 113
entomed 47
Entomological Society of Pennsylvania Insects 22
entomology: cultural and literary 1–6, 26–28; Dickinson 104–105, 114–115, 138; Muir 162; as a science 28–29, 34; 36; Thoreau 71–74, 78–79, 85, 103, 115; *see also* bugs; ecocriticism; Harris; insects; nature; science
Esch, Harald 13
eternity 80, 89, 105–106, 126, 143, 149, 166; *see* also lake; mountains; nature; universe
Eucharist 150
Evangelism 107, 115
"Everybody's Sermon" 65
eyes 2, 5, 18, 21, 70–72, 78, 83, 87–92, 102–106, 109–124, 133, 141, 143, 151, 157, 160, 165, 169; all eye 151; bee 166–171; childish 109–111; cow 173; earth 88–91; glacial 145, 155–158, 162–165, 170; god 2–3, 16, 24–26, 89, 150, 155, 160; heaven 89, 91, 102; lake 157–158; microscopic 22, 86, 103, 145, 156; nature 146; poetic 103, 106, 113; reflected 2, 23–24, 35, 86, 90–92, 95; scientific 29, 89, 103, 114, 118; squall 89; terrestrial 124; transparent 86, 145, 150, 156, 160; Walden 23, 88–89; *see also* insects; nature; voice; Walden

Fabre, Jean-Henri 28
fabric 22, 51, 53; *see also* silk
faith 17, 21, 25, 48, 65, 104–118, 132, 136–143, 151–152, 156, 169; Scientist of Faith 104, 113; *see also* balance; divine; god; nature; prayer; spirit; universe
fall 30, 92 95, 100, 136, 139; *see also* autumn
Farmers' Almanac 30
Farr, Judith 104, 116
"'"Fascination" is absolute of Clime': Reading Dickinson's Correspondence with Higginson as Naturalist" 114
fashion 5, 22, 28, 31, 40, 50–54
feathers 105, 133, 136, 141, 148; Eider 133; *see also* birds; nests; wings

fecundity 5, 94, 107, 123
Federal Drug Administration 55
"Feed on the Mystery" 64
feminism 7
Fernald, Mrs. C. H. 43
fertilization 37, 120, 117, 118, 158
Field, D.D. 101–102
fireflies 53–54
Fireflies, Honey, and Silk 44
fish 16, 50, 56, 92–94, 148; gills 16; minnow 72; perch 89, 92–93; pickerel 88–91
"The Flea" 63
fleas 58–59, 63–64, 68
flies 2, 6, 25, 47, 49, 53, 58, 60, 64–68, 87, 115, 130, 135, 157, 164, 167
flowers 24–25, 53, 105, 111–116, 119–130, 135, 138, 148–153, 158–175; annuals 172; floral timeline 168, 170–174; flower-beam 159; *see also* bees; blossoms; botany; gardens; insects; nature; plants; pollination; seeds
"The Fly" 64
folklore 6, 28–30, 46, 48–50; fairy tales 11; Muir as folk hero 146; superstition 11
forest 89, 101, 148, 152, 160–168, 174; egg of 141; folk 127, 136; redwood 170; *see also* trees
fountain 92, 159–161
Fouts, Roger 12–13
Fowler, Emily 116
Franklin stoves 115
frost 71, 93, 120, 140, 141; frostbite 45; *see also* ice
fruit flies 47
funeral 50, 130; *see also* coffin; death; tomb
fungi 10, 120; mushroom 122

gadfly 68
galls 47, 52, 96, 102
Garber, Frederick 7
gardening 28–31, 116–118
gardens 2, 34, 42, 104–105, 116–121, 130–135, 152, 158, 163, 170–173; bee-gardens 165–175; Dickinson as gardener 2, 24–29, 104–105, 115–135; Harvard Botanical Garden 34; honey-garden 172; *see also* blossoms; botany; crops; cultivation; flowers; horticulture; insects; nature; pesticides; plants; seeds
The Gardens of Emily Dickinson 116–117
Gardner, Allen 12
Gardner, Beatrix 12
Gatta, John 155
Gay Studies 9
gems 54
Gender Studies 9
geology 104, 113
Georgic 4 69
Gerhardt, Christine 112, 118–119

Index

glaciers 145–146, 153–158, 162–165, 170–172; lifecycle of 149; *see also* birth; creation; lake; mountains
Glotfelty, Cheryll 7, 9
glowworm 135
gnat 2, 24, 86, 88, 119, 126, 128, 135, 145, 163
God: armies of 32; as Artist 58, 117; benevolence 112; as Creator 2, 20, 24, 64–65, 96, 100–102, 109, 146–151, 156, 160–162, 166; fountain 160; judgment 109, 144; as Maker 20, 72, 81, 89–90, 166; as mother 110–111; patriarchal 107, 109; *see also* creation; divine; insects; nature
God's Wilds: John Muir's Vision of Nature 147
"Good News" 65
gossamer 91, 133
grasshoppers 2, 25, 49, 53–58, 62–64, 82, 120, 145–146, 162–166; as food 42, 56–58; plagues 42, 62; tobacco spit 49
Gray, Asa 34
Gray, Peter 68
grubs 24, 96, 100–102; as food 56–57; *see also* human insect; larvae
Gudger, E.W. 44
Gunn, Giles 19
Guthrie James 113

Harding, Walter 101–102
harp 80–84, 161
Harris, Thaddeus William 29, 34, 36, 39, 73–74, 103, 115
Harrison, Lucinda 39
Harvard Natural History Society 115
hatching 51, 59, 94–103, 139, 141; *see also* birds; eggs; human insect; metamorphosis; ova; shell
Heaven 2, 106–108, 111, 118, 126, 132–134
heaven 23, 42, 54, 60, 63, 81, 85–91, 94, 102–103, 106–107; eye 89, 102; *see also* divine; faith; prayer; resurrection; salvation; soul
Heaven of Delight 54
Hedges, James 79
hell 64–65
hellfire 153
herbs 57, 61
Herman, Louis 14, 16
Hessian fly 40
hieroglyphics 53, 156
Higginson, Thomas Wentworth 29, 34, 67–68, 113–116, 135
"Higginson the Entomologist" 114
hills 86, 111, 132, 159, 171, 174; hill people of Burma 45; hillside 94; hilltops 87, 90, 95
History of Berkshire County, Massachusetts 101

Hitchcock, Edward 113
hive 13–14, 28, 31–32, 37–39, 57, 63, 68–69, 97–100, 135, 168–169, 174; bee gums 37; bee logs 37; bee space 37; box 37; skeps 37–38; symbolism 37; *see also* beekeeping; bees; honey
The Hive and the Honeybee 39
Hive of Pandemonium 69
Hogue, C.L. 27, 28
Hold, Vincent M. 31
Holder, Mark 14
Hollingsworth, Christopher 28, 32, 68–69, 97
Holt, Vincent M. 55–57
Holy Ghost 160–161
homeopathy 46–47
Homer 62, 68–69, 82–83
honey 29, 38, 40, 50, 57–58, 61, 63, 97, 133, 135, 167–174; medical uses 46; *see also* beekeeper; bees; hive; industry
honeycombs 38–39, 61, 72, 168
honeypot ants 57
Horn, Tammy 37, 39
hornets 47, 50, 58–61, 64–65
horse-fly 76, 167
horticulture 28–29, 36, 104, 115–118
hospitality 123, 127
houseflies 2, 163
Howard, L.O. 43
Hoyt, Erich 27
Huber, François 100
Huckleberry Finn 49
human insect 95–97, 106, 101, 123, 101; *see also* metamorphosis; ova
Hunter, R. 66
Huxley, Julian 16

ice 71–72, 93–94, 147, 153, 157, 159, 166
identity: American 35, 57; Dickinson 116, 144; nature 8, 16, 121; spider as symbol 124; Thoreau 75
immortality 106
"Imperfect States: Thoreau, Melville, and the 'Insectivorous Fate'" 28
imps 95
Indiana State Beekeepers Society 39
industry 48, 98; beekeeping 172; fashion 22, 31; printing 22, 52; silk 43, 51; symbols for 37, 59, 97, 167; Thoreau 83, 97–100
infestations 22, 28–29, 36–45
ink 52
Insect Fact and Folklore 48
Insect Lives: Stories of Mystery and Romance from a Hidden World 27
Insect Poetics 28
Insecta 21
insects: alienation from 40, 46; bias against 6, 26; body parts 22, 53–56, 73, 78, 100,

Index

148; cabinets 22, 137–138; citizens 2, 5, 26, 84, 87, 105, 121, 127, 130, 133, 138, 145, 149, 158, 162, 166, 175; classification 21–24, 33–35; collections 28–36, 54, 68; collectors 22, 35, 68; corpse 130; ecological role 7, 24, 26–27, 105, 119, 136–137; function 6, 20, 21, 32, 70, 117–118, 121, 127, 130, 148, 163, 165; OED 21, 178; as people 2, 25, 59, 105–106, 119, 127–128, 133, 146, 162–166; pinning 29; social 68, 71, 97–98, 100; specimens 22, 29, 31–35, 53–54, 69, 73, 130, 138, 149; *see also* bugs; choir; entomology; eyes; individual insects; music; nature; universe; voices
Insects at Home 67
Interpretation of Otherness: Literature, Religion, and the American Imagination 19
Introduction to Entomology (Comstock) 35
Introduction to Entomology (Kirby and Spence) 22
ISLE Reader 9

Jackson, Helen Hunt 135
Janovy, John, Jr. 18
Jenkins, Sally (Katy Did) 133
Jesus 59, 108–111
jewelry 31, 51–54; cages for live insects 22, 54
jewels: beetles 54; dew 122; ice 71
John the Baptist 58
Johnson, Rochelle 9
justice 42

Kale, Marilyn 54
Kansas State Agricultural College 35
Keane, Patrick J. 111, 115
Keats, John 68
Kellert, Steve 40
Kher, Inder Nath 105
Kirby, William 22, 34, 53, 100
Kirchner, Wolfgange 13
Kuczaj, Stan 14

lac insect 31, 51–52
lace 133
Ladies' Home Journal 39
ladybugs 6, 49, 130
Laertias philenor 115
lake 92–93, 145, 148, 154–166; *see also* birth; divine; eyes; glaciers; mountains
landscape 8–9, 17–25, 37, 69, 72–75, 84–86, 97, 111, 114, 119, 131–132, 146–174; *see also* divine; eyes; nature; text
Langstroth, Lorenzo 38–39
Langstroth hive 38–39, 174; *see also* beekeeping; bees; hives; honey
language 9–26, 95, 132–133; American Sign Language (ASL) 12–14; animals 11–20; Dickinson's experiments 113; of god 24–26, 145, 163, 165; of insects 163; scientific 67, 113; of storms 152; transcendence through 77; of universe 24; Victorian symbolic 67, 113; *see also* divine; ecocriticism; landscape; nature; voices
"Language" (Emerson) 18
larvae 24, 38, 41, 47, 51, 54, 56, 94–96, 102, 136–141, 169; *see also* bugs; cocoons; entomology; insects
larval therapy 45–46
leaves 5, 20–21, 26, 30, 51, 70–72, 76, 84, 88, 96, 102, 120, 125, 135, 137, 146, 148, 156, 161, 169, 170, 172; *see also* divine; plants; trees
LeConte, John Eaton 34
leeches 45
lice 47, 49, 58, 60, 68; as food 56
The Life and Death of King John 63
The Life of Henry the Fifth 63
lightning bug 49; *see also* fireflies
Linnæus, Carl 21, 33
Literary and Philosophical Repertory 101
Living Free 16
Lockwood, Jeffrey A. 42
locust 61–62, 81–82, 97, 162; as food 61–62; hooved locusts (sheep) 167, 171, 173; plagues 61–62; 97; Rocky Mountain 40–42, 55
"Looking at the Overlooked: Four Essays on Still Life Painting" 18
Love, Glen 8
Love's Labor's Lost 63

macroscopic 26
maggot therapy 30, 45–46
maggots 64, 96
malaria 44
Manes, Christopher 9, 10
Mann, John S. 128
manna 58
mantids 49–50, 66
Marble, Annie Russell 75–76
Martin, Wendy 105
Mass 131
Massachusetts Historical Collections 101
Masson, Jeffrey Moussaieff 11
McCarthy, Susan 11
McDowell, Michael J. 17
McGowan, Tony 28
McIntosh, James 106–108
Medical Entomology Centre 47
medicine 6, 28, 30, 40–50, 163
Medicine Man 47
Medihoney 46
Meeker, Joseph 8
Mehring, Johannes 38
Melsheimer, Frederick Valentine 34
Melville, Herman 101–102
The Merchant of Venice 63

metamorphosis 24–29, 67–71, 85, 94–103, 106, 135–144; *see also* butterflies; cocoons; hatching; human insect; insects; soul; transformation
Michelsen, Axel 13
microbes 2, 163, 166
microcosms 19–20, 23, 86–87, 91, 149; *see also* eyes; insects; universe; Walden
microscope 33, 113, 153, 156
microscopic 26, 58, 85, 103–104, 113, 138, 145, 149, 155–156, 165; environment 1; eye 22–26, 86, 103, 145; *see also* insects; particles
midges 68, 126, 135
A Midsummer Night's Dream 63
Mill Brook 76
Milton, John 62
"Milton, a Poem in Two Books" 64
Mitchell, Domhnall 115–116
mock epic 83, 99
Moody, Dwight Lyman 65; *see also* individual titles
moon 90, 121–122; 137; lunar cycle 30
mosquitoes 23, 32, 40, 44, 71, 79, 82–86, 90–94, 145, 148
moss 10, 22, 157
mote 63, 89, 137
mother 42, 49, 66, 107–110, 118, 157, 175; *see also* birth; god; nature
moths 48–49, 54–66, 148; British gipsy 43; as food 56–57; *Schinia thoreaui* (Thoreau's Flower Moth) 74; wax 38; White Moth of Amherst 133, 135; *see also* butterflies; cocoons; metamorphosis
moulting 100
Mt. Ktaadn 150, 164
Mt. Ritter 149, 153–156, 159
Mt. Shasta 175
Mt. Yosemite 166–167
mountaineers 165
mountains 2, 25, 40–42, 146–161
MRSA 46
Muir, John: baptism by light 159–161; Emersonian eye 150; as environmentalist and nature writer 146; glacial eye 145, 155–158, 162–165, 170; God's eye 162; proto-awareness 165
music 24, 27, 32, 80–85, 90, 98, 122, 131, 134, 152, 154, 163
myriapods 27
Myrmidons 32, 99
mythology 6, 11, 32, 46; Dickinson 135; environmental myth 8; Myrmidons 32, 99; mythic landscape 119

Nagel, Thomas 16
natural history 5, 9, 26, 29, 33–35, 66, 69, 73–75, 104–105
nature 88–89; attitudes toward 5–11, 17–21, 26, 48, 78, 82, 106, 118, 132, 147–152, 163–165; book of 154, 156, 164; citizens of 2, 5, 26, 84, 87, 105, 121, 127, 130, 133, 138, 145, 149, 158, 162, 166, 175; as community 75–77, 88, 127, 166; divine writing 3, 117, 146, 154–156, 164, 166; insects in 5–6, 21, 26, 65, 79, 105; language of 95–96, 158, 166; as Mother 110, 118; people of 2, 105–106, 128, 133; voice of 1, 7, 9–19, 25, 72, 76–77, 84–92, 102, 145, 150, 154, 162–166
"Nature and Silence" 9
nature writing 1, 7, 25–28, 69, 72, 146
necrotizing fasciitis (flesh eating bacteria) 46
nematodes 130
nests 110, 133, 142; as adornment 22; ants' 29; bees' 169; hornets' and wasps' 47, 50, 52; Thoreau nesting 77; *see also* birds; cocoons; eggs; hatching
Next of Kin: My Conversations with Chimpanzees 12
Nissenbaum, Stephen 22
North Star 76, 127

ocean 15, 170; *see also* sea
O'Connell, Patrick 99
OED 21
"Of Insects" 64
"'Often seen — but seldom felt': Emily Dickinson's Reluctant Ecology of Place" 112
"On a Flea on His Mistress' Bosom" 63
On the Banks of Plum Creek 42
"On the Lives of Insects in Literature" 68
"'One Unbroken Company': Religion and Emily Dickinson" 107
ornithology 33–34, 162
Othello 63
the Other 9, 13, 16–17, 77, 160
Otherness 18–19
ova 23, 95–97, 102; *see also* eggs; hatching; human insect; shell

paradise 3, 69, 134, 138, 171
Paradise Lost 69
Paré, Ambroise 45
Paris green 30, 41–43
Part of a Man's Life 67
particles 2–3, 20, 26, 123–126, 149, 155–162; of god 150, 154, 165; *see also* god; microscopic; universe
"pathetic fallacy" 17–18, 154
Patterson, Daniel 9
Paul, Sherman 150
Payne, Daniel G. 8
pebbles 125–126, 157
Peck, William D. 34–35, 74
Pepys, Samuel 68
personification 11, 16, 122

pesticides 30, 37, 42–43
Peterson, Katie 131
physiognomy 124–125, 128
Piping Up: A History of Women and Bees 39
plagues 30, 32, 40, 42, 59–62; Wilder's account 42
plants 2, 24, 36, 51, 95, 102–105, 112–22, 130–136, 140–141, 148, 157–166, 170–74; adenostoma 173; alfalfa 170; annuals 172; bell-flower, blue 164; buttercup 129, 137, 174; castilleias 171; chaparral 161, 170; clover 127, 130, 133, 137–138; compositae 159, 171; daffodils 141; daisy 126; eriogonums 172; gentian 130, 157; geranium 140; gilias 171, 174; grass 2, 24, 86, 101, 119–122, 126–132, 136–137, 157; harmony 20; hay 2, 41, 122, 137; hellebores 41; *Hemizonia virgata* 172; honeysuckle 170; huckleberries 86, 174; lady slippers 126; liliaceous plants 171–172; lilies 116, 160, 175; manzanitas 173–174; mints 140, 171; mulberry 51; nemophilas 171; Orchis 114; peony 105; as people 27, 146; quassia 41; roses 30, 129, 137, 170; spiræa 173; spring beauty 126; tulips 141; violets 126, 171; wheat 40–42; *see also* botany; bulbs; flowers; gardening; horticulture; leaves; seeds; trees
Pliny 56
pods 56, 140–141, 139; dolphin 15; *see also* cocoons; seeds
The Poetics of the Hive: The Insect Metaphor in Literature 28, 32
pollen 122, 133, 148, 174–75
pollination 29, 33, 40, 131, 135; *see also* bees; flowers; plants
pollinators 14, 121, 137
ponds 1, 10, 23, 26, 72, 86–95, 103, 149
Popular British Entomology; Containing a Familiar and Technical Description of the Insects Most Common to the Various Localities of the British Isles 66
Porter, David 106
powdery mildew 120
"The Power of an Endless Life" 65
prayer 88, 99, 108–110, 130–134; *see also* balance; faith; god; nature; soul; spirit; worship
Presbyterian 148
pupae 94–95, 136
Purgatory 49
Puritanism 107

"Queen of Calvary: Spirituality in Emily Dickinson" 107
Quimby, Moses 38
quire 23, 72, 79, 80, 82; *see also* choir; chorus; crickets; dance; insects; music; universe

Racial Studies 9
rain 50, 120, 123, 137, 139, 153, 171
rainbow 54, 93
raindrops 149, 162
"The Rape of Lucrece" 63
Rashid, Frank D. 114–115
Reading the Earth: New Directions in the Study of Literature and the Environment 9
Reaumur, René Antoine 21
regeneration 93–94, 96, 136, 140–144
Report on the Insects of Massachusetts, Injurious to Vegetation 34
resin 52
resurrection 25, 103, 106, 121, 124, 136, 138–142, 172
Richards, Douglas 14
Riley, Charles Valentine 41
rills 157, 162
Robbins, Cassandra 39
Robertson, Frederick William 65
rocks 2, 10, 60–61, 65, 146, 149–159, 163–166, 170; rock berry 12; rock-man 146
Romantic imagery 222
Romantic indulgence 16
Romanticism 104
Romeo and Juliet 62
Root, A.I. 38, 39
Ross, Francis D. 99
Rossetti, Christina 68
Rutledge, Louis C. 135

Sacrament 130
sacred 46, 53, 71, 80–82; acorn 141; bee garden 167; crickets 131; nature 105, 114; texts 46; time 157, 166; Walden 71, 86, 89–91; *see also* creation; divine; god; nature
St. Armand, Barton Levi 135
salvation 65, 80, 107–108, 117, 124, 127, 134, 139, 143, 156; *see also* divine; faith; god; heaven; resurrection; soul; spirit; transformation
San Jose scale (pernicious scale) 43
sand 88, 121, 125, 157
Sattelmeyer, Robert 71
Savior 109
Say, Thomas 34
scale insects 40, 43, 52, 55, 58
Schultz, Ted 27
science 1, 5, 11, 17, 20–37, 69, 73, 78, 81, 100–106, 112–120, 130–138, 150, 163, 165; entomology as 26–29, 33–39, 115
scientific community 11–13
scientific observation 5, 19, 21, 72, 78, 95, 114, 120
scientists 1, 14–17, 21, 27, 30, 44, 46, 58, 62, 69, 74; Dickinson as 104–107, 112–120, 136–138; Thoreau as scientist-saunterer 34, 70–79

scorpion 57–59
Scripture Natural History 32, 58
Scudder, Samuel H. 73
sea 111, 132, 134, 137, 165, 170, 174; *see also* ocean
seedlings 122, 139
seedpods 136, 138–139, 143, 172
seeds 30, 40, 96, 118, 105, 120, 122, 130–131, 139–144, 172; Dickinson's italic 105, 120; Thoreau's seedtime 95; wings 148; *see also* flowers; plants; pods
"Sermon IX: The Connection Between Present Holiness and Future Felicity" 65
Shakespeare, William 32, 62–63, 68
shell 54, 102, 135, 139, 141
shellac 31, 51–52
Shelley, Percy Bysshe 68
Sierra Club 146
Sierras 3, 146, 168–171
silk 31, 43, 51–52, 136; Damask 136
silkworms 31, 43, 47, 51–52
sin 11, 64–65, 147
singing 2, 82, 119, 121, 163; crickets 132
sinners 65, 107, 153
"Sinners in the Hands of an Angry God" 64–65
sky 86, 89–94, 111, 125–127, 142, 155, 159–164; sky-man 146; sky water 93; Walden 3, 23, 53
Slovic, Scott 9
slugs 55, 57, 64
Smith, Jerome V.C. 98
snails 57, 162
snow 137, 152–153 162, 164, 170, 174
snowflake 156
Sorenson, W. Connor 33, 34
soul 49, 53, 65, 80, 84–85, 89, 102, 111, 114–116, 123, 133, 144; Divine 161; of flower 120; *see also* divine; faith; prayer; resurrection; salvation; spirit; transformation
Spence, William 22, 53, 100
"'Spider' Letter" 64
spiders 21, 24, 49–50, 58–59, 62–64, 106, 115, 121, 123, 130
"Spiders in the Attic: A Suggestion of Synthesis in the Poetry of Emily Dickinson" 123
spirit 2, 37, 43, 53, 58, 68, 93, 100, 109, 111, 121, 150, 159, 164, 166; kindred 103; *see also* divine; faith; prayer; resurrection; salvation; soul; transformation
spirituality 1, 6, 17–26, 76, 79, 102–108, 119, 123, 134–136, 141–142; *see also* divine; god; nature
Spooner, David 70, 73, 95–96, 101, 103
spring 50, 72, 76, 94–95, 101–102, 117, 121, 130, 136–141, 172
Spurgeon, Charles Haddon 65

star 138, 146, 160, 166; star-dust 161
storms 49, 111, 121–122, 146, 150, 152, 155, 160
Stout, Kathy 54
streams 72, 95, 148, 151, 157–158, 163–164, 169
"A Stroll through the Woods of Animals and Men" 17
summer 59, 72, 79, 81, 86, 102, 110, 130–141, 159, 163
sun 1, 24, 42, 52–53, 81, 91–92, 111, 119–120, 125–126, 131–132, 138–143, 151–152, 156–161, 173, 175; crickets set 1, 24, 111, 131–132
sunbeams 156–164
sunlight 143, 149, 158–163, 175
sunrise 108, 125, 127, 142
sunset 86, 117, 137
sunshine 122, 151, 157, 159–163
"Surround Sound: Dickinson's Self and the Hearable" 131
"Surveying the Emergence of Ecocriticism" 9
Swanson, Diana J. 97–98, 100
swarms 1, 23–26, 32, 41, 49, 61, 79, 149, 167, 173–174; *see also* insects; plagues
"'Sweet Skepticism of the Heart': Science in the Poetry of Emily Dickinson" 113
Systema Naturæ 33

Taming of the Shrew 63
tapeworm 64
Tennyson, Alfred 68
text: Divine 26; inscribed on nature 145, 154, 158, 178; living 102, 154; water-skater 92; *see also* divine; landscape; language; nature
thaw 72, 76, 137, 153, 159
thorax 54
Thoreau, Henry David: ecologist 103; entomology 71–74, 78–79, 85, 103, 115; flying cat 87; hatching 94–103; industry 48, 98; saunterer 34, 70–79; *Schinia thoreaui* (Thoreau's Flower Moth) 74; scientist-seedtime 95
Thoreau's Alternative History: Changing Perspectives on Nature, Culture, and Language 74–75
Thoreau's Morning Work: Memory and Perception in "A Week on the Merrimack Rivers," the "Journal," and "Walden" 74
Thoreau's Redemptive Imagination 75
"Thoreau's View of Science" 78
Thoreau's Vision of Insects and the Origins of American Entomology 73
"The Three Crosses on Calvary" 65
thrips 55
tomb 102
Torrey, Bradford 77
Tracking Thoreau: Double-Crossing Nature and Technology 77

Transcendentalism 20, 107, 146
transformation 24–25, 63, 66–67, 71, 94, 99–100, 106, 117, 124–126, 135–144, 147; butterflies; cocoons; hatching; human insect; insects; metamorphosis; soul; spirit
Travels in New England and New York 101
trees 2, 10, 25–26, 30, 40, 43, 54, 56, 61, 76, 91–96, 101–102, 119, 141, 146–162, 168–169, 173; acorns 141, 169; bee-tree 168; cherries 40, 174; firs 174; fruit 40, 101–102, 170; locust 20; *Magnolia grandiflora* 173; Muir in treetop 152; oak 30, 141, 168–169; orchards 40, 43, 103, 134, 170; peach 40; pine 76, 86, 101, 146, 148, 158, 176; plums 40; podcassia 56; redwood 170; sequoia 146, 160; spruce, douglas 152; spruce, hemlock 158; tree-man 146; willows 174
Tuskegee and Its People: Their Ideals and Achievements 39
Tuskegee Beekeeping Ladies 39
Twain, Mark 49
Twenty Hills Hollow 159–160
Tyack, Peter 15

Umwelt 17
universe 23–24, 58, 73, 76, 79, 84–95, 101, 103, 125–126, 134, 137, 148, 154–157, 160, 165; currents 160; joy 1; lyre 84; medicine 46; miniature 86; order 26, 78–79, 126, 148; peace 167; plan 96; rhythm 78–79; Universal Being 150

"Values and Perceptions" 40
Victorian 53
Virgil 62, 68–69, 97
voices: bee 117; carried on wind 145, 150, 154, 164; creation 84, 88, 94, 132, 145–146, 162; crickets 131; earth 79; god 81, 106, 134, 146; insects 23, 79–85, 90, 92, 145, 154, 162; mosquito 83; nature 1, 7, 9–19, 25, 72, 76–77, 84–92, 102, 145, 150, 154, 162–166; *see also* divine; eyes; god; insects; landscape; language; nature; text
von Frisch, Karl 13
von Uexkull, Jacob 17

Wade, J.S. 73
waggle dance 13
Waldbauer, Gilbert 44, 46, 51–52, 55
Walden: circles on surface 24, 70, 92, 102, 154; eye of 23, 88–89; frozen 2, 23, 93–94; insects on 88–95; sacred 71, 86, 89–91; sky 3, 23, 53; surface 2, 23–26, 70–71, 79, 82, 85, 88–94
Washington, Booker T. 39
Washington, Margaret James Murray 39
Washoe 12–13
wasps 50, 63–64; as food 57; jewel 47; paper 52; *see also* nests
water-bugs (*Gyrinus*) 90–95
water-skater 2, 23–26, 70, 85–94, 102, 154, 163
weaving 51–52, 59, 92, 94, 123–124, 130, 133, 136
webs 59, 63–65, 80, 88, 91, 94, 117, 123–124, 133, 163
weevils: cotton boll 40, 43; curculio 40; palm 56
Wenner, Adrian 13
"What Is It Like to Be a Bat?" 16–17
When Elephants Weep: The Emotional Lives of Animals 11
White, Fred D. 113
White, Lynn 8
Why Not Eat Insects 31, 55
Wilder, Laura Ingalls 42
Williams, Dennis C. 147–148, 151–155, 164–168, 170–174
Williams, JoAnne De Lavan 123–124
Wilson, Alexander 34
Wilson, Edward O. 28
wind 2, 24, 26, 76, 84, 95–97, 120–127, 136–139, 145–154, 161, 164–166; *see also* divine; language; voices
wings 16, 22, 33, 42, 48, 49, 63, 72, 100, 105, 118, 141–142, 148, 153; *see also* birds; feathers
Winhusen, Steven 106
winter 30, 50, 93, 95, 137, 140–141, 169, 172; cricket 63; migration 130; overwinter 136–137
Woltz, James 14
Wood, John George 67
Wordsworth, William 27, 68
worm 2, 51, 57, 60, 63, 65, 106, 120, 121, 123, 141, 165
worship 2, 117, 134, 141, 148, 158
Worster, Donald 102
Writing Nature: Henry Thoreau's Journal 75

Yosemite National Park 151

www.ingramcontent.com/pod-product-compliance
Lightning Source LLC
Chambersburg PA
CBHW032058300426
44116CB00007B/802